Financial innovation and monetary policy

How far is it beneficial to try and control the supply of money while the financial system is changing and evolving so rapidly? With the development of financial innovation and the rapid re-regulation of the financial institutions in the UK, the effects on monetary policy are far reaching. Looking at the context of both banks and building societies, this study characterizes financial innovations in order to illustrate the way they behave in the monetary system and show how they have played an important part in the inability of economists to forecast the economy in the 1980s and 1990s. Covering such topics as credit liberalization, market-led interest rates, consumers' expenditure function, definitions of money, internationalization and demand for money, this study offers a comprehensive account of monetary policy. This examination of the changes in the behaviour of financial institutions draws out important theoretical implications for monetary theory and policy. Using empirical data and econometric models to test his conclusions, Michael Pawley questions the fundamental tenets of monetarism.

This book will be invaluable to final-year undergraduates and postgraduates in finance and economics. It raises important questions which will be of interest to economists and policy makers.

Michael Pawley has held a number of academic posts, including that of senior lecturer at Birmingham Polytechnic. He is now acting as a consultant.

Financial innovation and monetary policy

Michael Pawley

ROUTLEDGE
London and New York

First published 1993
by Routledge
11 New Fetter Lane, London EC4P 4EE

Simultaneously published in the USA and Canada
by Routledge
29 West 35th Street, New York, NY 10001

Typeset by Leaper & Gard Ltd, Bristol
Printed and bound in Great Britain by
Biddles Ltd, Guildford and King's Lynn

British Library Cataloguing-in-Publication Data

A catalogue record for this book is available from the British Library.

ISBN 0-415-07503-3

Library of Congress Cataloging in Publication Data
has been applied for.

ISBN 0-415-07503-3

Contents

Figures

Tables

1 Introduction

The objective of this book is to analyse the efficiency of monetary policy in relation to financial innovation by building societies and banks, with particular reference to the period 1970–90. The major underlying theme is the extreme importance of the nature and developments of the financial system for the efficient operation of monetary control. A central thematic argument implicit throughout is that the analysis and application of monetary policy cannot be divorced from the financial system within which it operates.

The central tenets of monetarism and monetary control are set out in Chapter 2, and contrasted with the opposing Keynesian school. The necessary and sufficient conditions for a monetarist policy of control of the money supply are outlined, alongside the Keynesian viewpoint as to the appropriate manner in which monetary policy should be conducted. Recognition is given to the institutionalist school which first warned of the lacuna that existed in the monetary economics literature as the result of an inappropriate paradigm within which to carry out an analysis of the monetary aspects of the economy. According to the institutionalists, the framework of a static institutional system, an unchanging market environment and the assumed passivity of financial institutions negated many of the central conclusions of the traditional monetary debate. A parallel is drawn between the strictures of the institutionalist school and more recent conjectures as to the effects of financial innovation on monetary control.

The viewpoint that financial innovation has in some way affected monetary policy appears widespread, and some authors would go further in emphasizing the revolutionary importance of innovation upon monetary economics:

As deposits come to bear competitive interest rates monetary

> theory – models of money supply and demand and of the transmission of control measures and shocks through financial markets to the real economy – will have to be rewritten.
>
> (Tobin 1983a: 162)

There has been a great deal of comment by the monetary authorities as to the effects of financial innovation and change on their policy instruments. Much of that conjecture centred upon the developments in the building society and retail bank sectors, under the broad umbrella terms of liberalization, innovation and financial change. In Chapter 3 the various attempts at characterizing the major determinants of financial innovation are surveyed and, for purposes of exposition, an analytical framework incorporating the process of financial innovation within the monetary system is adopted. It is noted that as yet there does not exist a comprehensive study of the form and nature of the financial innovations that have occurred, the reasons for their occurrence, their effect on the efficiency of monetary control or their effect on the conduct of policy.

Attention is paid to the twin constraints of regulation and monetary control upon the activities of the building societies and the banks, and the manner in which the market environment shaped and delineated the operational policies of these institutions. Particular note is made of the dynamic interaction between changes in the authorities' regulatory and monetary policies and changes in financial innovation. The possibility of regulatory-induced innovation is examined with reference to changes in monetary control and the Medium Term Financial Strategy (MTFS). Sustaining the debate as to the effects of the monetary authorities' own monetary and regulatory policies upon the degree of financial innovation and change, evidence is assimilated as to the degree to which the activities of building societies and banks have become less demarcated as a result of regulatory-induced innovation.

The manner in which specific institutional factors, such as the mutuality of building societies and the building societies' recommended rate system, shaped the nature of competition between the mix of price and non-price factors, and hence limited the degree of financial innovation, is fully analysed, as is the effect of the cartel on the desired portfolio balance of the personal sector.

The operation of the building societies' cartel is examined, and attention is drawn to the effect it had in smoothing building society interest rates and creating an excessive demand for mortgages that varied with movements in general interest rates. An analysis is made of the expected effects of the abolition of the cartel, in terms of both finite stock adjustments and more continuing effects such as structural changes in building societies' interest rate setting policies. Chapters 5 and 6 deal largely with the stock adjustment effects of the abolition of the cartel and financial liberalization on the effectiveness of monetary control, and Chapter 7 examines in more detail the long-term effects in relation to interest rates.

One of the major economic conundrums of the 1980s was the fall in the income velocity of circulation of the broad monetary aggregates. Having detailed the major innovations introduced by the building societies and banks in Chapter 4, in Chapter 5 we examine the effect of these innovations in stock adjustment terms upon the growth rates of the monetary aggregates relative to nominal incomes. The fall in the income velocity of circulation is examined in terms of the effects of financial innovation on the personal sector's willingness to hold interest-bearing money balances.

The voluminous literature as to the meaning and definition of money is reviewed from the angle of the innovations introduced by building societies and banks, with detailed comment as to the changing motives for holding money. The problems and difficulties of interpreting monetary growth and controlling the money supply when the motives for holding money alter are synthesized with reference to the experience of monetary targeting in the MTFS.

An investigation into the regulatory convergence of building societies and banks and the consequences for the delineation of building society and bank activities leads to an assessment of the homogeneity and substitutability of their deposit liabilities and an analysis of the necessity for changing the monetary target for purposes of monetary control.

The analysis in Chapter 5 of the stock effects of financial innovation upon the growth rates of the monetary aggregates relative to nominal income leads to the contention that the payment of interest on extremely liquid accounts at building societies and banks has been a major contributory factor in the breakdown of demand for broad money equations.

Attention is drawn to the dichotomy between monetary theory, which emphasizes money balances in the transmission process, and reality, where the money and credit markets interact to determine the transmission mechanism. In Chapter 6 the growth rates of the monetary aggregates relative to nominal incomes are examined in terms of the demand for credit, with particular attention to the personal sector's demand for credit and stock adjustment effects that may have caused temporary instability.

Special consideration is placed upon the effect of the abolition of the building societies' cartel, the entry of the banks into the mortgage market and the liberalization of credit to the personal sector. The importance of the freeing-up of the mortgage market is isolated, and particularly the impact of the temporary stock adjustment to the personal sector's demand for money balances. Polar views as to the exogeneity or endogeneity of money are judged with reference to the behaviour of the building societies and banks under contrasting market conditions, and conclusions are drawn as to the monetarist assumption of exogeneity. The preliminary general contention that financial innovation has in some way altered the money–income relationship is extended to include the idea that financial innovation and liberalization have also altered the credit–income relationship.

Parallels are drawn between the attempt of competition and credit control (CCC) to promote control of the money supply in a freely competitive system and the attempt of the MTFS. It is argued that the lessons from the CCC approach were not taken into account in the design and implementation of the MTFS, particularly in the form of the likely activities of the building societies and banks in a highly competitive market system. It is also argued that the changing financial system during the period of the MTFS enforced a move away from a dogmatic approach to monetary control towards a far more eclectic approach that recognized the existence of institutional change.

The more continuing effects of financial innovation upon the effectiveness of monetary policy are assessed in greater detail in Chapter 7. Specifically, it is expected that the demand for money became less elastic with respect to interest rates, while consumers' expenditure became more elastic as a result of the greater flexibility and importance of interest rates following the abolition of the cartel.

The ability of the monetary authorities to control the money supply given the innovations outlined is analysed with reference to the effectiveness of interest rates as a monetary instrument.

In Chapter 8 the salient econometric literature on the demand for broad money function and the demand for credit in the UK is critically examined. Earlier econometric models of the demand for money are surveyed, with explicit consideration given to those studies that have attempted to model financial innovation as part of the function, and to both the econometric formulation and econometric methodology employed.

Chapter 9 sets out a theoretical model for evaluating the effects of financial innovation by building societies and banks. Standard error-correction and cointegrating models of the demand for money function for the non-bank private sector are estimated in order to analyse the earlier stated argument that financial innovation led to instability of the demand for money and that the demand for money became less elastic to interest differentials and less elastic to general rates of interest. The question of whether or not wealth has become an important variable in the demand for money function as the result of money becoming more popular for investment purposes is also examined.

Given the analysis of Chapter 5 which emphasizes the homogeneity of building society and bank deposit liabilities, the M4 aggregate is used in the demand for money specification, rather than the M3 aggregate which excludes building society deposits.

The expectation that expenditure became more sensitive to interest rates as a result of more flexible and market-related interest rates is econometrically evaluated using both error-correction and cointegration models. The area of analysis as set out above covers the major issues isolated by Akhtar as being of prime importance in the examination of financial innovation:

> The process of financial change may exert significant influences on the empirical definition of money, the money supply process, the demand for money and the role of interest rates in the transmission of monetary influences to the rest of the economy. More generally, changes in the financial system raise questions about the meaningfulness of monetary and financial aggregates and may lead to shifts or (further) instability in the relationship of those aggregates to economic activity.
>
> (Akhtar 1983: 6)

In Chapter 11 the impact of the exchange rate mechanism (ERM) on the mode of operation and importance of monetary policy is analysed, and conclusions are drawn regarding the future of monetary policy given the twin constraints of financial innovation and the ERM.

2 Monetary control – theory, practice and financial change

2.1 INTRODUCTION

Monetarist theory, long espoused by academic economists, has provided the major basis for macroeconomic policy in the UK since the mid-1970s. Section 2.2 outlines the underlying theoretical rationale of monetarism and the opposing theoretical basis of the Keynesian school of thought. The necessary and sufficient conditions needed for a monetarist policy of control over the money supply are detailed, as are the theoretical deficiencies in the monetarist standpoint. Section 2.3 explains the *modus operandi* of *practical* monetarist policy in the UK, how it differs from mainstream theoretical monetarism (as detailed in Section 2.2) and the reasoning behind adopting such a form of policy. The experience and results of monetary control in the UK are examined in Section 2.4, including an appraisal of the contention that financial change and innovation may be responsible for both the breakdown of previously stable relationships upon which theoretical monetarism rests, and problems encountered with practical monetarism and its subsequent abandonment. The similarity is noted between the warnings of the institutionalist school over two decades ago as to the effects of financial change on monetary policy, and subsequent official statements as to the reasons behind the failure of practical monetarism. In Section 2.5 the views about the effect of financial change on the *conduct* of monetary control and how financial change is expected to modify the early theoretical monetarist policy prescription are analysed.

2.2 THE BASIC POSTULATES OF MONETARISM

The modern quantity theory, or 'monetarism'[1] as it has come to be known, is firmly based on the work of Friedman (1956). According to Friedman, the quantity theory is in essence a theory of the demand for money.[2] It is argued that the demand for money should be analysed in the same manner as the demand for real goods, as money yields a flow of services or utility to its holder. Friedman emphasized the active role of money in income determination with two statements. First, he argued that the demand for money bears a stable relationship to money national income. The velocity of circulation is assumed to be a stable function of a small number of variables. Second, Friedman argued that the supply of money is exogenously determined either because it is fixed by policy or because it is independent of the variables which determine the demand for money (Friedman 1970a).[3]

It is possible to use the post-Keynesian IS–LM framework along the lines of Poole (1970) to show the relative importance of monetary policy, and the vital importance of a stable demand for money for control of the money supply. In the familiar IS–LM diagram (Figure 2.1), consider the situation whereby the IS curve is subjected to random shocks and may lie anywhere between IS_1 and IS_2. If, as monetarists claim, the money demand function is stable and if the

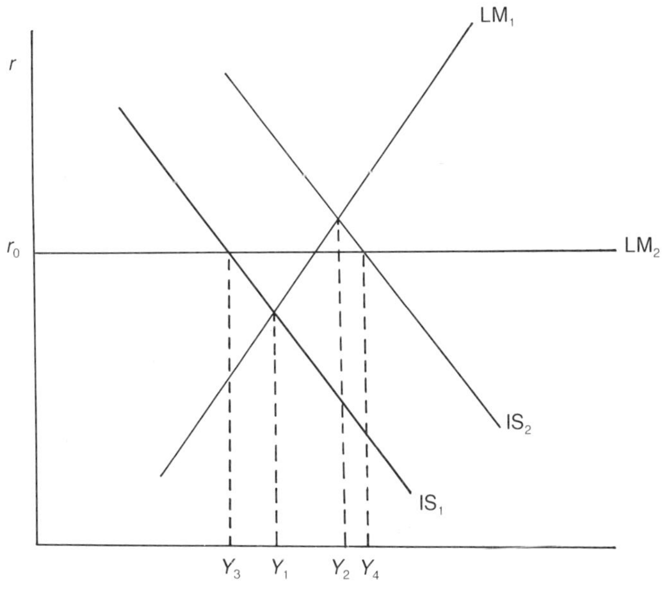

Figure 2.1 IS–LM analysis

stock of money is fixed, income may end up at any position along the horizontal axis between Y_1 and Y_2. If, on the other hand, the rate of interest is held constant, there will be fluctuations from Y_3 to Y_4.

From this it can be seen that shifts in the IS curve whilst holding the quantity of money constant lead to smaller fluctuations in income than whilst holding the rate of interest constant. Thus, it is argued that, if there is a stable demand for money, control of the money supply is a more effective policy than controlling interest rates.[4] Furthermore, the authorities can only observe and therefore influence a *nominal* rate of interest, whereas the *real* rate of interest is the relevant one for the IS curve. For the two rates of interest to be equal, expectations of inflation on the part of the private sector must be zero.

The stability of the demand for money is crucial to monetarist propositions as to the appropriate conduct of monetary policy. If there is a stable money demand function the implication is that money has a predictable influence on the economy and hence control of the money supply by the monetary authorities is a powerful instrument of economic policy (Judd and Scadding 1982). If the relationship between the monetary aggregates and nominal incomes is reasonably stable and predictable, the conduct of policy should involve a declared emphasis on control of the growth of the money stock and monetary policy should be based on quantitative monetary targets (Desai 1981). If there is a stable relationship between the monetary aggregate and the goal variable, it is possible to set a target growth path for the monetary aggregate which will be consistent with the desired growth rate of the goal variable. Thus, if monetary aggregates are to be used as targets, it is a necessity that there should be a stable relationship between the monetary aggregate and the goal variable (nominal income).

Keynes and Keynesian monetary theorists, on the other hand, dispute that the demand for money is a stable function.[5] Keynes (1936) recognized the importance of the transactions motive for holding money in order to bridge the gap between planned regular payments and receipts of money, and the precautionary motive for sudden unexpected expenditures. The main importance of Keynes's analysis of the demand for money is found, however, in the emphasis on the 'speculative' demand for money, and the notion of uncertainty. Keynes highlighted uncertainty in terms of the variability of the rate of interest and hence the vital importance of the speculative motive to the stability of the demand for money.[6]

Keynes argued that, at certain times, money will be held in

preference to an alternative interest-yielding asset. Such 'speculative' holdings of money would be over and above that held for precautionary motives. Money is a capital-certain asset, the nominal value of which does not vary. The alternative to holding money is to hold an asset (bond), the market price of which varies according to the rate of interest.[7] When choosing between the alternative of holding money or bonds, the expected rate of interest is taken into account. If the rate of interest is expected to fall, capital gains may be made; if rates are expected to rise, capital losses may be faced on bonds. The demand for money is relatively low when the rate of interest is expected to fall, and greater when the rate of interest is expected to rise. At any one time, wealth-holders have an opinion as to the 'normal' rate of interest relative to the current rate of interest. It is assumed that different individuals will have different expectations, such that in the aggregate a smooth speculative demand for money function is obtained which is a negative function of the current level of the rate of interest.[8]

One assertion of Keynes's speculative motive is that the rate of interest as perceived by wealth-holders will change over time. So, rather than being constant as argued by monetarists, Keynes argued that velocity is both unstable and volatile. An increase in the money supply, he argued, would lead to an increase in holdings of speculative balances, such that any increase is offset by a reduction in velocity.

The implications of an unstable demand for money function upon the operation of monetary policy can be seen in the IS–LM framework. Figure 2.2 shows the relative stability of the IS curve,[9] whilst the demand for money is unstable and may vary from LM_2 to LM_3. This results in variations in income from Y_2 to Y_3.

According to this analysis, large fluctuations in income may occur, such that Keynesians favour control of the interest rate. For example, consider the case where a rise in the demand for money occurs, causing the LM curve to shift from LM_1 to LM_3. This will force up interest rates, from r_1 to r_3, and reduce income, from Y_1 to Y_3. If an interest rate policy (i.e. a policy of trying to keep interest rates constant) is being followed, the money supply will be increased to allow for the increase in the demand for money, such that income returns to Y_1. Thus, variations in the level of income will be minimized. The policy implications of the Keynesian model of money demand are thus distinctly different from the monetarist framework. Keynes, through the introduction of the speculative demand for money which explicitly outlines uncertainty, was able to argue that

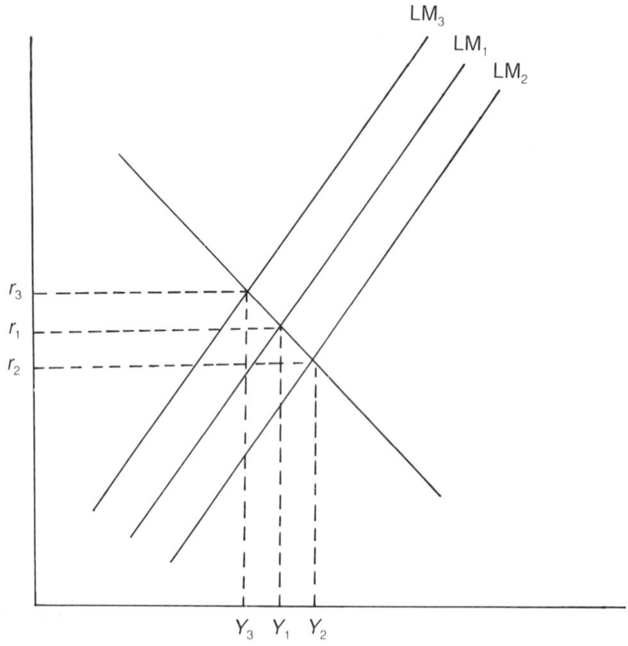

Figure 2.2 IS–LM analysis

volatile expectations may cause instability in the demand for money function. This implies that monetary policy via control of the money supply will be ineffective.

Apart from the assertion that the demand for money is, in reality (i.e. not constrained to a simplified theoretical construct but in real-world terms), a stable function of a few measurable variables, a further assertion appears to distinguish clearly Friedman's approach. Money, he argues, is a unique asset, and is therefore not a close substitute for any other asset, real or financial. Changes in the quantity of money will thus have an impact which is spread widely among a number of assets, causing a pervasive change in all planned expenditures both on goods and on financial assets; portfolio equilibrium is only restored after large changes in asset yields. All forms of expenditure will be affected, thus significantly affecting nominal income.

The monetarist view, therefore, is that the interest elasticity of the demand for money is low, and hence monetary policy will be effective. The underlying rationale for this position is that, if the authorities are able to reduce the supply of money, there will only be a small volume of idle balances which may be induced into the pool of active funds (through an increase in the level of interest rates) in order to support the existing level of expenditure. Indeed, it would require relatively large increases in the level of interest rates to significantly undermine the impact of the initial reduction in the money supply (through raising the velocity of circulation of money), and this adjustment in itself would tend to depress the level of credit-financed expenditures within the economy. In addition, a significantly higher level of interest rates would be expected to reduce the demand for bank loans and may depress the volume of bank-created deposits.

In Figure 2.3, if the money supply is reduced, national income will fall further (from Y_1 to Y_3), and interest rates will increase further (from r_1 to r_3), when the demand for money is relatively interest inelastic. Therefore, the lower the interest elasticity of the demand for money is, the higher is the change in the rate of interest needed to

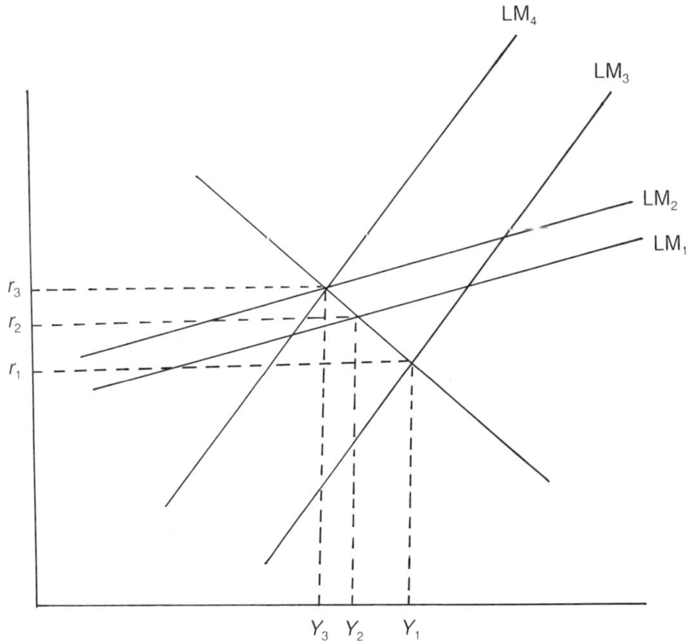

Figure 2.3 IS–LM analysis

restore equilibrium, and the stronger the monetary policy. Thus, an important element in the monetarist/Keynesian debate lay in differing opinions as to the substitutability of money and real assets. Empirical studies on the degree of substitution as measured by the interest elasticity of the demand for money have not, however, provided results which show whether the monetarist or Keynesian theories are most valid. The only effect that empirical work has had on this point is to contradict the more radical assertions of both protagonists. The results show that there is a negative relationship between changes in interest rates and money balances, but that the interest elasticity of the demand for money seems to be quite low. The special cases of zero-interest elasticity assumed by the monetarists and the infinite-interest elasticity of the Keynesians as represented by the liquidity trap are both disproven (see Chapter 8 for an analysis of researchers' econometric results on interest elasticity).

Monetarist theory asserts that, although a rise in the money supply will increase nominal income, monetary policy will not have a permanent effect on the level of real output. A rise in the money supply will affect output after approximately six to nine months, and affect the price level after about twelve to eighteen months, after which output will return to its previous level. According to the expectations-augmented Phillips curve the rise in output is only sustained until the accompanying increase in inflation becomes fully anticipated. At this time output returns to its natural level, the rise in the money supply leading only to an increase in the rate of inflation.

Thus, real income, argued Friedman, is determined by supply-side considerations. If changes in the rate of growth of the money supply do not impinge on long-term real income, then the price level will change in order to restore equilibrium between the supply of money and the demand for money. So, changes in the money supply affect real income only in the short run, and prices in the long run. This received further theoretical support from the rational expectations school[10] (Muth 1961; Lucas 1972, 1976). The adaptive expectations hypothesis implicit in Friedman's work maintains that individuals will continuously make systematic errors as to their estimates of future inflation. Rational expectations contradicts this, however, and argues that expectations are based on *all* available information, including past errors in expectations of inflation and the effects of policy actions which may themselves alter expectations. Sargent and Wallace (1975, 1976) show that, under conditions of rational expectations, there will be instantaneous adjustment of the economy to an anticipated increase in the money supply. Monetary policy will have no effect on real output.[11] Instead, prices will rise with no long-term effect on real income. Sargent and Wallace thus come to the same conclusion as Friedman, that monetary policy should follow a money supply growth rule rather than be used for active stabilization policy[12] (Friedman 1960).[13]

2.3 MONETARY CONTROL IN THE UK – POLICY PRESCRIPTION

Friedman's assertion of a stable demand for money became the central issue in debates on monetary economics. Indeed, Laidler (1971) has suggested that the stability of the demand for money over time is capable of reflecting the whole argument between Keynesians and monetarists as to the role of money in the economic system. In the USA, Friedman and Schwartz (1963) claimed to be able to show that real money balances and real income were connected in a reasonably predictable way, arguing that changes in the rate of growth of the money stock are a necessary and sufficient condition for changes in the rate of change of money income (Friedman and Schwartz 1963: 676).[14] The theoretical arguments of Friedman and his empirical work on the demand for money were corroborated by empirical research in the UK which suggested that the demand for money function was stably related to income and interest rates (Dow 1958; Paish 1958; Kavanagh and Walters 1966; Fisher 1968; Goodhart and Crockett 1970; Laidler and Parkin 1970; Laidler 1971). It did seem that in the late 1960s there was a general consensus as to the existence of a stable demand for money (Laidler 1971: 43).

The implications of such a finding were thought to be substantial. Through a stable demand for money, controlling the monetary aggregates would have a major and determinate effect on the economy (Parkin 1978: 252–3; Freedman 1983: 103–4). At the time, a stable function suggested to some economists that monetary policy would be effective, that a particular policy could be chosen and monitored and that desired levels of the monetary aggregates could be achieved by varying the level of interest rates (Goodhart 1984: 46). A stable demand for money thus appeared to provide empirical support not only for the *ability* of the monetary authorities to control the money supply, but also for the *desirability* of so doing in terms of the information value of monetary aggregates (Courakis 1981: 306).

The econometric investigations in the UK were carried out on M3,[15] and from the monetarist standpoint appeared to suggest a direct link between the rate of change in the money supply M3 and the rate of change in nominal incomes. The line of causation, it was claimed, ran from money to income, with a lag. Thus, to bring about a reduction in the rate of growth of the price level, it was deemed necessary to bring about a reduction in the rate of growth of the money supply M3. The econometric evidence also seemed to suggest that, as there was a link between M3 and nominal interest rates, control of that aggregate could be achieved by manipulation of interest rates. Moreover, it was believed at the time that control of the aggregate could be achieved without recourse to unacceptably high interest rates (Bank of England 1983a: 202).

The belief in the ability of the authorities to control money supply growth via interest rates was seen to be an important factor in placing greater emphasis on the manipulation of interest rates in competition and credit control (CCC).[16] If interest rates could be used as an instrument to control monetary growth, then there would be no need for the use of direct controls over banks' financial intermediation activities, which had proven largely ineffective and with hindsight were seen to inhibit competitive efficiency in the banking system (Bank of England 1983a).[17]

The reliance on the econometric evidence as to the stability of the demand for money relationship was soon seen to be unfounded, however (Hacche 1974). Econometric models based on data from the 1960s could not explain the monetary movements of the early 1970s, in particular the fast growth of M3 after the removal of direct controls in 1971 under the aegis of CCC and the abandonment of the retail banks' interest rate agreements. Yet, the argument that the previously held relationship had been distorted by structural change in the financial system also led to the notion that, once the changes were over, the link between money and nominal income would return to a reliable stable relationship. Despite the fact that it did not return to such a state, the monetary authorities believed that, after the aftermath of CCC, the growth rate of M3 could be influenced by a mixture of direct control and debt management (Bank of England 1983a: 203).

Despite the conjecture as to the effects of structural change in the financial system upon the growth of the money supply, the institutional background in which policy actions take place seems to have been inadequately considered by the monetary authorities. Despite the breakdown of the money–income relationship as shown by econometric demand for money equations, targets were published for the growth of M3 in 1976, partly in response to the conditions on a loan from the International Monetary Fund (IMF) to maintain domestic credit expansion within certain limits.

Although it was recognized that, in econometric terms, the money–income relationship had broken down, it was still maintained that monetary growth over and above the rate of growth of nominal incomes would result in inflationary conditions (Bank of England 1984e: 54).

This belief that the money supply was still the dominant impulse affecting the price level, despite the breakdown of demand for money functions, gained theoretical support from the emerging 'buffer stock' or 'disequilibrium money' school.

In the buffer stock model it is argued that economic agents may be temporarily moved off their demand for money functions by credit-side shocks. This may lead to holdings of excess money balances, which will be slowly dissipated (Artis and Lewis 1974, 1976). The applicability of the buffer stock model in a period of financial innovation is examined in Chapter 6.

The theoretical standpoint of the rational expectations school (see earlier) was to be emphasized in practical policy operation through published money supply targets. It was hoped that inflationary expectations would be reduced if people were convinced of the monetary authorities' conviction to restrict the rate of growth of the money supply (Bank of England 1984e: 46). In particular, it was hoped that this would lead to wage claims being in some way linked to the future publicly announced rate of growth of the money supply. This, it was thought, would reduce the impact of possible high unemployment under a tight money policy. This is because it was maintained that, if wage claims grew faster than the rate of growth of the money supply, it would lead to increased unemployment. By keeping expectations of the rate of growth of the money supply low, it was hoped to reduce wage claims and stop unemployment rising (Green Paper 1980: paragraph 8).

It was noted that problems had occurred in the past with the M3 aggregate, but it was not felt that these problems were insuperable; indeed, it was felt that it was the *method* used to control the money supply that was at fault, rather than problems with the aggregate itself (Bank of England 1983a: 204).

The Medium Term Financial Strategy (MTFS) also maintained that there was a close link between the money supply, the public sector borrowing requirement (PSBR) and interest rates. It was argued that an increase in the PSBR would lead to an increase in the rate of growth of the money supply or would push up interest rates.

This occurs because a large PSBR, which results in the government borrowing from the banking system, necessarily increases the money supply. On the other hand, it can borrow from the non-bank private sector, which, it was believed, would occur at steadily rising rates of interest (Treasury and Civil Service Committee 1980: 21). Thus, in order to reduce the money supply without resorting to high levels of interest rates, it was argued that the PSBR had to be reduced. The combined tools of monetary control were thus to be short-term interest rates and debt management. It is important to distinguish this *modus operandi* from a strict monetarist policy prescription of control of the monetary base. Indeed, Friedman himself was incredulous as to the proposed method of control in the UK in his (oft quoted) evidence to the House of Commons Treasury and Civil Service Committee:

> I could hardly believe my eyes, when I read, in the summary chapter [of the Green Paper on Monetary Control] 'the principal means of controlling the growth of the money supply must be fiscal policy – both public expenditure and tax policy and interest rates.' Interpreted literally this sentence is simply wrong. Only a Rip Van Winkle, who had not read any of the flood of literature during the last decade and more on the money supply process, could possibly have written that sentence.

He continued:

> Direct control of the monetary base is an alternative to fiscal policy and interest rates as a means of controlling monetary growth. Of course, direct control of the monetary base will affect interest rates ... but that is a very different thing from controlling monetary growth through interest rates.
>
> (Treasury and Civil Service Committee 1980: paragraph 11, 57)

The force of Friedman's argument is evaluated in Chapter 7 with reference to the effects of financial innovation on the efficiency of both interest rates and monetary base control as methods of controlling the money supply.

2.4 FINANCIAL INNOVATION AND MONETARY CONTROL IN THE UK

The experience of the monetary authorities in carrying out a policy of control of the money supply in the early 1980s was not, however, a happy one. In 1986, the governor of the Bank of England admitted that the Bank's ability to use an estimate of the relationship between monetary growth and the rate of growth of nominal incomes for setting targets, and then to hit those targets, had been 'unimpressive' (Leigh-Pemberton 1986: 500).

The Bank of England did appear to have considered the problems of financial change at the introduction of the MTFS. It noted in 1980 that, although targets were set, it was possible that structural change may affect the relative growth rates of aggregates, but that the problem was not insuperable. It was recognized that substitutability between near money just inside or outside particular aggregates meant that a number of monetary measures needed to be used (Green Paper 1980).

In view of the events of the 1980s, however, it appears that the problem of financial change was underestimated. In contrast to the initial confidence of the authorities as to the insignificance of changes in the financial system for the operation of monetary control, the monetary authorities progressively emphasized the importance of financial institutions during the MTFS and subsequent analyses of the MTFS.

Official publications increasingly tended to cite the effects of change in the financial institutional framework as the major factor in the problems experienced with monetary control, yet the Bank of England's conclusion that monetary policy is affected by financial change is not a new viewpoint. Indeed, the notion that the behaviour of financial institutions needs to be taken into account when examining the efficacy of monetary controls has a long, although perhaps not popular, pedigree. The 'institutionalist' school (comprising, *inter alia*, Gurley and Shaw 1955, 1956, 1960; Minsky 1957; Radcliffe Committee 1959; Tobin 1963; Brainard 1964) first warned of the possible dangers of 'traditional' monetary theory, which promulgated the view that the financial system is essentially a static equilibrium system, a mere unchanging backdrop against which policy operates (see Brainard 1964: 95–6).

Opposed to this, the institutionalist school takes the actions of financial institutions as being of central importance in the conduct of policy. It is recognized that observed statistical relationships may change over time because of changes in financial markets. Even if a policy of controlling the money supply may be optimal at present, if previously held relationships break down under rapid financial change, then the rationale for controlling the money supply may disappear. The IS–LM apparatus used earlier, and, indeed, often used by monetarists in demonstrating the conditions under which control of the money supply is superior to control of interest rates, is dependent on an unchanging financial system if the authorities are to be *able* to control the money supply. With financial innovation, traditional instruments may become obsolete in influencing the money supply, as has been recognized by Poole (1970: 178).

Under circumstances of deregulation and financial change it is instructive to be reminded of Minsky's concern that:

> If a period of rapid changes in the structure or in the mode of functioning of financial markets occurs, then the efficacy of central bank actions has to be re-examined.
>
> (1957: 171)

The Radcliffe Committee (1959) emphasized in stronger terms the problems associated with financial change, and concluded that the supply of money could not reliably be used as a policy measure (paragraph 504).

Moreover, the Radcliffe Report maintained that it is impossible to define money, because there is no clear criterion with which to determine those assets that are part of the money supply.[18] Obviously, if it is impossible to define the money supply, it is impossible to control it. This view has since been reflected in official commentary during and after the MTFS. The impact of increased competition between building societies and banks has been blamed as a major determinant of the observed change in relationships among the various monetary aggregates, and between them and nominal incomes. The activities of building societies and banks have been given prime consideration when assessing the appropriate definition of money and the problem of implementation of monetary control:

> There are other structural changes to come, some of which we can discern in advance, some of which we cannot foresee. Among those that we can expect are the changes that are arising, and may well accelerate, from the changing role and operations of the building societies. The extent and nature of competition among building societies, and between them and banks, is already changing, and this will give that yet further impetus. In these circumstances, all the aggregates, not only the various definitions of narrow and broad money, but also the wider liquidity measures, are liable to be subject to unforeseen distortion.
>
> (Bank of England 1984d: 476)

One of the main reasons cited has been the importance of liberalization of credit markets and the introduction of new types of financial assets:

> the gathering pace of innovation under the spur of competition is leading to new channels of finance and new financial instruments. A statistical series for any monetary aggregate, compiled on static definitions, is thus liable to shift in meaning.
>
> (Bank of England 1982a: 6)

The authorities have given special emphasis to the new financial instruments offered by banks and building societies:

> a number of developments currently taking place or in prospect could significantly affect the aggregates: these include the possible introduction by the clearing banks of interest-bearing current accounts, expansion of the payments facilities offered by building societies, and increasing provision of withdrawal facilities for building society term shares.
>
> (Bank of England 1982a: 21)

Even a cursory examination of the developments in the building society industry indicates that there has been considerable evolution and innovation, a detailed examination of which is carried out in Chapter 4.

2.5 FINANCIAL INNOVATION AND THE CONDUCT OF MONETARY POLICY

The integration of monetary economics and financial innovation by specific institutions is by no means an easy undertaking. Indeed, some would argue that traditional modes of analysis are incapable of providing the correct framework for research. Phillips (1981: 267) maintains that the main economic paradigm used to analyse monetary economics cannot be properly utilized in many Western economies because the competitive behaviour of financial institutions and the changing regulatory structure have affected interest rates, the supply and demand for money and relationships between money, income and employment.

Whilst acknowledging that the combined analysis of financial innovation, financial change and monetary economics represents a blending of macro and micro aspects of economics, it is argued in this book that the standard tools of economic analysis *are* useful in analysing the monetary effects of financial change (see Llewellyn 1985b: 19).

To the author's knowledge there has been no systematic attempt to assess fully the alleged impact of financial structural changes upon the operation of monetary control.[19] Many of the opinions reported are based largely on informed but speculative comment. It remains unclear as to exactly *how* financial change has actually affected monetary control. Without detailed knowledge as to what the effects upon monetary control are, and without a grasp of the *magnitude* of such effects, theories as to the appropriate *conduct* of monetary policy are also based on informed but speculative comment.

Although little detailed research has been carried out on the effects of financial innovation and structural change on the appropriate conduct of monetary control, it appears that there is a consensus of opinion that the effects of financial change necessitate that monetary policy be conducted in a *discretionary* manner (Goodhart 1986a: 101).

Not only may policy have to be carried out in a discretionary approach, but the authorities may be constrained to 'muddling through in a discretionary, but unrigorous manner'. (Goodhart 1986a: 101).

It is argued by some that institutional change vitiates the strict form of monetarism. Laidler (1981: 23) points out that financial innovation which affects the demand for money means that it is impossible to impose an *ex ante* growth rule as championed by Friedman (1960). He even argues that it may be necessary for wholesale change in the financial institutional structure to ensure the ability of the monetary authorities to control the money supply (Laidler 1981: 23).

Monetarist writers have long since accepted that it is not plausible to appease opponents with the argument that if the rate of growth of one monetary aggregate is held down then in the long term the other aggregates will behave consistently (Laidler 1981: 23). The movement of the monetary aggregates under conditions of financial innovation suggests that this can no longer be held as a tractable position.

But where did this leave policy? Should the monetary authorities have attempted discretionary control? Did they have the ability to control the money supply? Was there a link between money and nominal income, and money and prices? The difficulty experienced by the authorities in interpreting the movements of the published monetary aggregates has shown that even taking account of several measures during a period of structural change may not necessarily provide accurate information upon which to make policy decisions.[20]

Indeed, the 'Legal Restrictions' or 'Libertarian' School (see Johnson 1968; Black 1970; Jao 1983; Wallace 1983) argue that the observed link between money balances and nominal incomes only exists because of certain legal restraints placed on the banking system. Moreover, it is argued that once these restrictions are abandoned, and/or financial innovation occurs, then such statistical regularities as the demand for money will break down (Jao 1983: 14).[21]

A conceptually similar argument is provided by those who suggest that the very operation of monetary control has led to instability of money demand. This is commonly referred to as Goodhart's law (Goodhart 1984: 96). Without the ability to forecast future financial innovations, the Bank of England may have to take discretionary action in the interpretation and control of the monetary aggregates (Bank of England 1986b: 506).

Although the way in which monetary control can be exercised may have changed, under certain conditions it may still be an effective tool of economic policy. It is possible that if, as some would suggest, growth in the money supply is still a necessary force for inflation, then there may still be an important role for monetary policy (abstracting from exchange rate mechanism considerations). This is dependent, however, on the ability of the authorities to control the money supply, and on knowledge of the effects of institutional change on the private sector's demand for money. Monetary policy may only be useful if the authorities have a detailed understanding of any relationship between financial innovation/structural change and observed breakdowns in previously stable economic relationships and any effects of financial innovation on the techniques of monetary control. If, as many commentators would argue, changes in financial institutions and the markets in which they operate *are* important factors in the operation of monetary management, then they need to be examined closely to determine any effects that institutional change may have on the operation of monetary policy and the appropriate conduct of monetary control. In particular, it is desirable to investigate fully the possible effects of the intermediation activities of building societies and banks upon the postulates necessary for a policy of controlling the money supply.

2.6 CONCLUSION

In assessing the experience of monetary controls over the past decade, the official stance has been to emphasize the deleterious effects of a changing financial system and increased competition in financial markets, and in particular the developments that have been occurring in the building society industry, which, it is argued, circumscribe the effectiveness of monetary control.

It has been pointed out (Section 2.5) that the choice of a monetary aggregate is not as simple as the monetarists claimed. If monetary aggregates are to be used as targets in a money supply targeting strategy, it is necessary that there should be a reasonably stable relationship between the policy instrument and the monetary aggregate(s) used and between the monetary aggregates and the ultimate goal. A reduction in the growth rate of the monetary aggregates implies a reduction in the amount of money available for carrying out expenditure decisions. As noted in Section 2.5, however, the evidence of practical experience has shown that these conditions are not always prevalent.

Speculation centred on the possibility that financial innovation by building societies and retail banks affected the growth rates of the various monetary aggregates in relation to nominal incomes, and even altered the meaning and function of money. It is thus unclear, when trying to cut down on private sector expenditure, precisely which definition of money or monetary aggregate (if any) expenditure decisions depend on. The effects of bank and building society developments and change upon the movements of the monetary aggregates and the meaning of money are analysed in Chapters 5 and 6.

The importance of a stable demand for money function, from the monetarist standpoint, has been emphasized in Section 2.2. Some commentators believed that instability was due to financial change and innovation, and in particular to the activities of building societies and retail banks. A notable gap in monetary research is the dearth of econometric evidence as to the importance or otherwise of the effect of financial innovation on the demand for money function. In Chapter 9 an attempt is made to estimate a demand for money function which takes into account those innovations noted in Chapters 3 and 4, in order to ascertain whether or not financial innovation has been responsible for the breakdown of the money-demand relationship.

The implications of building society developments for Keynes's speculative demand for money and for the buffer stock model are explored in Chapter 6.

It has been suggested that, with rapid financial innovation, traditional monetary policy instruments for influencing the money supply may be inadequate for the task. The *ability* of the authorities to control the money supply in relation to building society developments is examined in Chapters 7, 9 and 10.

An analysis of these arguments may determine the appropriate *conduct* of monetary control and monetary policy, and may serve to alter or modify the divergent opinions of one or both of the monetarist and Keynesian schools. This is examined in Chapters 7 and 11.

3 Building society and bank developments, 1970–9

3.1 INTRODUCTION

It was noted in Chapter 2 that there has been substantial speculation and assertion that the core of the Medium Term Financial Strategy (MTFS) – control of the money supply – was in some way inhibited by financial innovation, particularly on the part of building societies and banks. Given this conjecture as to the possible detrimental effects of the activities of building societies and banks on the operation of monetary control, it is germane to examine the operations of these intermediaries and the developments and innovations that have occurred.

Little substantive work has been carried out into building society and bank innovation and, importantly, why innovation occurs. To ascertain the effects of financial innovation on monetary control (if any), it is vital to isolate the main innovations and the factors motivating them. If innovation has in some way altered the efficiency of monetary control, it is important for future policy considerations to have an understanding of why innovations occur, and what conditions are necessary or sufficient for innovation. It is also of importance to ascertain whether or not they are a one-off short-term phenomenon or an inexorable process. These considerations are vital to an understanding of the development of financial innovations and financial change and their possible impact upon monetary control.

It is possible to divide the period of study, 1970–90, into two periods, pre-1980 and post-1980. It is recognized that bank and building society changes have not occurred overnight, and hence a dividing line is in some senses an inappropriate categorization. Of course, change involving building societies and banks has occurred extremely fast, yet it has also been in an evolutionary rather than revolutionary manner. The use of 1980 as a delineator is therefore rather arbitrarily chosen, given that innovation and financial change occur over a period of time, yet a number of factors outlined below appear to provide the necessary justification for the delineation of building society and bank activities according to these broad time periods.

The literature on the definition and process of financial innovation is analysed in Section 3.2 and used to set out a broad framework in which to examine building society and bank developments. The way in which institutional features have affected the objectives of building societies is examined in Section 3.3. The combined factors of mutual status and the operation of the interest rate cartel are analysed in relation to their effects upon the manner in which building societies have conducted their business. An analysis is made of the operation of the cartel, with emphasis on the manner in which it created a variable excess demand for mortgages that tended to be variable over the interest rate cycle. Also, the degree to which mutuality and the cartel impinged upon the type of competition in terms of the mix of price and non-price factors is evaluated. The operation of the cartel is compared with traditional economic models of cartels, with special reference to the interest rates on shares and deposits and on mortgage loans. The relationship between the degree of financial innovation and the twin constraints of mutuality and recommended interest rates is also examined in Section 3.3. The effect of extensive non-price competition upon the variety of financial instruments offered by building societies and banks is detailed, and the link between cost efficiency and financial innovation in the building society sector is examined.

The nature of competition between banks and building societies in terms of the effects of monetary control and the banks' ability to compete in the personal sector retail financial market is analysed in Section 3.4. The asymmetry of monetary control is outlined, as are the relative non-neutral tax considerations applied to building societies and banks. The effect of these asymmetries upon the relative market share of banks and building societies is shown, as is the effect on the degree of financial innovation by these institutions.

3.2 THE DEFINITION OF FINANCIAL INNOVATION AND FINANCIAL CHANGE

It is necessary to define precisely what is meant in this book by the terms 'financial innovation' and 'financial change'.[1] Llewellyn (1985a, b) categorizes the former as the *types* of financial instruments introduced, the growth of new financial markets and the methods by which financial services are provided. The latter is related to the area of business activity that financial institutions are prepared to move into, and hence is a factor in laying down both the demarcation lines between different groups of financial institutions and the degree of competition involved. This appears to be a logical classification and is the one adopted in this book.

Whilst 'financial change' in terms of changing areas of activity can be identified, it is not easy, in practice, to identify 'financial innovation', as Desai and Low point out:

> In oligopolistic markets with product differentiation, it is a standard selling strategy to describe products as 'new, improved'. A handful of firms each providing a similar if not identical range of products may continuously announce new, improved, super versions of their products which may only be new in trivial aspects of product design. A bank providing its customers with cheque books in different colours may claim to be innovative, but it is when a rival bank/non bank offers higher interest rates for the same withdrawal facility that one would say that we have an important innovation. This implies, of course, *a priori* ordering of characteristics by their importance. Such ordering may be revealed by consumer preference but this is not guaranteed.
>
> (1987: 114)

There have been numerous attempts to specify the *underlying causal factors* affecting the nature and degree of financial innovation. An analysis of the literature shows that technological, market and regulatory factors are maintained to be the major determinants of financial change and financial innovation, although the emphasis placed on each tends to differ somewhat between authors (and there is no precise standardization of terminology). For example, Kane (1983) categorizes technological, market and regulatory factors as *environmental constraints*, a change in any one of which may lead to a restructuring of a financial institution's product line, organizational structure, production process and demand for financial services. Bain (1986) classifies the factors influencing the changing variety of financial instruments available as structural, legislative and market. The first includes the location of surplus and deficit units in the economy, portfolio preferences of the users of financial services and the economic and political environment. Legislative influences include taxation considerations and monetary and supervisory controls, whilst market factors involve the stage of development of financial institutions and markets in the economy, particularly in the form of the competitive relationships between different financial institutions.

Smithin (1984) categorizes financial innovations by distinguishing those that are *caused* by technological, institutional and regulatory factors, and from a slightly different perspective (commenting on the American situation) Tobin (1983a) also cites technological, institutional and regulatory factors as being prime determinants of financial innovation and change.

A slightly different approach is taken by Rybczynski (1986). Changes in financial markets are differentiated by Rybczynski according to whether they are changes in 'internal' or 'external' frontiers. The former refers to the elimination of traditional demarcation lines as to the activities carried out by financial institutions. These he outlines as the payments mechanism (preserve of the banks), the collection of savings (provided by non-bank financial imtermediaries) and the underwriting of securities and fund management (investment banking). The external frontiers he establishes as the number of clients for services, the geographical area over which services are available and the provision of new financial services both by incumbent institutions and new entrants.

The main factors affecting these 'internal' and 'external' frontiers, according to Rybczynski, include economic factors (under which technological innovation is subsumed) and the regulatory framework, the latter cited as the main cause of shifting the frontiers.

Perhaps the most comprehensive classification of the factors affecting financial innovation is that of Llewellyn (1985a, b). The analytical framework for considering the evolution of the financial system consists of six major elements (which are set down here verbatim):

1 the volume and structure of the flow of funds of *users* of the financial system which determine the demand for financial intermediation;
2 their portfolio preferences which determine the type of services and instruments demanded;
3 the 'efficiency' of different financial intermediation mechanisms which determines the terms that can be offered by institutions to both savers and borrowers;
4 institutions' own portfolio strategies and preferences;
5 the dynamics of financial innovation;
6 the portfolio and regulatory constraints on financial institutions.

Furthermore, all these factors can be influenced by general economic and monetary influences. Llewellyn maintains that it is the mix of the above factors that determines financial change and financial innovation in the financial system.

Whilst not wishing to prejudge the analysis of building society and bank financial innovation and change by outlining any one analytical framework, the above conjectures as to the determinants of financial change provide a useful initial structure within and around which to analyse the developments involving the above institutions.[2]

3.3 THE EFFECT OF THE CARTEL ON BUILDING SOCIETY OPERATIONS

The roots of the building society movement as self-help mutual institutions had greatly affected the manner in which the movement as a whole had conducted its affairs.[3]

The relatively simple role of building societies in the pre-1980 period is adequately summarized by the Building Societies Act 1962:[4]

> The purpose for which a society may be established under this Act is that of raising, by the subscription of members, a stock or fund for making advances to members out of the funds of the society upon security by way of mortgage of freehold or leasehold estate.
> (chapter 37, part 1, section 1(1))

The status of building societies as mutual institutions means that defining their precise business objectives is somewhat more problematic.[5] Nevertheless, there is general agreement that during the post-war period, at least until the early 1980s, a major business objective of many societies was the pursuit of balance sheet growth. In other words, it appears that many societies aimed explicitly to maximize, in the long term, the volume of their on-lending within the constraints of prudent fund management and their ability to attract deposits.

The existence of the recommended rate system[6] tended to encourage balance sheet growth as the major objective of building societies. The recommended rate system effectively formed an interest rate setting cartel within the sector. Whilst most cartels operate in order to keep prices up by reducing the supply of their product–service, it appears that the building society recommended rate system operated a policy of keeping prices down. The cartel tended to keep lending rates below the market clearing level such that there was a deliberate rationing of mortgage loan supply (for empirical results of the rationing of mortgage demand see Anderson and Hendry 1984). This pricing policy was adopted largely in connection with the perceived role of societies as providers of low-cost housing finance.

The status of building societies as mutual institutions has also been a factor however, in the operation of the recommended rate system. The building society industry viewed itself as a self-help movement for the benefit of its members. Each building society appeared to be a constituent part of the movement, all involved in the same goal. The building society cartel aimed to limit interest rate competition amongst societies partly to protect the smaller more inefficient societies. The cartel appeared to run counter to the traditional economic model of a price setting cartel. Most cartels function in order to distribute income from consumers to industry and to drive out smaller firms. The concentration of a large proportion of total building society assets in the hands of a few building societies (Table 3.1) seems to suggest ideal conditions for the larger societies to form a cartel to 'drive out' the smaller societies. The recommended rate system, however, had the effect of transferring income from depositors to borrowers (Llewellyn 1985a) and of protecting smaller inefficient building societies (Gough and Taylor 1979). Although it may have kept building society lending rates below a market clearing level, many home-buyers paid an effective rate above this level. As Boleat (1986: 177) points out, the availability of loans must also be considered as part of the cost of house purchase. If a borrower cannot obtain a full loan at the building society rate of interest because of mortgage rationing, the result may be that he or she obtains a small

Table 3.1 Degree of concentration in the building society industry, 1970–9

Year	*Largest 5*		*Largest 10*		*Largest 20*	
	Total assets (£m)	*Share of total (%)*	*Total assets (£m)*	*Share of total (%)*	*Total assets (£m)*	*Share of total (%)*
1970	5,416	50.1	6,955	64.3	8,369	77.4
1975	12,797	52.9	16,498	68.2	19,930	82.3
1976	15,144	53.7	19,401	68.8	23,344	82.8
1977	18,391	53.6	23,715	69.2	28,571	83.3
1978	21,489	54.4	27,901	70.6	33,220	84.0
1979	25,192	55.0	32,390	70.7	38,489	84.1

Source: *BSA Bulletin* October 1987

loan at that rate of interest and 'tops up' with a larger loan from 'other' financial intermediaries at a higher rate of interest.

The cartel had a marked effect on the mix of price and non-price competition in the market for retail funds. Whilst the cartel was in operation, changes in the price competitiveness of building societies' services could only be initiated through changes in the recommended rates and hence a deliberate change in interest rate differentials by a large majority of building societies relative to other retail financial institutions. This resulted in a lower level of price competition than might be expected under a free market system.

The effect of the cartel can be seen in Figure 3.1. The Building Societies Association advised the level of interest rates on shares and deposits (e.g. I_D) and mortgages (e.g. I_M). The Stow Report (Building Societies Association 1979) argued that the effect of operating with low interest rates that are at an uncompetitive level is that there are insufficient funds to meet mortgage demand. For example, if the mortgage interest rate is I_M, there is excess mortgage demand of $Q_1 - Q$ at an interest rate of I_D on shares and deposits, whereas the market clearing level for mortgages is I_{M_1}.

The cartel operated such that the supply of mortgages was largely determined by the supply of deposits. This meant that there was

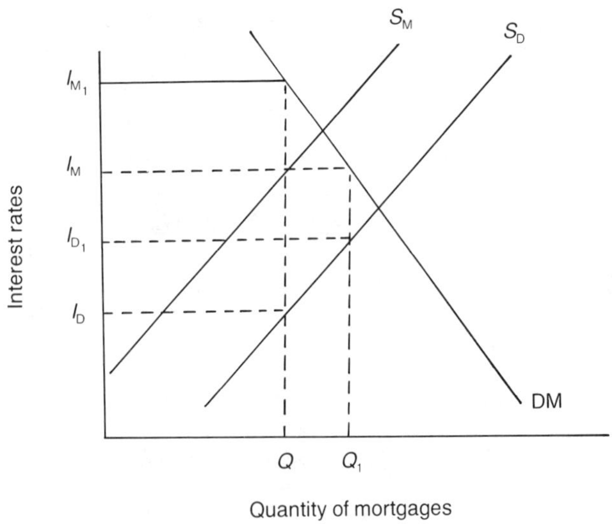

Figure 3.1 Effect of the cartel on mortgage supply: SM, supply of mortgages; SD, supply of shares and deposits

variable excess demand for mortgages over the interest rate cycle. Building societies' interest rates on deposits tended to lag behind any increase in the general level of market interest rates, resulting in a loss of competitiveness and a reduction in inflows to shareholders' accounts. With a fall in inflows of funds, the building societies, as they would not push up mortgage interest rates to market clearing levels and as running down liquid assets could not occur indefinitely, employed non-price rationing devices to limit mortgage supply. At such a time, excess demand for mortgages tended to be high.

Conversely, when the general level of market interest rates was falling, the building societies enjoyed greater competitiveness and as a result interest rates were sticky, deposit inflows were strong and mortgage rationing declined. Thus, when general interest rates were falling the excess demand for mortgages tended to be low. These effects can be seen in Figure 3.2. When general market interest rates as represented by the London Inter-bank Offer Rate (LIBOR) rose, excess demand for mortgages as measured by Meen (1985) tended also to rise, and when market rates fell, excess demand for mortgages fell. Overall, the cartel tended to operate in such a way as to stabilize and smooth out the fluctuations in building society interest rates compared with general market rates, and the role of price effects in

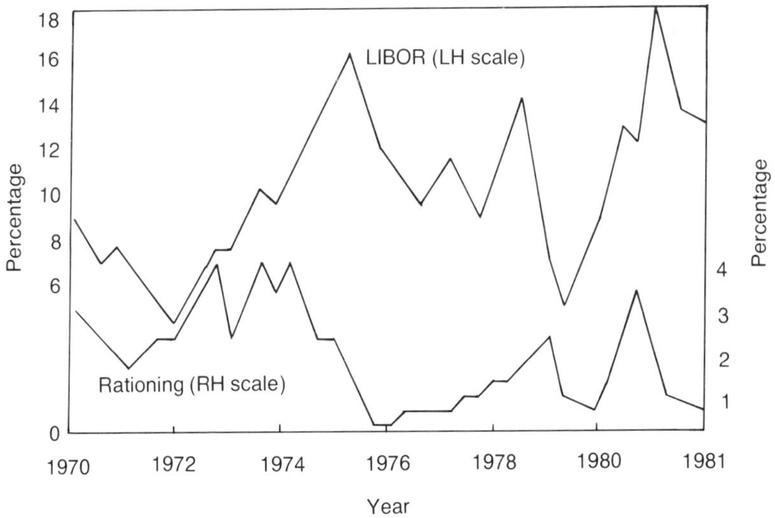

Figure 3.2 LIBOR and mortgage rationing

equilibrating the demand for and supply of mortgage funds was reduced. The Wilson Report (1980: 113) expressed the view that the cartel led to inefficiency and was a hindrance to competition, and argued that the abolition of the recommended rate system would lead to higher interest rates on shares and deposits (e.g. I_{D_1}) and the ability of societies to meet mortgage demand. It also noted that one likely impact of greater competition would be to encourage mergers by smaller societies transferring their engagements to larger ones and also mergers between larger societies (see Chapter 4 for more detail on this point).

The investigation of the National Board for Prices and Incomes (NBPI) (1966) into recommended rates argued that the cartel determined a spread between investment and lending rates that was greater than might be expected under a more competitive system. This tended to deter efficiency by allowing the less efficient societies to survive, whilst at the same time discouraging innovation by providing the more efficient societies with wide margins.

Furthermore, the cartel meant that in general, whilst price competition was stifled, competition for retail funds was largely effected through the rapid growth of advertising and the dramatic increase in the number of building society branches (Table 3.2).

There was also, however, scope for more efficient societies to circumvent the constraints of the recommended rate system. In particular, some small societies with low management expense ratios were able to offer premia above the recommended rate.

Table 3.2 Building society branching

Year	*Number of societies*	*Number of branches*	*Growth (%)*
1970	481	2,016	11.6
1971	467	2,261	12.2
1972	456	2,522	11.5
1973	447	2,808	11.3
1974	416	3,099	10.4
1975	382	3,375	8.9
1976	364	3,696	9.5
1977	339	4,130	11.7
1978	316	4,595	11.3
1979	287	5,147	12.0

Source: *BSA Bulletin* December 1985

It would thus appear that the building societies' ov strategies and objectives were a major determinant of the n which business was conducted. The building societies' objec tended to outweigh the portfolio preferences of the members of the building societies and their demand for financial intermediation services. With deposit rates kept artificially low, inflows of funds were lower than would have been expected under a competitive market clearing system, and hence this affected the ability of the societies to meet mortgage demand.

3.4 MONETARY CONTROL, COMPETITION AND INNOVATION

The mode of operation of monetary control was perhaps the single most important factor affecting the relative competitive positions and degree of innovation by banks and building societies over the period 1970–9.

Initially the broad approach of monetary control under competition and credit control (CCC) was towards free operation of the price mechanism and free competition in the financial system, with the level of credit to be determined by cost, and away from quantitative monetary control which tended to lead to disintermediation, distortion and a lower level of competition than would be expected under a less restrictive system.

As explained below, however, it was soon deemed necessary by the monetary authorities to impose more restrictive monetary control arrangements on the banking system, controls which effectively then hampered the ability of the banks to compete in the personal sector financial markets for the rest of the 1970s.

The clearing banks, similarly to the building societies, had operated an interest rate cartel since 1955, whereby the seven-day deposit rate was fixed at 2 per cent below the bank rate and lending rates were informally linked to the bank rate. There was therefore an effective limitation to the degree of interest rate competition between the retail banks and between the retail banks and other financial institutions.

Both the NBPI (1967) and the Monopolies Commission (MC) (1968) criticized the operation of the cartel, arguing that it led to an over-emphasis on non-price rather than price competition, in particular in the form of the rapid expansion of the branch network in the 1960s (Table 3.3). The call by the NBPI and the MC for the abolishment of the cartel was given impetus by changes in the broad

Table 3.3 Committee of London Clearing Banks[a] branch network, 1960–88

Year	*Number of branches*
1960	10,886
1962	11,250
1964	11,804
1966	11,972
1968	12,315
1970	12,137
1972	11,838
1974	11,807
1976	11,659
1978	11,107
1980	11,964

Source: Committee of London Clearing Banks; *Abstract of Banking Statistics* May 1988
Note: [a]Barclays, Lloyds, Williams and Glyn, Midland, National Westminster.

ethos and practical methods of monetary control introduced under the CCC regime (September 1971). The previous policy of direct controls, particularly in the form of quantitative ceilings on bank lending, were seen to be inefficient and a constraint on competition in the financial system. Moreover, the interest rate cartel acted as an encouragement to secondary banking institutions to develop at the expense of the clearing banks.

Also, quantitative controls led to large-scale disintermediation through the growth of the secondary money markets: flows of funds outside the banking system which avoided the quantitative monetary control ceilings and confused interpretation of monetary conditions (further analysis of aspects of disintermediation is carried out in Chapter 7).

Initially, it was thought that under CCC two main instruments would be sufficient: reserve requirements and special deposits. Banks were required to keep reserve ratios of 12½ per cent between eligible reserve assets and eligible liabilities.[7] Also, the banks were obliged to place special deposits with the Bank of England when called for (normally called as a percentage of eligible liabilities).[8] A call for special deposits was expected to have the effect of placing pressure on the banks' reserve ratios, forcing them to sell eligible assets. Goodhart (1981) maintains that the decision to impose a reserve ratio arose out of the monetary authorities' uncertainty as to the banks' reaction to operating in a less constrained, more competitive market environment. The reserve ratio could act as a pivot against which the monetary authorities could apply pressure through calling for special deposits.

The attitude of the banking industry in the competitive system was indeed dramatic. As would be expected, greater competition led to a reduction in the administratively maintained margin between deposit and lending rates and an increase in absolute deposit and lending rates. In effect, with quantitative lending controls abolished, the banks actively competed for deposits on price terms, pushing up the average rate paid on deposits at banks. The shift from non-price to price competition by the retail banks is partly evidenced by the rationalization of the branch network in the 1970s compared with the expansion of the 1960s (see Table 3.3). There was a tremendous 'reintermediation' effect after the abolition of quantitative controls in September 1971, with funds previously maintained outside the banking system being re-channelled through the banks. The growth of bank deposits and bank lending was particularly fast after the removal of the quantitative controls. As can be seen from Figure 3.3, bank lending to the non-bank private sector (NBPS) grew by over 50

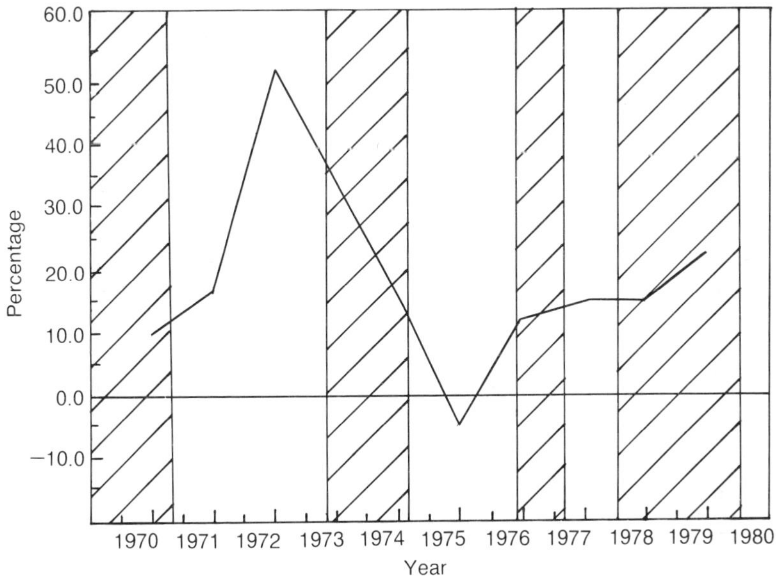

Figure 3.3 Bank lending to the NBPS (percentage change on previous year)

per cent between the end of 1971 and the end of 1973 (from £11.2 billion to £17.1 billion; see Table 3.4), and doubled over the two-year period from the end of 1971 to the end of 1973 (from £11.2 billion to £22.9 billion). The shading in the figures shows the periods of quantitative controls.

Deposits of the NBPs held with the banking system also showed fast growth after the removal of quantitative controls – by over 30 per cent in each of the years 1972 and 1973 (see Figure 3.4 and Table 3.5). As can be seen from Figure 3.5 and Table 3.6, bank lending to the personal sector showed particularly fast growth over the period 1971–2.

Interestingly, the banks also increased their lending for house purchase, thus competing directly with the building societies for market share, although bank lending for house purchase still accounted for only a small proportion of total mortgage lending. Net new loans for house purchase increased by over 280 per cent during 1972 (Figure 3.6), although the absolute figures were relatively small compared with those for building societies (Table 3.7).

The extent to which the banks were able to attract retail deposits is shown in Figure 3.7 and Table 3.8. Personal sector deposits held by the monetary sector grew by over 25 per cent in 1973, although it is clear that most of the growth in money balances in 1973 and 1974 was at the expense of the 'other' category rather than the building society sector.

Table 3.4 Bank lending to the non-bank private sector[a] (end period)

Year	*Amount (£billion)*	*Growth (%)*
1970	9.6	10.0
1971	11.2	16.7
1972	17.1	52.2
1973[b]	22.9	33.9
1974	26.7	16.3
1975	25.3	−5.0
1976	28.4	12.3
1977	31.9	15.0
1978	36.7	15.0
1979	45.3	23.0

Source: *Financial Statistics*, various issues, Table 6.6

Notes: [a]All banks in the UK plus National Giro, the discount market and the Bank of England Banking Department.

[b]The end of the first quarter of 1973 includes new contributors to the series.

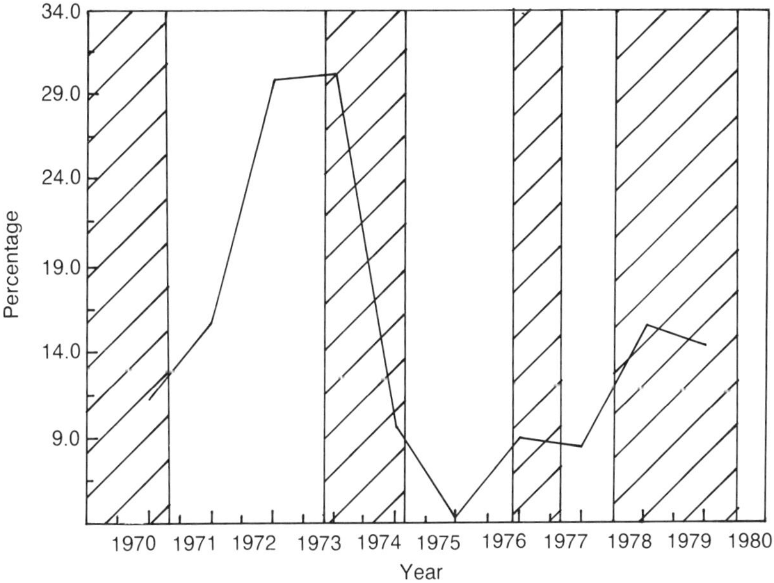

Figure 3.4 NBPS deposits with the banking sector (percentage change on previous year)

Table 3.5 Bank deposits held by the non-bank private sector (end period)

Year	*Amount (£billion)*	*Growth (%)*
1970	13.8	11.2
1971	16.0	15.4
1972	20.7	29.8
1973	26.9	29.9
1974	29.6	9.7
1975	30.8	4.1
1976	33.5	9.0
1977	36.3	8.3
1978	41.8	15.2
1979	47.7	14.1

Source: *Financial Statistics*, various issues, Table 6.6

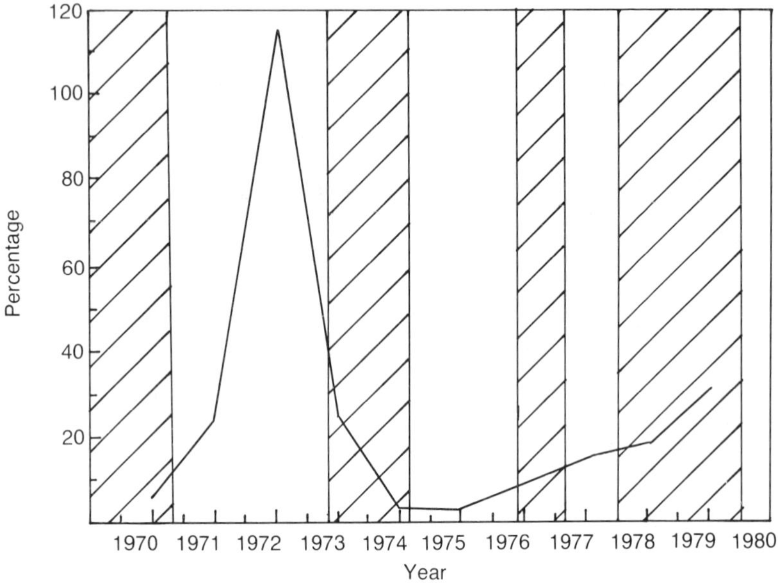

Figure 3.5 Bank lending to the personal sector (percentage change on previous year)

Table 3.6 Bank lending to the personal sector[a] (end year)[b]

Year	*Amount (£billion)*	*Growth (%)*
1970	2.0	6.1
1971	2.5	25.0
1972	5.4	116.0
1973[c]	6.7	24.1
1974	6.9	3.0
1975	7.1	3.0
1976	7.7	8.5
1977	8.9	15.6
1978	10.5	18.0
1979	13.8	31.4

Source: *Financial Statistics*, various issues, Table 10.3
Notes: [a]See Table 3.4, note a.
[b]Includes loans for house purchase.
[c]See Table 3.4, note b.

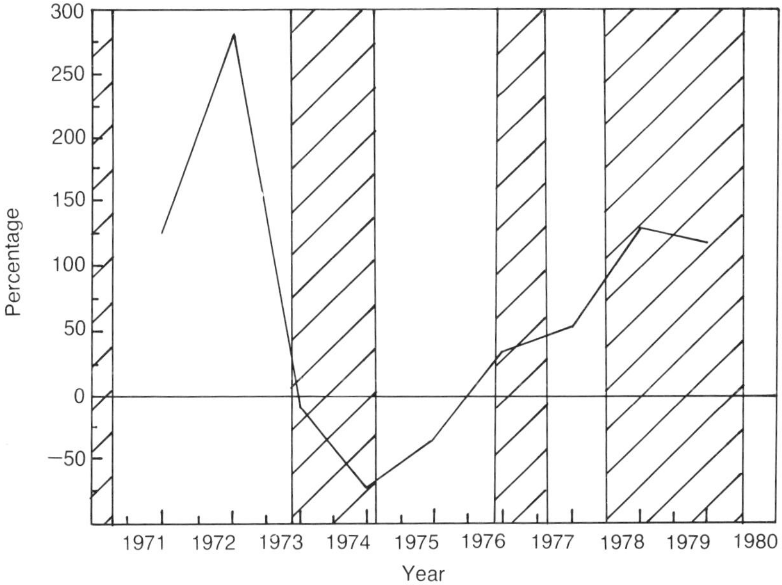

Figure 3.6 Net new bank loans for house purchase (percentage change on previous year)

Table 3.7 Net new loans for house purchase (end period)

Year	*Building societies (£m)*	*Banks (£m)*	*Other*[a] *(£m)*
1970	1,088	40	181
1971	1,600	90	227
1972	2,215	345	475
1973	1,999	310	584
1974	1,490	90	859
1975	2,768	60	902
1976	3,618	80	230
1977	4,100	121	141
1978	5,715	275	47
1979	5,271	597	593

Source: *Financial Statistics*, various issues, Table 9.4
Note: [a]Local authorities, insurance companies, pension funds, other public sector.

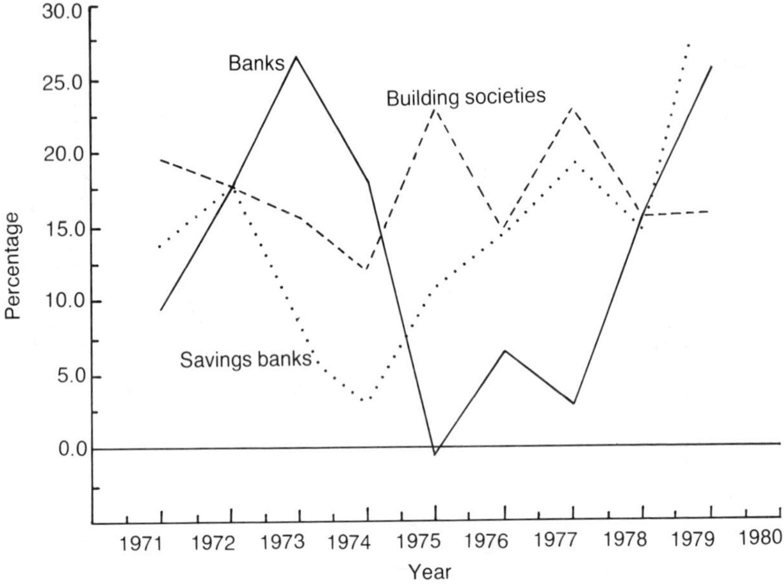

Figure 3.7 Personal sector holdings of selected liquid assets (percentage change, year end)

Table 3.8 Personal sector holdings of liquid assets (end period)

Year	*Deposits with monetary sector*			*Deposits with building societies*	*Deposits with savings banks*
	Sight (£m)	*Total (£m)*	*Time (£m)*	*(£m)*	*(£m)*
1970	n/a	10,062	n/a	10,059	1,772
1971	n/a	11,015	n/a	12,020	2,013
1972	n/a	12,901	n/a	14,159	2,367
1973	n/a	16,317	n/a	16,347	2,533
1974	n/a	19,290	n/a	18,316	2,595
1975	n/a	19,206	n/a	22,477	2,866
1976	n/a	20,461	n/a	25,778	3,281
1977	10,372		10,646	31,710	3,892
1978	12,010		12,164	36,609	4,463
1979	13,209		17,148	42,442	6,896

Source: *Financial Statistics*, various issues, Table 9.5

Given the rapid growth of lending and deposits, the chosen monetary control system appeared to be a failure:

> clearly the standard control mechanism had not worked; the first need was to discover why this was. An important factor, in my view, was that we had failed to foresee the likely course of bank behaviour in an unconstrained system (a failure which may be more easily understood since the British banks had not had the chance of operating in such a *milieu* in living memory). In particular, in an oligopolistic banking system, with a large element of 'endowment' profits accruing on assets held against zero-yielding current accounts, the extent to which the banks might take the expansionary and competitive bit between their teeth and gallop off was unexpected.
>
> (Goodhart 1981: 123)

Under CCC, there were two major transmission channels by which interest rates were expected to affect the money supply. First, an increase in interest rates on public sector debt was expected to result in funds being transferred by the NBPS out of bank deposits and into holdings of public sector debt. Increases in rates on public sector debt were not expected to be matched by increases in rates on bank deposits, as the latter were presumed to be stickier.

However, under the competitive aggressive system unleashed by CCC, the banks competed strongly for deposits (particularly wholesale) so that there was not such a decisive change in interest differentials between public sector debt and bank deposits when rates on the former were raised. Thus a policy of raising interest rates to induce a shift out of deposits into public sector debt would have no effect on interest differentials, and hence no effect on monetary expansion.

This placed much more emphasis on the second main channel, the effect of interest rates on the demand for bank borrowing, which appeared to be a relatively weak relationship (Bank of England 1984e: 44).

The main problem, as far as monetary control was concerned, was the liability management policies of the commercial banks. The advent of liability management meant that the retail banks were largely credit driven rather than deposit driven, i.e. the banks granted credit and then changed their liability portfolio in response to this increase in assets, rather than vice versa (Goodhart (1986a: 88). Traditionally, equilibrium between assets and liabilities was maintained by buying or selling marketable government securities; with the advent of a robust inter-bank market the retail banks increased the tendency to rely on raising wholesale deposits at short notice. Such 'liability side liquidity' allowed the retail banks to fulfil the demand for credit.

To counteract the banks' aggressive bidding for funds through liability management, the supplementary special deposits (SSDs)[9] scheme was introduced, colloquially known as the 'corset'. The SSDs scheme represented an attempt by the monetary authorities to inhibit the banking sector from utilizing the practice of liability management in the face of a strong demand for credit. Under the scheme, non-interest-bearing SSDs had to be placed at the Bank of England if a bank's interest-bearing eligible liabilities (IBELs) grew faster than the specified penalty-free rate, which was a percentage figure of the base level of IBELs. The periods during which the corset applied are shown in Table 3.9.

The underlying motive of the corset was to force the banks into a decision-making process limited to the choice of accepting lower profits on any additional lending undertaken or widening their margins. The incentive to widen margins was provided by the fact that the opportunity cost of placing non-interest-bearing SSDs with the bank was greater than the cost of acquiring extra reserve assets (Bank of England 1982b).

Alongside the corset, the Bank of England also imposed qualitative lending guidelines on the banking system. The Bank of England consumer credit notice of 17 December 1973 requested the banks to exercise restraint on lending to the personal sector and to property companies. The request was reaffirmed in subsequent credit control notices, such that the banking sector was effectively constrained in its lending policies to the personal sector throughout the 1974–9 period.[10] This had a major effect on the banks' ability to compete in the personal sector retail financial markets. Furthermore, the retail banks were also requested to restrict the interest rate paid on deposits of less than £10,000 to 9½ per cent between September 1973 and February 1975. Thus, for a time, the retail banks were constrained in their ability to compete with the building societies for personal sector deposits.

Largely as a result of the SSDs scheme and the qualitative lending guidelines that inhibited the banks' potential for competition, the building society movement faced a favourable market environment over the majority of the period 1974–9. Bank lending to the NBPS dropped dramatically during the first phase of the SSDs scheme (see Figure 3.3) and remained stable over the second and third phases.

Total bank lending to persons and lending solely for house purchase were also curtailed, particularly in 1973 and 1974 (Figures 3.5 and 3.6). In addition the retail banks were unable to compete effectively for retail deposits during the operation of the corset and the enforced lending guidelines, and the rate of growth of bank balances held by the personal sector declined rapidly from 1973 to 1977.

The periodic imposition of direct monetary controls between December 1973 and June 1980, aimed at reducing the banks' deposit bases, thus restricted a major element of the potential competition for retail funds, strengthening the competitive position of the building societies. Table 3.10 shows clearly the rapid growth in personal sector holdings of money as a proportion of gross financial wealth over 1971–4, and the decline after 1974 as a result of stringent portfolio controls on the banks.

Leigh-Pemberton, then the Chairman of the National Westminster Bank, put forward the objections of the banking community to the asymmetry of monetary control by arguing that non-bank financial institutions' liabilities were very close substitutes for bank deposits but fell outside the scope of the instruments in use. These institutions, he argued, could thus gain market share at the expense of the banks. According to Leigh-Pemberton, the changing nature of building society deposits necessitated placing building societies under the same controls as were placed on the banks (both in terms of fairness to banks and in terms of efficiency of monetary control) (1979: 9).

It would be expected, according to traditional economic theory, that the building societies would have taken advantage of the monetary controls on the retail banks. Gurley and Shaw (1955: 532) pointed out the opportunities for non-bank financial institutions to compete more actively against the banks when the latter were constrained.

Building societies represented a special case, however, in terms of their mutuality and the existence of the cartel. The building societies did not actively compete with one another on price terms, and hence probably did not attract as many deposits from the banking system as they might have done if they were price competitive.

The growth of building societies over the period 1974–7 was largely at the expense of the retail banks, whilst the corset was in operation (Table 3.11). The evidence appears to indicate that the corset has a major effect on the ability of the banking sector to compete with the building societies. The banks lost market share to societies particularly over the period 1974–7, a time of heavy corset restrictions.

Table 3.9 The supplementary special deposits scheme

1 The scheme applied in principle to all 'listed' banks and deposit-taking finance houses; but small institutions and (because of the special circumstances there) institutions in Northern Ireland were exempt.
2 Institutions were required to lodge non-interest-bearing deposits with the Bank of England if their IBELs grew faster than a specified rate. The rate of deposit was progressive from 5 per cent to 50 per cent as the amount of excess growth increased.
3 The liability to pay SSDs was calculated monthly, on a moving three-month average of IBELs.
4 The precise details which applied to each activation of the scheme are shown below.

Scheme announced	*Base period*[a]	*Allowable growth*	*Rate of deposit*	*Exemption*[b]	*Scheme terminated*
17 Dec. 1973	Oct.–Dec. 1973	8% over first six months; $1\frac{1}{2}$% per month thereafter	Until Nov. 1974: 5% in respect of excess of up to 1% 25% in respect of excess of 1%–3% 50% in respect of excess of over 3%	£3 million	28 Feb. 1975
			From Nov. 1974: 5% in respect of excess of up to 3% 25% in respect of excess of 3%–5% 50% in respect of excess of over 5%	£5 million	

18 Nov. 1976	Aug.–Oct. 1976	3% over first six months; 1/2% per month thereafter	As above	£5 million	11 Aug. 1977
8 Jun. 1978	Nov. 1977–Apr. 1978	4% over period to Aug.–Oct. 1978; 1% per month thereafter	As above	£10 million	18 Jun. 1980[c]

Notes: [a]The base level was the average level of IBELs over the period shown.
[b]The scheme did not apply to institutions with IBELs below the amount shown.
[c]The announcement of the termination of the scheme was made on 26 March; final deposits were repaid in August.

Table 3.10 Personal sector holdings of gross financial wealth by asset type as a percentage of the total (end period)

Year	*Money*[a] (%)	*Building society shares and deposits* (%)	*National Savings* (%)	*Others*[b] (%)
1970	13.7	10.8	7.1	70.4
1971	12.5	10.7	6.3	70.6
1972	12.8	11.2	5.9	70.1
1973	16.5	13.5	6.3	63.6
1974	21.7	16.9	7.0	54.4
1975	17.2	16.0	5.7	61.1
1976	17.1	16.8	5.5	60.6
1977	14.4	16.7	5.1	63.7
1978	15.2	17.5	5.4	61.9
1979	16.0	17.6	4.5	61.9

Source: *Financial Statistics*, various issues, Table 14.4
Notes: [a]Notes and coin plus sterling and foreign currency sight and time deposits at UK banks.
[b]Local authority temporary loans, savings bank deposits, UK stocks and shares, public sector long-term debt, trade credit, equity in insurance and pension funds, accrual of taxes and interest and other overseas and domestic assets.

Table 3.11 Deposits of the personal sector: changes in market share (end period)

Year	*Banks* (%)	*Building societies* (%)(%)	*National Savings*
1963–72	+0.3	+16.2	−16.3
1972–4	+5.5	+0.2	−5.1
1974–7	−8.5	+9.5	−0.7
1977–9	+0.4	−0.4	–
1963–79	−2.3	+25.5	−22.1

Source: Vittas and Frazer 1980

Building societies thus faced little effective competition for retail funds, reflected in their product variety and product range (Lewis 1987) (Table 3.12). Throughout the 1970s the building societies' funds were dominated by the ordinary account. Ordinary shares represented over 87 per cent of total savings at building societies in

Table 3.12 Distribution of savings accounts at building societies, 1974–9

End year	*Ordinary accounts (%)*	*Term accounts (%)*	*Regular savings + SAYE (%)*	*Other (%)*
1974	87.2	5.6	3.8	3.5
1975	85.7	7.3	3.6	3.4
1976	84.6	8.5	3.6	3.3
1977	83.2	9.4	3.4	3.9
1978	83.1	9.9	3.5	3.5
1979	80.5	13.0	3.4	3.0

Source: Boleat 1986: 21

1974, falling slightly to 80.5 per cent by 1979 as a result of the limited growth in term shares.

Some commentators would argue that a major factor affecting the competitive environment was the lack of competitive neutrality (Llewellyn 1986a, b, 1987b). In particular, the Committee of London Clearing Banks complained that building societies have enjoyed various unfair artificial competitive advantages (Committee of London Clearing Banks 1977: 189).

In relation to the supply of funds to building societies, it has often been argued that the existence of the composite rate tax system[11] gave them a competitive advantage relative to the retail banks (until the extension of that system to the retail banks in April 1985). The composite rate system works so that, for example, with an ordinary share rate of 9.75 per cent, a basic tax rate of 30 per cent and a composite rate of 25.25 per cent, the gross effective yield to tax-paying investors is 13.93 per cent, but the gross cost to societies of their funds is only 13 per cent. Thus the composite rate system allowed building societies to maintain a lower mortgage rate than would be necessary under tax procedures applied to the banking system at the time (Building Societies Association 1972). The banks complained that this represented a fiscal advantage in that it acted as an inducement to those paying income tax to deposit with building societies rather than the retail banks. In the example above, to an investor liable to the basic rate of tax the gross equivalent yield is 13.93 per cent, whilst for an investor not liable to tax the gross equivalent yield is the same as the net yield, 9.75 per cent. According to the Committee of London Clearing Banks, building societies benefited to the extent that tax-paying investors are more sensitive to differentials in interest rates between institutions than are non-taxpayers. Thus the portfolio preferences of the users of the financial system were being affected by the non-neutral taxation considerations between building societies and banks. Boleat (1986) points out, however, that the relative competitive advantage is dependent on the elasticities of demand for building society shares and deposits for basic rate taxpayers and those not liable to tax. He disputes the point that those liable to the basic rate of tax are more interest sensitive than those not liable to tax. Also, it should be noted that, whilst the composite rate may mean that societies gain a competitive advantage by attracting money from taxpayers, at the same time they may suffer a disadvantage in attracting money from non-taxpayers.

It has also been argued that building societies have received favourable treatment in respect of their corporation tax liability (formerly it was set at a rate of 40 per cent, as opposed to the standard 52 per cent rate applied to the clearing banks) and the exemption from taxation of the capital gains on their gilt-edged securities transactions (provided they have been held for more than twelve months). It should be noted, however, that because of leasing arrangements banks rarely paid the full 52 per cent corporation tax; in fact more commonly banks pay effective tax rates of about 20 per cent.

The main factors affecting the activities of the building societies and banks can be seen in terms of a regulatory matrix (Table 3.13, after Llewellyn 1987b) ('regulatory' here is used to mean any form of regulation, official or unofficial, that in some way constrains the operations of building societies and banks). The functions or business areas which the banks could undertake were largely prohibited by the monetary controls examined earlier, and they were unable to compete actively in the personal sector savings market or the mortgage market. Their pricing policies were also affected to the extent that they were effectively restrained from actively competing for deposits. In addition, moral suasion was at times used to affect the lending and pricing policies of the banks.

The building societies, by contrast, were not included in the portfolio monetary controls and hence were unrestrained in this manner in terms of their pricing activities. However, the building societies, as emphasized earlier, influenced their own pricing by operating the self-imposed interest rate setting cartel, so that they too faced pricing constraints, but as a result of unofficial regulation. On their functional side, the building societies were not constrained by portfolio controls as the banks were, but were more strictly regulated

Table 3.13 Regulatory matrix for banks and building societies, 1974–80

	Geographical	*Functional*	*Ownership*	*Pricing*	*Standards*	*Business operations*
Portfolio controls		Y_1		Y_2		
Moral suasion		Y_3		Y_4		
Legal		X_1Y_5	X_2Y_6			
Self-imposed				X_3		
Self-regulation					X_4Y_7	X_5Y_8
No regulation	XY					

Notes: X, building societies; Y, banks; Y_1, monetary controls affecting the banks' ability to compete in the mortgage market; Y_2, monetary controls affecting the banks' ability to compete on price terms for deposits; Y_3, moral suasion by the Bank of England on the sectors to which the retail banks should lend; Y_4, moral suasion by the Bank of England on maximum deposit interest rates of the retail banks; Y_5, legal restrictions on permitted activities of banks; Y_6, legal restrictions on banks' ownership of insurance companies; Y_7 and Y_8, self-regulation by the Bank of England upon capital and liquidity requirements and standards; X_1, legal restrictions on permitted activities of building societies; X_2, legal restrictions on ownership of building societies and building societies' ownership of other financial institutions; X_3, self-imposed cartel; X_4 and X_5, self-regulation by the Building Societies Commission on liquidity, reserves and standards.

in terms of the areas of business allowed under the Building Societies Act 1962.

3.5 CONCLUSION

The mix of institutional features and asymmetric monetary control were important determinants of the *modus operandi* of building societies and banks pre-1980, and hence major factors in both the nature of competition between these financial intermediaries and the degree of financial innovation.

The recommended rate system operated by the building societies ran counter to the traditional economic model of a cartel. Whilst most cartels aim to raise prices, the building societies' cartel maintained deposit and mortgage interest rates below market clearing levels. It has been shown in Section 3.3 that the existence of the cartel had a marked effect on the form of competition for retail personal sector financial business and subsequently on the level of innovation. As a change in interest rates was only carried out en masse, price competition was effectively stifled. The mix of competition in terms of price versus non-price aspects was thus aimed almost exclusively at non-price initiatives. The fast growth of building society branches was a major non-price competitive element, as was the degree of advertising.

The cartel tended to encourage the building society industry to adopt balance sheet growth as its main objective. The existence of fixed wide margins led to large surpluses for the more efficient societies, which tended to provide further impetus to non-price forms of competition and stifle any need for product innovation on the part of building societies.

The cartel smoothed and stabilized building societies' interest rates compared with general market rates, causing a high level of excess mortgage demand when interest rates were rising, and lower excess mortgage demand when interest rates were falling. The price effects of the abolition of the cartel on the effectiveness of monetary control are examined in detail in Chapter 7.

A major factor in the degree of competition and innovation in the personal sector retail financial market lay in the degree of asymmetry of monetary control with regard to the retail banks. The effect of monetary control, in particular the SSDs scheme, was to inhibit the retail banks from entering the mortgage market on any significant scale or from effectively competing for personal sector deposits. This lack of competitive neutrality had a significant effect on the mortgage market and the way in which building societies operated. The cartel could only be operational if the building societies faced no effective competition from other financial institutions. With no competition from the banks the building societies were able to maintain deposit and mortgage rates below market clearing levels and operate a policy of rationing mortgage supply. Lack of financial innovation reflected in the simple and homogeneous nature of building society and bank deposit accounts was determined by the mutuality ethos, the cartel, restrictive monetary controls placed on the banks and the subsequent low level of competition.

4 Re-regulation, competition and innovation by building societies and banks, 1980–90

4.1 INTRODUCTION

One of the main factors affecting the degree of competition and innovation by the building societies and retail banks in the 1970s has been isolated as regulatory constraint. Monetary controls affecting the banking sector and creating a regulatory asymmetry tended to limit competition for personal sector retail financial business for most of the 1970s. The building societies' recommended rate system could only really exist in such an environment characterized by ineffective competition. Regulatory constraint, lack of competition and the cartel were the major determinants of the low level of innovation during this period. To the extent that building societies did not come under the aegis of monetary control, they enjoyed a major competitive advantage over the banks.

Given the above constraints on competition and innovation, an obvious starting point for an analysis of the main catalysts of financial change and innovation would be to concentrate on structural change involving the above factors – regulation, competition and the cartel. The immediate effect of re-regulation in terms of changes in the *modus operandi* of monetary controls upon the competitive aspect of the personal sector retail financial services market is assessed in Section 4.2, and the importance of regulatory-induced financial change is analysed. The effects of changing monetary controls upon the operations of the retail banks are detailed, including an analysis of the effects upon the market for mortgage loans. It is of some importance to the monetary authorities if changes in monetary control procedures *stimulate* financial innovations which may subsequently affect the very same controls.

The implications of a change in market structure and competition upon the operation of the building societies' recommended rate system is considered in Section 4.3. The effects of a competitive financial market on the degree of financial innovation are investigated in terms of both economic theory and events that occurred in practice. The particular innovations introduced by building societies and banks are analysed, as is the changing mix of price and non-price competition that has occurred over time.

Special emphasis is placed on the change in interest rate strategy adopted by the building societies. The average mortgage rate and deposit rates in the more competitive dynamic system are compared with average interest rates in the 1970s for evidence of policy change. The fluidity of interest rate movements is analysed to investigate whether or not building society interest rate changes became less 'sticky' as economic theory would tend to suggest. An analysis is also made of the effect of competition on building society and bank margins. Given that one of the major policy instruments of monetary control is the manipulation of interest rates (see Chapter 7), it is of some importance to establish whether there has been a change in interest rate policy by the financial institutions concerned.

Section 4.4 examines the relative market shares of building societies and banks, and the changing competitive advantage over time, and assesses the impact of regulatory convergence on the activities of these financial intermediaries. An analysis is made of the degree to which building societies and banks have become less differentiated in their activities as a result of regulatory change (particularly as a result of new powers given to building societies under the Building Societies Act 1986) and increased competition and innovation. The extent to which building societies and banks became more homogeneous may be of some importance to the operation of monetary control (this point is raised in more detail in Chapter 5).

4.2 RE-REGULATION AND COMPETITION IN THE PERSONAL SECTOR RETAIL FINANCIAL MARKET

Since the beginning of the 1980s the building societies sector has undergone considerable evolution, in terms of both the innovative financial services offered and the apparently more commercial orientation of business objectives (Llewellyn 1985a: 29).[1]

It is possible to isolate the major factors that have brought this about: regulatory change, competition and technology appear to have been the main influences affecting the personal sector retail financial market.[2] An analysis of the determinants of financial change by building societies and banks is obviously of some importance, particularly if it is found that new modes of monetary control result in innovation by financial intermediaries.

Changes in the UK monetary control framework, introduced at the beginning of the 1980s, appear to have been the major catalyst in stimulating increasingly competitive conditions within the retail financial sector. Many of the subsequent innovations by building societies and banks appear to have resulted indirectly from this change in monetary control through the increased level of competition. Recently, Hester (1981), commenting on the US financial system, has pointed to the possible link between regulation and institutional change, and the fact that changes in monetary policy may lead to financial innovations.

Indeed, the effects of competition and credit control (CCC) upon the activities of the retail banks (isolated in Chapter 3) appear to be a classic example of this form of regulatory-induced innovation. Monetary controls, placed on the retail banks in the 1970s, effectively precluded them from entering the personal sector financial market on any significant scale. This meant that the building societies sector faced relatively little competition from the retail banks. Re-regulation via a change in the system of monetary control had a particularly immediate effect on the competitive aspect of the mortgage market. Whilst the corset was in operation, the banks were largely inhibited from competing for mortgage business. The direct monetary controls acted as an artificial constraint on the banks' ability to expand into this area, by creating a restrictive environment in which they could operate. The abolition of exchange controls in October 1979 heralded the demise of the corset with the possibility that banks could bypass the corset controls by disintermediation through the Euro sterling market.

Official recognition of the inefficiencies in *direct* monetary controls (outlined in detail in Chapter 8 – disintermediation, hard arbitrage, competitive non-neutrality) came with a series of publications: the Green Paper on *Monetary Control* (1980), 'Background note on methods of monetary control' (Bank of England 1980a), 'Monetary control – provisions' (Bank of England 1981c) and 'Monetary control – next steps' (Bank of England 1981d). The main details of the changes in monetary control and their effectiveness are assessed in Chapter 8. In essence, short-term interest rates were to be maintained within an (unpublished) band and would be the sole instrument of monetary control. The abolishment of the corset and subsequent new arrangements for the operation of monetary control meant that banks and building societies came under the same instrument of control – interest rates (Congdon 1979), and so the arguments put forward by Leigh-Pemberton (see Chapter 3) and Turnbull (1979) concerning the asymmetry of monetary control could no longer be applied. Once interest rates were used to restrain monetary growth, there was ultimately no competitive disadvantage to the banking system, as recognized by Rose (1978: 7).

Removal of the corset constraint in 1980 correspondingly removed the artificially created environment. The changed conditions meant that retail banks could increase their lending for house purchase if they so wished. The initial competition between banks and building societies was thus on the assets side of the balance sheet, stimulated by a change in monetary control.

There was a substantial readjustment on the part of the retail banks to rectify a loan portfolio imbalance once the inhibiting controls were removed. In effect, the banks merely adjusted their portfolios to a level that they would have preferred had controls not been implemented.[3] It thus partly represented a once-and-for-all portfolio adjustment. With the building societies offering mortgage rates below the market clearing level, there had previously existed a mortgage queue, with demand outstripping supply, and hence a certain amount of non-price rationing by building societies. The banks were also able to concentrate on large mortgages (over £30,000) as a result of the building societies' reluctance to lend at the higher end of the market.

Under such circumstances, there was scope for profitable lending by the retail banks (Figure 4.1). Once direct controls were removed, the prime reason for the growth of bank lending for house purchase was that of profitability. Another facet of the banks' rationale for entering the mortgage market can be explained in terms of their overall strategy, which was aimed at the ultimate objective of offering a complete package of financial services to the personal sector. Mortgage lending was thus used as a device for introducing other business such as insurance, home improvement loans and unsecured lending, both to extend their customer base and to offer new services to existing customers. The underlying factor, however, was that of profit. Mortgage lending and total lending to the personal sector tended to be a growth area for the retail banks, in view of the relatively slower growth in the demand for bank loans by the companies and overseas sectors (Bank of England 1988b: 81).

The Bank of England recognized the importance of regulatory changes which might affect the degree of competition and financial innovation in financial markets (Bank of England 1986d: 529).

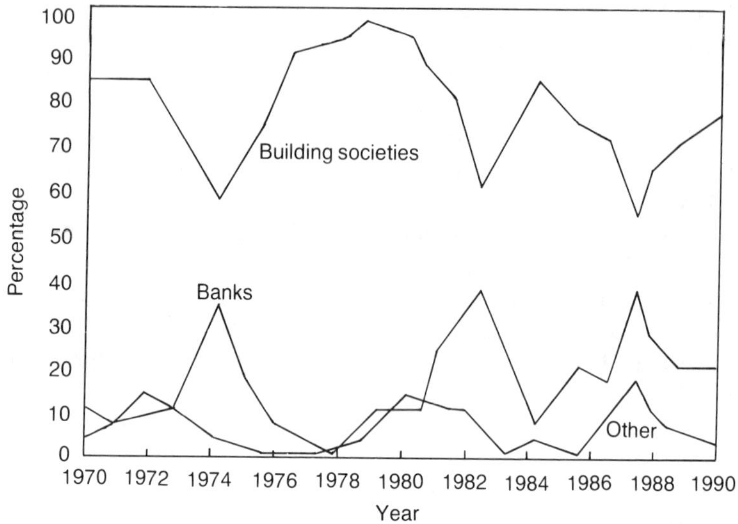

Figure 4.1 Market share of net mortgage advances

Although an increase in bank intermediation was expected after the removal of controls in 1980, it appears that the Bank of England was surprised at the subsequent market effects, in that the initial stock adjustment was just the tip of the competitive iceberg (Bank of England 1986b: 501).

The entry of the retail banks into the mortgage market precipitated an increased level of competition for personal sector funds, and led to an increase in the attractiveness of personal liquid assets compared with other assets. It appears that there was a change in the retail banks' funding strategy in terms of the retail–wholesale mix. The banks placed greater emphasis on raising funds from the retail market, resulting in a slowdown in the earlier 1970s trend of increasing wholesale funds. This change in funding mix is in large part a result of the change in competition between banks and building societies in the 1980s (Llewellyn and Drake 1987).

Traditionally banks did not perceive the building societies as being major competitors because they were not in competition for lending and because funds attracted by building societies are maintained within the banking system (only the ownership of deposits changes, the total volume of deposits at banks remaining unchanged). However, once banks and building societies were competing for mortgage and other business, it became logical to compete for deposits. Funds held or attracted by the retail banks at the expense of building societies will tend to reduce the societies' ability to lend for mortgage purposes. Moreover, it became advantageous to attract deposit customers as this allowed customer relationships to develop and the customer base to grow, with substantial opportunities for increasing fee income and cross-selling financial services.

The entry of the retail banks into the mortgage market expedited the breakdown of the building societies' cartel. Several smaller societies had already been offering interest rate premia above the cartel rate. The Abbey National Building Society, then the largest in the UK, formally announced its withdrawal from the cartel in 1983. For a short period of time (October 1983 to November 1984), the Building Societies Association issued 'advised' rather than 'recommended' rates of interest, although this also was later abandoned in November 1984.[4] A further significant factor in forcing the breakdown of the cartel was the increasing reliance placed by the government on funding the public sector borrowing requirement (PSBR) through National Savings. Attractive interest rates were offered on National Savings investment accounts, representing a further increase in competition for building societies.

Of course, the government has a competitive advantage over the banks and building societies in the collection of funds through National Savings. It has no liquidity or capital adequacy constraints, and can choose the returns on National Savings necessary to attract the desired inflow of funds. Furthermore, the government can place favourable tax arrangements on National Savings in order to raise funds.

The importance of regulatory change can be seen from the regulatory matrix for banks and building societies for post-1980 (Table 4.1). In contrast with the earlier regulatory matrix, it is obvious that portfolio controls and moral suasion now constrain neither banks nor building societies. The retail banks' functional areas are no longer limited by monetary controls as they were earlier, and they have been able to enter the mortgage market. Similarly, they can now compete on price terms with the abolition of the corset and the abrogation of moral suasion on lending to the personal sector.

Although the building societies were granted substantial new powers in terms of the functional areas of business they are empowered to carry out, they were nevertheless still legally hindered by the Building Societies Act 1986, as outlined earlier. It may well prove to be the case that the removal of the remaining legal constraints on building societies' functional activities will be the main catalyst for

Table 4.1 Regulatory matrix for banks and building societies, 1980–90

	Geographical	*Functional*	*Ownership*	*Pricing*	*Standards*	*Business operations*
Portfolio controls						
Moral suasion						
Legal		X	X			
Self-imposed						
Self-regulation					XY	XY
External agency		Y			XY	XY
No regulation	XY		Y	XY		

Note: X, building societies; Y, banks.

financial innovation and change in the future. It is also noticeable that there are no official or unofficial regulations affecting the pricing policies of the building societies or the banks, the former having abandoned their self-imposed constraint of the cartel in 1983.

Finally, it is of interest that both building societies and banks are regulated to a far greater degree than before by external agencies in the form of the Securities and Investments Board (SIB) and the various Self-Regulatory Organizations (SROs) established under the Financial Services Act 1987.

4.3 FINANCIAL INNOVATION BY BUILDING SOCIETIES AND RETAIL BANKS

According to economic theory, in a competitive market system with no cartel restrictions, the entry of a large new competitor will have significant effects upon both the price and output of the incumbent's product/service.

One major effect of banks competing for retail deposits has been a change in the intensity and mix of price and non-price competition. Prior to 1980, building societies competed against each other almost exclusively on non-price terms, in particular through the extension of the branch network rather than through innovating their share and deposit accounts. The entry of the retail banks into the mortgage market and the more aggressive competition for retail deposits entailed a shift towards more explicit price competition and innovation in the types of account being offered by both banks and building societies. Indeed, the rapid development of the branch network in the 1970s slowed considerably in the 1980s as building societies concentrated more on innovative accounts and interest rate competition. The rather simple homogeneous nature of building society ordinary shares, which dominated building societies' funding in the 1970s, declined dramatically in the 1980s.

This provides an interesting extension to Kane's 'regulatory dialectic' which argues that regulation causes regulatory avoidance and hence a new cycle of regulation, and so on (1981: 355). Indeed, Kane argues that many firms judge the success of innovations according to their ability to circumvent regulations (1981: 358).

An example of this regulation–innovation cycle in the UK was the 'bill leak' outlined in Chapter 3: the growth of banks' bills held outside the banking system in order to facilitate off-balance-sheet lending and hence avoid the corset restrictions. It appears, however, that the events after the release of the banks from the corset were qualitatively different from the cycle described by Kane. In 1980, re-regulation led to innovation in that it engendered an increase in competition. Re-regulation of banks, in the form of the ending of the corset and subsequent competition in the mortgage market, led to innovation by those institutions *not* previously regulated (the building societies) *and* by those previously regulated (the retail banks). Rather than restrictive controls leading to regulatory avoidance through financial innovation, the *liberalization* of controls through re-regulation contributed to competitive financial innovations.

Figure 4.2 gives some indication of the degree of innovation by building societies[5]. It indicates the relative movements in the distribution of balances held at building societies.

Pre-1980, most societies limited the investment choices available to members. Ordinary shares accounted for 87.2 per cent of shares and deposits at year-end 1974, falling slightly to 79 per cent in 1980. The period 1980–6 saw the greatest fall in ordinary accounts in terms of the share of retail deposits held at building societies (63 per cent in 1981 as opposed to 16.5 per cent in 1986 – see Figure 4.3).

Ordinary share accounts were superseded in terms of net inflow by *term shares*. First introduced in 1973, these accounts offered a guaranteed differential over ordinary share rates in return for investing for a fixed time period. Pre-1980 term shares tended to be relatively restrictive in that they were less liquid than both existing building society share accounts and bank seven-day deposits. Money could not be withdrawn from term shares before the original term to maturity had expired, often a period of between two and five years. In terms of balances held at building societies, term shares grew relatively slowly from 5.6 per cent in 1974 to 9.9 per cent in 1978. During the 1980s many of these restrictions were considerably reduced in severity, in particular by the introduction of term shares with withdrawal facilities (but often with an interest penalty). Subsequently, there was a greater rate of growth of term shares as a proportion of total balances, from less than 10 per cent in 1978 to 23.4 per cent in 1982.

The relative decline in the growth of term shares after 1983 is largely a result of a new innovation, the *high interest account*. From 1983 onwards there was an outflow of deposits from all types of accounts except high interest accounts. These were first offered in 1980, paying premia over ordinary shares with varying withdrawal periods (usually seven days) and minimum deposits (sometimes only £500). These accounts gradually became increasingly flexible, especially in terms of accessibility, many societies offering immediate withdrawal facilities. There was little difference between many high interest accounts and ordinary accounts except in terms of the former's higher return. Less than 10 per cent of balances were held in high interest accounts in 1981, growing swiftly to over 70 per cent by the end of 1987.

The growth of high interest accounts at building societies increased the average rate for all building society deposits above the interest rate on ordinary shares (Figure 4.4). A premium of approximately 2 per cent above the ordinary share rate was paid on high interest accounts. In many cases, the withdrawal terms and minimum balance requirements to qualify for premium rates were scarcely more onerous than the restrictions on ordinary share accounts. Moreover, it appears that building society accounts were being treated more like transactions accounts, according to Figure 4.5 which shows the number of accounts and transactions at a representative building society, Bristol & West, typical of most large building societies.

Technology played a major part in building societies' financial intermediation activities. The invention of the automatic teller machine (ATM) could be argued to be an advantage to the building society industry (Bank of England 1983b: 372–3).[6]

The advent of new technologies provided a spur to the level of competition in the retail financial market, and technological innovation had a major effect on the nature and degree of competition in the personal sector financial markets. Technology enhances the ability of institutions to offer new financial services through lowering the cost of providing such services, and also promotes efficiency in existing financial services. Prohibitive barriers to entry in the form of high costs tend to be eroded by technology – hence the increased attractiveness to building societies of joining the money payments system as a result of cost reductions (Revell and Barnes 1984; Revell 1986).[7] Some building societies took their financial innovation much further and announced the introduction of *interest-bearing cheque accounts*. Such a strategy confirmed the aggressive nature of building societies' operations and further eroded the distinction between building societies and banks.

The effect of the building societies offering cheque books and being part of the money transmission system may have considerable effects. In particular, if the building societies' market share of the money payments system increases, as seems likely, the greater will be the redepository ratio of the building societies. Quite simply, a greater proportion of funds paid out of building society accounts will tend to

(a)

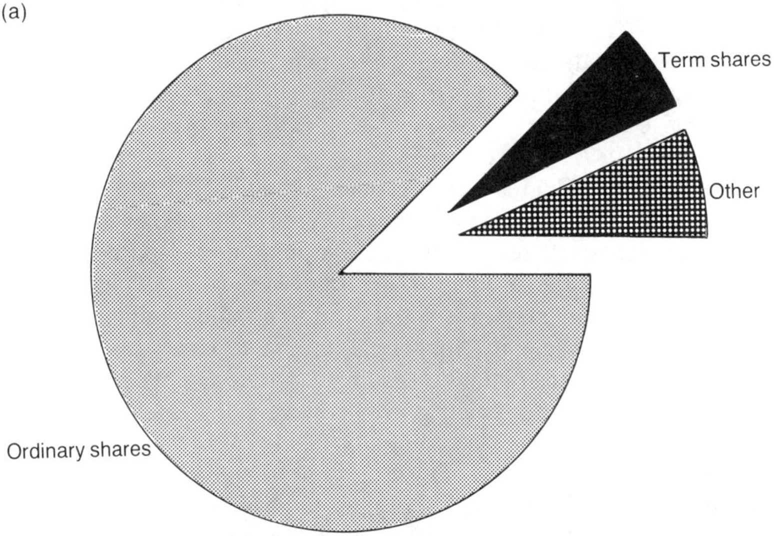
Term shares
Other
Ordinary shares

(b)

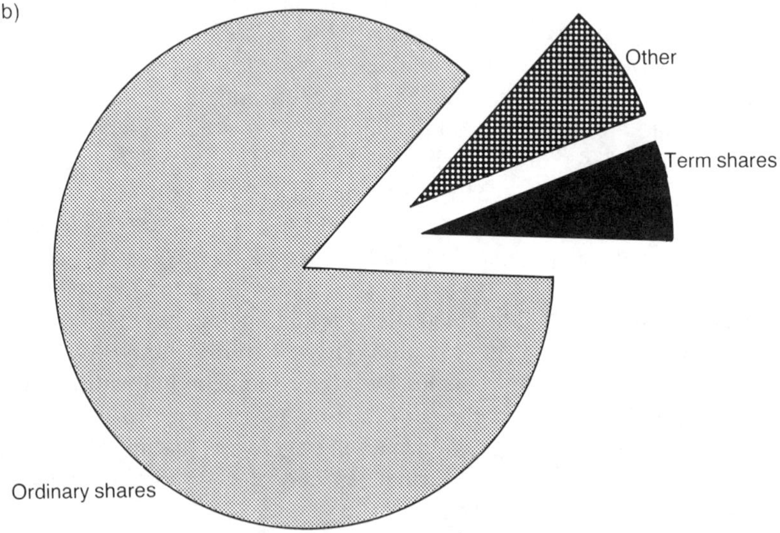
Other
Term shares
Ordinary shares

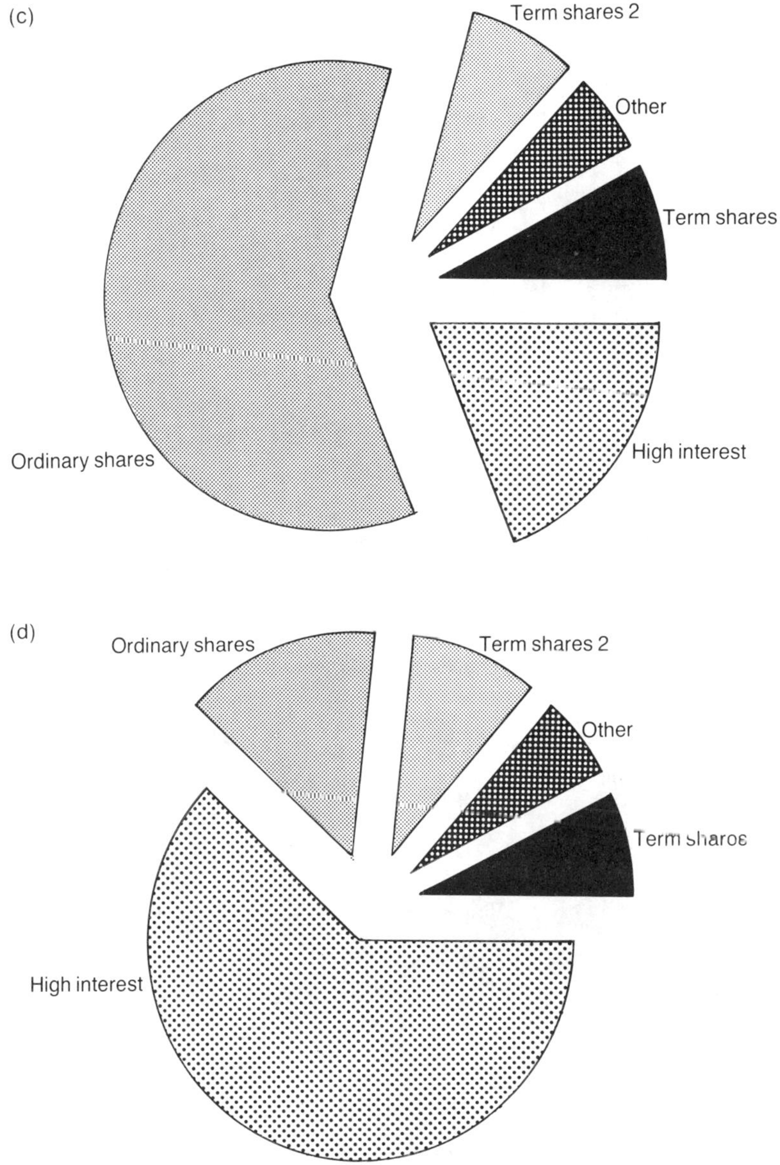

Figure 4.2 Financial innovation: (a) 1974; (b) 1978; (c) 1982; (d) 1986

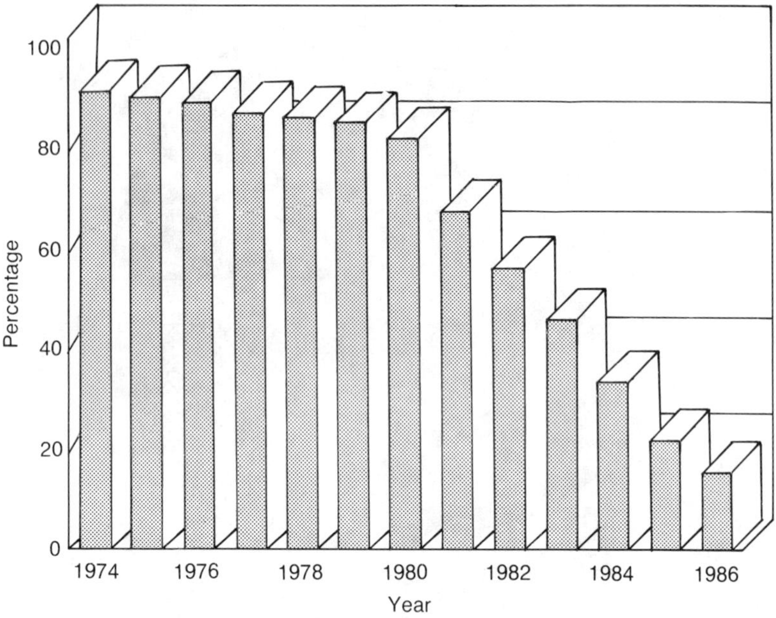

Figure 4.3 Percentage of balances in ordinary accounts

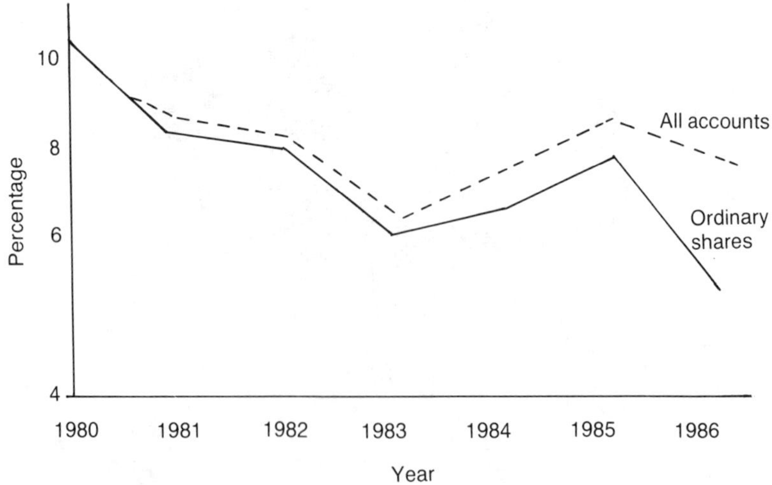

Figure 4.4 Interest on ordinary share accounts and average for all accounts
Source: Bristol & West 1987

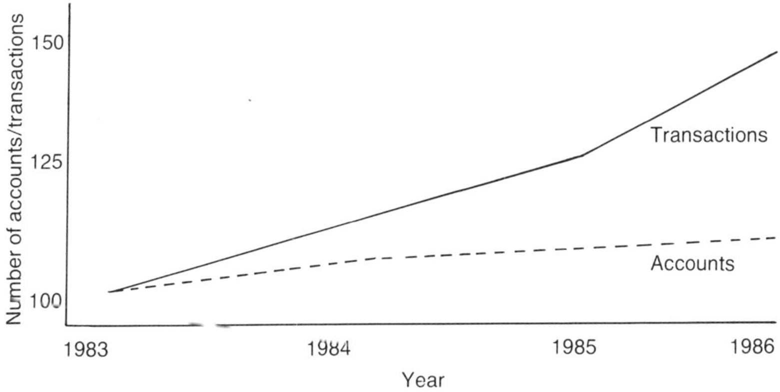

Figure 4.5 Growth in accounts and transactions (1983 = index of 100)
Source: Bristol & West 1987

return directly to building societies, such that at the extreme they will have the same ability as banks to create credit (Rose 1986: 24).[8]

Unfortunately, comparable figures on financial innovation by the retail banking industry are not available. However, it is possible to identify substantial changes in the retail banks' funding structure. The clearing banks started offering interest-bearing sight accounts in 1983–4 and higher rate sight deposit accounts in 1985. The main innovation of the banks was the introduction of *high interest sight deposits.* Table 4.2 shows the growth of high interest personal accounts compared with current accounts and total sterling sight deposits. From the available evidence, it can be seen that high interest personal accounts grew considerably from 3.2 per cent of total sight deposits in 1984 to 23.2 per cent in 1990. *Non-interest-bearing current accounts,* by contrast, fell as a proportion of total sight deposits from 1980 onwards.

Seven-day deposit accounts also declined (Table 4.3), from 20.8 per cent of total time deposits in 1985 to 5.1 per cent by 1990. The decline in both non-interest-bearing current accounts and seven-day deposit accounts will be partly as a result of switching towards high interest sight accounts, although the extent of this is difficult to determine given the available data.

An analysis of the residual maturity of bank deposits (Table 4.4) reveals that the proportion of sterling sight deposits as a percentage of total sterling deposits grew from 34.6 per cent in 1981 to 43.6 per

Table 4.2 Committee of London Savings Banks deposits, analysis by type: sterling sight deposits

Year	*Total* (£m)	*Current accounts* (£m)	*Proportion* (%)	*High interest accounts* (£m)	*Proportion* (%)
1978	17,747	14,547	82.0	N/A	–
1979	20,936	16,068	76.8	N/A	–
1980[a]	19,989	15,879	79.4	N/A	–
1981	22,664	16,956	74.8	N/A	–
1982	26,609	18,424	69.2	N/A	–
1983	30,808	19,810	64.3	N/A	–
1984[b]	36,491	21,705	59.5	1,156	3.2
1985[c]	47,810	22,850	47.8	6,279	13.2
1986	67,960	30,173	44.4	10,779	16.0
1987[d]	78,677	34,110	43.4	13,698	17.5
1988	88,112	36,705	41.7	19,658	22.3
1989	104,454	33,091	31.7	24,238	23.2
1990	114,281	31,111	27.2	N/A	N/A

Source: *Abstract of Banking Statistics* May 1991
Notes: N/A, not available.
[a]Change from banking sector to monetary sector.
[b]Formation of Committee of London Savings Banks (CLSB) including Standard Chartered Group.
[c]Inclusion of TSB Group in the CLSB and change from banking month to calendar month reporting.
[d]Excludes Clydesdale Bank and five other subsidiaries.

cent of the total in 1990. This appears to be mainly as a result of the decline in deposits with a residual maturity of less than eight days. Short-term deposits at retail banks thus became far more liquid in the 1980s.

Substantial change also occurred in the mortgage market, with the abandonment of the cartel and greater competition. The mortgage queues that existed as a direct result of the building societies' policy of rationing mortgage supply largely disappeared as supply was increased to meet demand. Mortgage loans became far more freely available, representing substantial liberalization in this market, particularly in 1981 and 1982 (Table 4.5). Loans were advanced for a greater percentage of the purchase price than previously, and higher multiples of income were accepted. The building societies' policy of charging different rates for loans over £35,000 was also competed away.

Table 4.3 Committee of London Savings Banks deposits, analysis by type: sterling time deposits

Year	*Total* (*£m*)	*Seven-day deposit accounts* (*£m*)	*Proportion* (*%*)
1978	24,448	N/A	–
1979	29,968	N/A	–
1980[a]	37,836	N/A	–
1981	45,876	N/A	–
1982	59,511	N/A	–
1983	63,757	N/A	–
1984[b]	68,433	N/A	–
1985[c]	74,437	15,004	20.8
1986	88,805	17,101	19.9
1987[d]	101,073	15,313	15.9
1988	130,212	14,203	10.9
1989	155,536	12,043	7.7
1990	171,667	8,667	5.1

Source: *Abstract of Banking Statistics* May 1991
Notes: see Table 4.2.

According to economic theory, the entry of banks into the mortgage market would have been expected to shift the demand curve for mortgages faced by building societies (e.g. from DM_1 to DM_2 in Figure 4.6) unless the banks cause the total demand for mortgage loans to increase in a manner which more than compensates for the decline in market share. The effective margin or spread faced by societies would be reduced by a shift in the supply of mortgages from SM to SM_1 and a shift in the supply curve for deposits (from SD to SD_1) as competition bids up the cost of funds. With the cartel removed, and with increased competition from banks (the new entrants), the previous non-market-clearing mortgage rate would also be expected to rise (e.g. to I_{M_1}).

In practice it appears that the building societies' rate setting behaviour did change. Building societies showed an increased willingness to accommodate demand for mortgage loans, whereas previously non-price rationing was in force. This entailed a new interest rate setting strategy that allowed higher mortgage rates, rather than the previously adopted policy of pegging mortgage rates below market clearing levels. Figure 4.7 shows the relationship between the mortgage rate of interest and the maximum retail rate of interest.

Table 4.4 Committee of London Savings Banks sterling deposits: analysis by residual maturity[a] (end October[b])

Year	*Sight*[f]	*Less than eight days*	*Up to one month*	*Up to three months*	*Up to six months*	*Up to one year*[g]
1981	23,515 (34.6)	24,381 (35.8)	6,984 (10.2)	6,710 (9.9)	2,914 (4.3)	1,591 (2.3)
1982	27,779 (32.3)	27,513 (32.0)	11,633 (13.5)	8,879 (10.3)	4,317 (5.0)	3,151 (3.7)
1983	32,246 (34.1)	27,906 (29.5)	12,239 (12.9)	10,707 (11.3)	4,502 (4.8)	3,644 (3.9)
1984[c]	38,191 (36.4)	27,703 (26.4)	15,511 (14.8)	11,907 (11.3)	4,753 (4.5)	3,396 (3.2)
1985[d]	50,198 (41.1)	27,391 (22.4)	17,131 (14.0)	14,714 (12.0)	5,489 (4.5)	3,408 (2.8)
1986	68,957 (44.0)	32,545 (20.8)	20,309 (13.0)	17,564 (11.2)	7,753 (4.9)	5,485 (3.5)
1987[e]	80,159 (46.4)	33,007 (19.1)	18,049 (10.5)	20,214 (11.7)	9,337 (5.4)	7,668 (4.5)
1988	95,254 (45.3)	38,515 (18.3)	29,748 (14.1)	24,070 (11.4)	10,787 (5.1)	7,741 (3.7)
1989	109,725 (43.0)	45,477 (17.8)	34,327 (13.5)	29,823 (11.7)	15,143 (5.9)	8,029 (3.1)
1990	118,419 (43.6)	39,109 (14.4)	44,877 (16.5)	29,013 (10.7)	18,720 (6.9)	9,102 (3.4)

Source: *Abstract of Banking Statistics* May 1991

Notes: [a]Analysed by residual period to earliest maturity date (which could be the first roll-over date or the shortest period of notice).
[b]Figures prior to 1986 are as at mid-November.
[c]Formation of CLSB including Standard Chartered Group.
[d]Inclusion of TSB Group in the CLSB and change from banking month to calendar month reporting.
[e]Excludes Clydesdale Bank and five other subsidiaries.
[f]Figures in parentheses are percentages of total.
[g]Deposits of over a year's maturity are excluded (thus the percentages do not sum to 100 per cent).

Table 4.5 Growth in total mortgage lending, net advances 1975–87

Year	*Total (£m)*	*Increase (%)*
1975	3,730	–
1976	3,928	5.3
1977	4,362	11.1
1978	5,437	24.6
1979	6,461	18.8
1980	7,333	13.5
1981	9,489	29.4
1982	14,141	49.0
1983	14,525	27.0
1984	17,072	17.5
1985	19,116	12.0
1986	26,581	39.0
1987	29,256	10.1
1988	40,050	36.0
1989	33,658	−16.0
1990	32,067	−4.7

Source: *Financial Statistics*

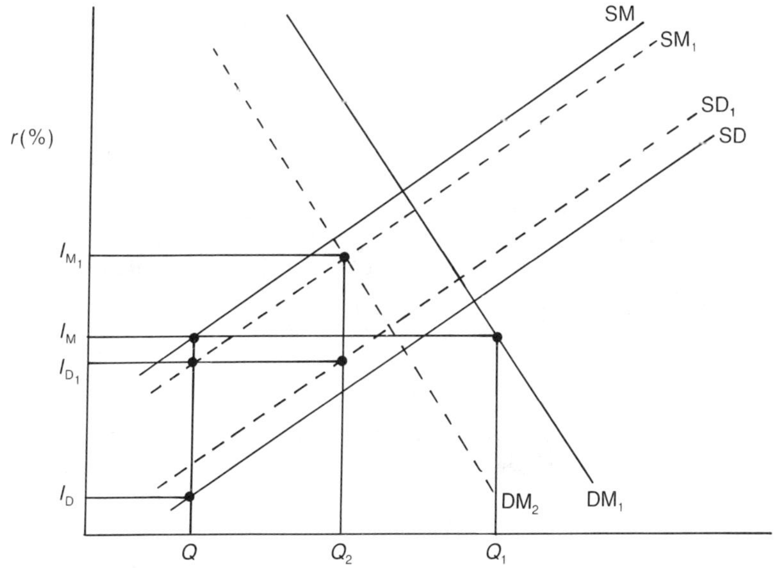

Figure 4.6 Competition and the mortgage rate
Source: Llewellyn 1987a

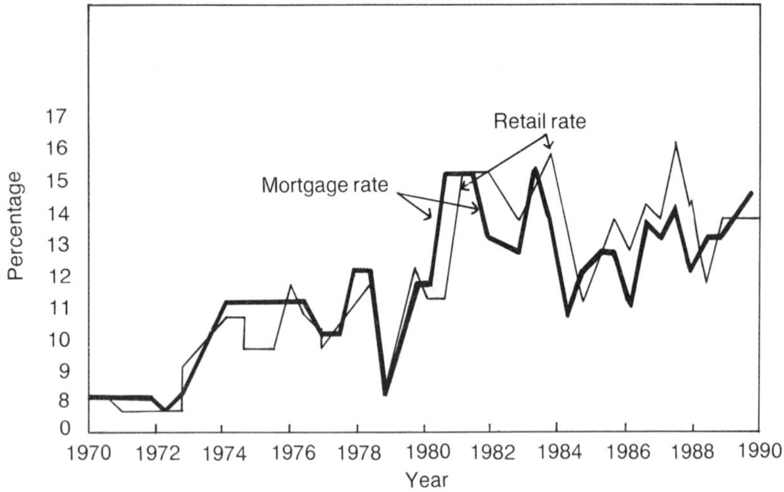

Figure 4.7 Mortgage rate and maximum retail rate at building societies

Mortgage rates were invariably above retail rates over the period 1970–80. In the 1980s, however, the difference between mortgage rates and deposit rates tended to decrease, with deposit rates exceeding mortgage rates at several times. So, as would be expected, the spread between building society mortgage lending and deposit rates was indeed reduced.

Furthermore, as expected, the mortgage rate rose relative to other market rates. Figure 4.8 shows the mortgage rate and a representative money market rate – the London Inter-bank Offer Rate (LIBOR). In general the mortgage rate was above LIBOR for much of the 1980s apart from 1981 and 1989. In contrast, LIBOR was generally above the mortgage rate prior to 1981. LIBOR only tended to be below the mortgage rate when money market rates were falling. Moreover, Figure 4.9 shows that for much of the 1980s retail funds were on average more expensive than wholesale funds.

Allied with an increase in competition, building society deposit rates tended to move more in line with other competing rates. Figure 4.10 shows the maximum retail rates at building societies and banks. It can be seen that building society rates were far more fluid and far more market related after 1980. In other words, interest on building society deposit accounts became less 'sticky', resulting in more flexible rates in relation to changes in competitors' rates (see Bingham 1985: 2). This tendency for financial institutions to pay

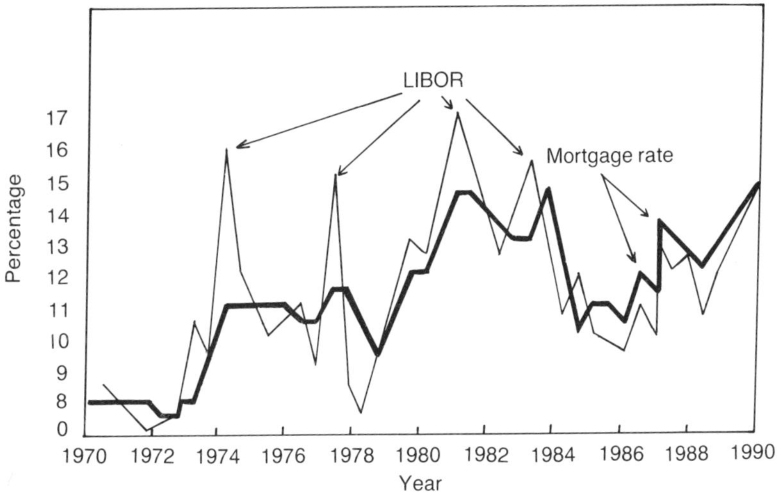

Figure 4.8 Mortgage rate and LIBOR (wholesale rate)

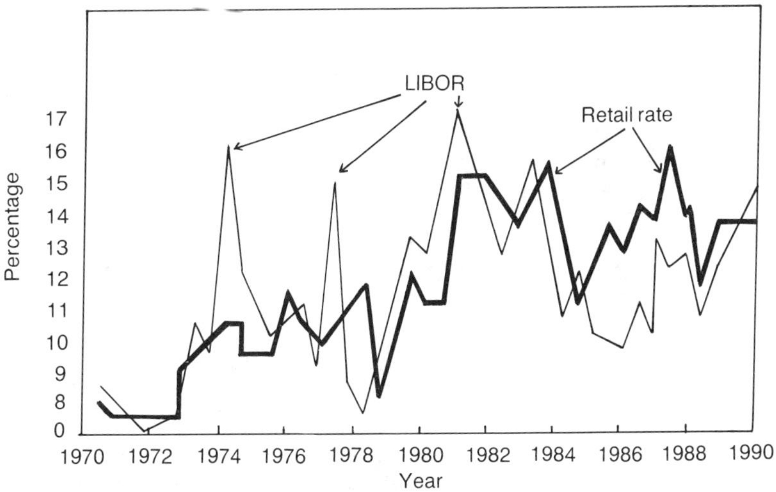

Figure 4.9 Maximum retail rate (net) at building societies and LIBOR

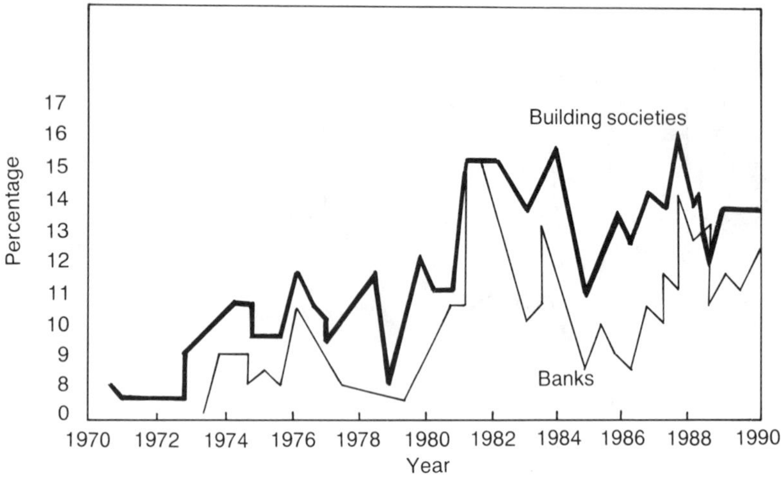

Figure 4.10 Maximum retail rate (net) at building societies and banks

market-related rates of interest has been termed 'marketization' by Bingham (1985).

Casual analysis of the data thus appears to show that building societies changed their interest rate structure in the 1980s. Llewellyn (1988b) attempted a more rigorous test to see whether there has been a structural shift in the relationship between the level of LIBOR and the interest differential between the maximum retail rate of societies and LIBOR. A regression of the differential against LIBOR (using ordinary least squares) tended to confirm that structural change was indeed taking place. The results show that building society retail rates became much more responsive to movements in market rates.

4.4 REGULATORY CONVERGENCE AND RELATIVE MARKET SHARES IN BUILDING SOCIETIES AND BANKS

The relative competitive positions of banks and building societies in the market for personal sector balances is shown in Table 4.6. After an initial setback by building societies in 1981 (largely at the expense of National Savings), the relative competitive advantage of building societies was reflected in their increasing share of personal sector liquid assets. The share of liquid assets at building societies increased from 46.8 per cent to 53.0 per cent over the period 1982–7, whereas the share held at banks fell from 38.3 per cent to 32.6 per cent. Over

Table 4.6 Relative shares in personal sector liquid assets

Year	*Building societies (%)*	*Monetary sector (%)*	*National Savings (%)*
1980	50.5	37.2	12.3
1981	46.8	38.3	15.0
1982	48.3	36.1	15.6
1983	49.7	34.4	15.8
1984	51.7	32.3	16.0
1985	53.1	31.4	15.5
1986	53.2	31.9	15.0
1987	53.0	32.6	14.4
1988	52.9	34.2	12.9
1989	44.4	44.9	10.7
1990	45.3	44.9	9.8

Source: *Bank of England Quarterly Bulletin*, various years
Note: From 1989 Abbey National plc is included as a bank.

the period 1988–90, however, the banks made up some of the lost ground.

The relative interest rate relationships between the mortgage rate and LIBOR examined earlier mean that it was profitable for new entrants to the mortgage market which were exclusively funded by wholesale money (such as the National Home Loans Corporation and the Household Mortgage Corporation). It has also been suggested that building societies suffered a competitive disadvantage in that regulation constrained the societies to funding the majority (60 per cent) of their mortgage lending in the relatively high cost retail market. Building societies have only been able to secure wholesale funds since 1981.[9] In view of the structure of interest rates prevailing since then (with mortgage rates and retail deposit rates generally above money market rates) it is hardly surprising that building societies increased their wholesale funding as a proportion of total funding (Table 4.7). It could be argued that the lack of competitive neutrality in terms of restraints on building societies' wholesale funding has increased the tendency for building societies to adopt an aggressive innovative strategy in the retail market. Paradoxically, it is partly this aggressive competitive strategy which has driven up the cost of retail funds relative to wholesale funds. In 1988, however, conditions reversed somewhat with wholesale rates rising above retail rates. Combined with the stock market crash in October 1987, which

Table 4.7 Building societies' wholesale and retail funding

Year	*Net inflow from wholesale sources (£m)*	*Net receipts of shares and deposits (£m)*	*Wholesale as percentage of total (%)*
1981	102	3,601	2.8
1982	252	6,466	3.8
1983	1,635	6,839	19.3
1984	2,228	8,572	20.6
1985	3,093	7,462	29.3
1986	6,141	6,635	48.1
1987	3,159	7,487	29.7
1988	5,471	13,554	28.7
1989	8,226	7,738	51.5

Source: *Building Societies Yearbook* (London: Franey, 1988)

led to substantial inflows to building societies, this gave building societies a considerable advantage in 1988.

It is interesting to note that there was some degree of convergence in the liabilities portfolios of the building societies and retail banks. Building societies increased their wholesale funding operations whilst banks attempted to increase their retail funding (Table 4.7). Thus these institutions became less differentiated in funding structures (within the confines of the Building Societies Act 1986).

Moreover, the previous stability of retail funds has tended to fall. The changing competitive positions of competing financial institutions and the increasing financial sophistication of the personal sector meant that retail funds could at times be extremely volatile (building societies are also particularly hit by outflows of funds for privatization issues). Thus the advantage of the stability of retail funds over wholesale tended to decline.

Furthermore, the marginal cost of retail funds to building societies was relatively expensive compared with the marginal cost of wholesale funds, because increasing the rate of interest on deposits to raise more funds increases the rate on funds already deposited with the building society (alternatively a rise in the rate for one type of deposit, e.g. term shares, may induce switching from lower rate accounts). Wholesale funds, by contrast, do not affect the cost of funds already held at the building society. Wholesale funds were thus extremely attractive to building societies.

Wholesale funds have the advantage that building societies could actively engage in liability management (as the banks did) which gives societies greater flexibility. Wholesale funds were generally readily available when needed, and could be used to stabilize mortgage lending flows. Indeed, the use of wholesale funds meant that building societies could reduce their average liquidity levels. Traditionally, building societies run down liquid assets at times of low fund inflows to stabilize mortgage lending. As wholesale funds could be used for this purpose, societies could reduce their holdings of low-yielding liquid assets. Building societies are expected to move towards an optimal mix of wholesale and retail funds that minimizes costs. Also, portfolio diversification into a greater variety of sources of funds should create greater stability of inflows. Given the advantages offered by wholesale funding, and the tendency for regulatory convergence (Llewellyn 1988b), it is likely that the funding mix of banks and building societies will tend to become even less differentiated over time.

A further factor affecting competition in the retail market was the stipulation that building societies' unsecured lending be limited to £10,000. Some would argue (Llewellyn 1987a) that banks could offer mortgages at the same rate of interest as building societies (despite building societies' lower operating expense ratios) because of their ability to cross-subsidize mortgage lending with their high-priced profitable lending business, such as consumer loans.

Llewellyn argues that this has also allowed the retail banks to offset the cost of their high interest retail deposits. The new legislation (Building Societies Act 1986) allowed building societies also to engage in such cross-subsidization with the ability to diversify into unsecured lending. The building societies faced a regulatory asymmetry, however, in the constraints imposed on the limits to their unsecured lending activities. The limit of £10,000 represented a lack of competitive neutrality *vis-à-vis* the ability of banks to lend unsecured only constrained by prudential limits.

It may be that this lack of competitive neutrality which curtailed building societies' ability to cross-subsidize high-cost retail funding was an important factor in the offering of non-price inducements, such as the increased liquidity of most balances held at building societies.

Increased competitive pressure was partly responsible for the increase in the rate of decline in the number of building societies in the 1980s (Table 4.8). The decline in the number of societies was due to mergers, rather than dissolution of societies. This had a marked effect on the degree of concentration in the building society industry

Table 4.8 Rate of decline in the number of building societies

Decade	*Average rate of decline (%)*	*Year*	*Annual rate of decline*[a] *(%)*
1900–10	2.8	1980	4.9
1910–20	3.0	1981	7.3
1920–30	2.1	1982	10.3
1930–40	0.7	1983	9.3
1940–50	1.5	1984	7.8
1950–60	1.2	1985	12.1
1960–70	4.0	1986	9.6
1970–80	5.5	1987	8.6
		1988	5.1

Source: *BSA Bulletin*, various years
Note: [a] Average 1980–7, 8.74.

in the 1980s, which affected its ability to compete. Notice that, when the cartel was in operation, large interest rate margins allowed inefficient societies to survive (See Chapter 3). Indeed, this was one of the stated objectives of the cartel. The abolition of the cartel and greater competition in the personal sector retail financial market, combined with a reduction in spreads, increased the pressure for smaller less efficient societies to transfer their business to large building societies. The majority of mergers since 1979 were of this type.

There was also an increasing number of mergers between large building societies in the 1980s, as predicted by the Wilson Report (1980) (See Chapter 3). Table 4.9 shows mergers between building societies which have more than 0.5 per cent of the industry's assets. The tendency to merge meant that the largest societies gained an increasing share of the industries' assets. By 1990 the largest twenty societies controlled over 90 per cent of the assets of the building society industry as a whole.

Moreover, it has been argued (Morgan 1988) that only building societies with an asset base of £10–15 billion will be likely to thrive by the end of the 1990s. Morgan foresees only six to ten large mutual societies existing in ten years' time. If correct, this means that there will be a rapid growth in mergers in the building society industry and a large concentration of assets. This is important given the evidence of increased efficiency and economies of scale due to size and growth

Table 4.9 Mergers involving large building societies, 1982–7

Year	*Merging societies*	*Assets as a percentage of industry assets (%)*
1982	Provincial	3.0
	Burnley	1.6
1983	Anglia	3.6
	London and South of England	0.7
1985	Alliance	3.1
	Leicester	2.9
1987	Nationwide	8.7
	Anglia	3.8

Source: *BSA Bulletin*, various years

through mergers (Drake 1986)[10]. It suggests that increasing concentration in the building society industry leads to a greater ability to compete through cost efficiency. Building societies have a major competitive advantage in the efficiency of their business over banks. Building societies can operate on a narrower spread between the average cost of funds and the average interest rate on mortgages. Their ability to do this stems from their relative 'efficiency' *vis-à-vis* retail banks. They can operate with a narrower interest rate spread largely because of their uncomplicated business. It is interesting to note that building society operating expense ratios were increasing until 1982 whereas they declined after that date. This was partly a result of the decrease in the annual growth rate of the number of building society branches (see Table 3.2), which, in turn, may have been a reflection of the increase in price competition instead of the previous predominance of non-price competition which resulted in a proliferation of building society branches. The reduction in building society operating expense ratios appears to justify Silber's (1975a, b) claim that cost-efficient firms are the main innovators. However, this comment must be treated with caution as there is a strong positive relationship between operating expense ratios and the rate of inflation, and thus the building societies have not had absolute control over this ratio. It is therefore not possible categorically to maintain that building societies have deliberately become more efficient in the 1980s as a matter of policy.

Moreover, the retail banks' 'endowment effect' decreased in the 1980s. The increasing importance of interest-bearing deposits at retail banks and the fall in non-interest-bearing sight deposits eroded the banks' source of traditionally cheap retail funds (non-interest-bearing sight deposits are not free as the banks provide for the costs of the payments system). Retail deposits have become increasingly expensive at the margin for retail banks, and the decline in the endowment effect reduces bank profitability. There was a decline in the banks' proportion of total income derived from their interest margin in the 1980s. The *Bank of England Annual Review 1988* points out that this largely results from a deliberate policy change towards fee income growth, particularly through diversification into insurance, asset management and estate agency.

Of course, the increasing cost of retail funds tended to have an effect on building societies' profitability as well. It must be remembered, however, that building societies have their own version of the 'endowment effect'. Building societies face a zero cost of reserve capital. This is because, as mutual institutions, they do not have to service their capital. Societies thus have free reserves, the level of which can affect profitability. A society with a large volume of free reserves will tend to be more profitable as it will have a relatively high proportion of capital on which interest does not have to be paid compared with the amount of its assets which are non-income-earning. This results in free reserve income, which provides an endowment effect when interest rates are rising. As interest rates rise, societies have an endowment effect as interest-bearing liabilities will be less than interest-bearing assets by the size of the free reserves. This was a powerful advantage to building societies during periods of rising interest rates.[11]

A further stimulus in the broadening of the similarities between building societies and banks was the Building Societies Act 1986. Under section 34 of the Act a building society or a subsidiary of a building society may provide the services listed in Schedule 8 of the Act (and the review of Schedule 8 in February 1988). The building societies were given the powers to undertake *inter alia* money transmission services, foreign exchange services, personal equity plans, unsecured loans, estate agency, administration of pension schemes, investment services, insurance and unit trust schemes.

The ability to diversify into these areas was a powerful example of the decreasing differentiation between building societies and banks. Indeed, the Act allows for conversion from mutual status to public limited company status, with the permission of the members.

Such a society (and at least one, the Abbey National, has taken this action) would be regulated by the Bank of England, rather than by the Building Societies Commission (BSC).[12] This may prove advantageous in view of the degree of regulatory asymmetry between retail banks and building societies – particularly concerning wholesale funding, unsecured lending and capital adequacy requirements – although it is likely that the BSC will eventually be superseded by the Bank of England (Llewellyn 1988b).

The constant evolution of the financial system is in this case likely to lead to both building societies and banks coming under the umbrella of one regulator – the Bank of England. In the extreme, there may be nominal or zero difference between the regulations of the two sets of institutions, and between their main operations and activities (notwithstanding the possibility of smaller building societies adopting specialist or 'niche' strategies according to their relative strengths and weaknesses).[13]

4.5 CONCLUSION

Section 4.2 analysed the main factors impinging upon the degree of competition in the personal sector retail financial market and the main determinants of financial innovation. Re-regulation via a change in monetary control was shown to be a major catalyst for an increase in competition and financial innovation. The removal of distorting direct monetary controls from the retail banks enabled a portfolio redistribution towards mortgage lending. The retail banks' entrance into the mortgage market precipitated the breakdown of the interest rate cartel. The effects on interest rates of the abandonment of the cartel and an increase in competition have been as would be expected from economic theory (see Section 4.3). Greater competition for personal sector retail funds was combined with innovation in the type and variety of deposit accounts offered by both building societies and banks. In particular, high interest easy access accounts were introduced by both sets of institutions. One major effect of increased competition and innovation was the change in the interest rate policies of the building societies and banks. First, the average rate of interest paid on retail funds at building societies and banks tended to increase. Second, the average rate charged on mortgage loans also increased. The combined effect, however, was a reduction in the 'spread' (or cost of intermediation) between mortgage and deposit rates. Third, building society interest rates tended to become less sticky, and now move more in line with other rates of interest.

This resulted in building society interest rates becoming more flexible and fluid in relation to competitors' rates.

There was also substantial change in the mortgage policies of the building societies. As would be expected, the higher mortgage rate charged for larger loans was competed away. The supply of mortgage loans, previously rationed, became more responsive to demand conditions, such that the mortgage queues disappeared. Large multiples of income were advanced for the purchase of houses, as were larger percentages of the sale price, 100 per cent advances not being uncommon. This resulted in substantial liberalization of credit conditions to the personal sector.

Section 4.4 analysed the relative market shares of building societies and retail banks of the personal sector retail financial market, with particular reference to the changing extent of heterogeneity between these institutions. Banks and building societies became and are still becoming less differentiated and more homogeneous in nature. This is especially noticeable in the more dynamic aggressive and innovative nature of building societies, exemplified by the decision of a number of building societies to offer interest-bearing cheque accounts, further eroding the retail banks' traditional monopoly of money transmission services and increasing the degree of similarity between these institutions. The range of services that building societies are empowered to adopt under the Building Societies Act 1986 further increased the areas in which banks and building societies are in competition. It is likely that the tendency for regulatory convergence will ensure that any regulatory asymmetries *vis-à-vis* banks and building societies will be altered over time, encouraging the tendency towards homogeneity.

5 Financial innovation and the monetary aggregates

5.1 INTRODUCTION

The criteria for defining 'money' assets are examined in Section 5.2, where it is noted that defining money is wrought with difficulty even without financial innovation. The institutionalist school argued over two decades ago that, given that financial institutions are constantly developing, new assets would at times be created which may act as substitutes for money. This was not seen as a new process but as an example of the evolution of financial institutions. It was argued that new assets which perform the transactions/medium of exchange function would evolve over time leading to an increase in the variety of assets that perform the role of money. Financial innovation was not, therefore, a phenomenon solely of the 1970s or 1980s, although the variety and pace of financial innovation and change in the building society and retail bank sectors was unprecedented.

In Section 5.3 the development of building society innovations is analysed in terms of their increasing similarity and apparently greater substitutability with bank sight deposits. The effects on the broad monetary aggregates of 'switching' of balances between building societies and banks is examined, as is the problem of redefining the monetary aggregates in the face of financial innovation.

The effect of financial innovation on the money-income relationship is examined in Section 5.4 in terms of the motives for holding money balances. It was noted in Chapter 4 that many building society and bank easy access accounts now bear interest, and it may be that financial innovations have led to money being held for reasons over and above the transactions and precautionary motives. If this is so, then money balances being held for other than transactions and/or precautionary motives may be responsible for the fast growth of the broad monetary aggregates relative to nominal incomes, as evidenced by the fall in the income velocity of circulation of broad money in the 1980s.

5.2 FINANCIAL INNOVATION AND THE DEFINITION OF MONEY

The basis upon which to define money has in the past aroused considerable controversy, even without the added complication of financial innovation. The functional criteria often stipulated as defining 'money' have not been sufficient to set out a definitive classification of 'money'. The *a priori* approach generally places weight on the specification of 'money is what money does' (Hicks 1967: 1) whereby money is defined by functional criteria. Anything that can perform in the capacity of fulfilling the function that money occupies is assumed to be a constituent part of 'money'.

The role frequently volunteered as distinguishing 'money' from other assets is that of a medium of exchange, or the transactions role. This is as a result of money performing the intermediary function between buyer and seller that nullifies the necessity of a double coincidence of wants. It is thus, according to this criterion, anything that is generally acceptable as a medium of exchange. This functional criterion does not, however, establish an unambiguous classification of assets according to whether or not they should be represented in that group of assets delineated as 'money'. Certainly notes and coin are generally acceptable in exchange, and most would further argue that bank deposits are a form of money, being subject to payment by cheque. As early as 1960, however, there was dispute about drawing the line there, with Sayers arguing that written instructions to a building society or Post Office Savings Bank to make a payment are as good as drawing a cheque on a current account at a bank (Sayers 1960: 711–12).

Indeed, the Radcliffe Committee (1959) fully rejected the view that money could be defined according to certain functional criteria, and the comments made in the report appear extraordinarily prescient in view of the effects of financial innovation in the 1980s.[1] A largely unquantifiable concept was expounded by the Committee, the very broad concept of 'liquidity'. According to the report, it is liquidity that determines expenditure decisions, rather than access to money holdings (media of exchange) *per se* (paragraph 389).

According to the Radcliffe Report, there is in existence a wide spectrum of assets, each of which contains to a different extent some of the features of 'moneyness'. It was further argued that there exist in a developed financial economy many highly liquid assets which are close substitutes for money. Money is thus only a constituent part of the much broader quantum 'liquidity' in the economy. It is therefore necessary to examine the whole liquidity spectrum when analysing spending decisions (paragraph 389).

The report does not, however, provide a clear, quantifiable, unambiguous definition of liquidity,[2] although an analysis of the 'whole liquidity position' would certainly involve, at the very least, looking at deposits held at the London clearing banks, building societies, Post Office Savings Banks and the Trustee Savings Banks (paragraph 478, Table 22).

Whether or not there is a variety of near-money assets highly substitutable for money is an empirical matter. Unfortunately, much of the econometric work has been carried out on American data and, moreover, has provided no clear consensus.

The substitutability of money issue is a complex one, compounded by the fact that many researchers have obtained conflicting results (or what they claim to be conflicting results). Feige and Pearce (1977) provide an invaluable survey of the pre-1977 work. Much of the problem lies with disagreement over what numerical magnitude of cross-elasticity should be taken as indicative of close substitutability, with many authors providing highly subjective interpretations of their results that imply a wide disparity, when in fact many of the results are very similar (Feige and Pearce 1977: 456).

Mills and Wood (1977), as far as is known, are the only authors to examine the issue of substitution of assets in the UK. They measure the elasticity of substitution by estimating a demand for money function and observing its interest elasticity. In doing so, they aim to test what they call the 'Radcliffe' hypothesis – that the liabilities of non-bank financial intermediaries (NBFIs) must be *perfect* substitutes for those of the commercial banks before NBFIs can *completely* frustrate monetary policy as described by the Radcliffe Committee. If the interest elasticity of the demand for money has become infinite, monetary policy cannot affect money market conditions. They found that the interest elasticity of the demand for money, for the period 1923–74 shows no upward trend, and they thus reject the Radcliffe hypothesis. These results must be viewed with caution, however, in view of the doubts as to the econometric specifications of the demand for money of that time and the much faster pace of financial innovation since 1980.

Despite the objections of the Radcliffe Committee, only the liabilities of banks were traditionally included in the monetary aggregates (along with notes and coin), largely because of the belief in the banks' 'uniqueness' in terms of their ability to create credit. Traditionally, theory has distinguished sharply between banks that *create* credit, and NBFIs which merely pass it on. Building societies, for example, have to attract a deposit before they can make a loan, and cannot lend more than savers deposit with them (Reifler 1959: 301), whereas banks have the ability to create 'virulent liquidity' (Holtrop 1959). Whilst it is true that building societies were not credit creators as they were not involved in the payments mechanism, a strict demarcation line was probably unhelpful in terms of classifying financial institutions for the purposes of monetary policy. It tended to propagate the view that NBFIs had no role to play in the monetary process. This was seen in the view that banks would not lose deposits to NBFIs (see Chapters 3 and 4 and Llewellyn 1979a) and in neglect of the point that NBFIs could increase the velocity of circulation of money by attracting deposits away from banks. This traditional viewpoint very much promulgated the notion that NBFIs such as building societies were passive institutions that did not affect the monetary process in any way, a standpoint which was challenged by Gurley and Shaw (1955: 521). This is backed up by the 'new view' of Tobin (1963) who argued that the differences between banks and other financial intermediaries was one of degree rather than of substance (p. 418).

The building societies have increasingly encroached upon the banks' credit-creating preserve, and as the attractiveness of building societies' liabilities increases, so does their redepository ratio and ability to create credit (Rose 1986: 24).

Of course, the increasing liquidity of building society accounts and, most importantly, the movement of the building societies into the payments transmission mechanism means that building societies are now also credit creators and cannot be ignored for purposes of monetary control.[3]

Given that changes in credit correspond quite closely to changes in the broad monetary aggregates, this should not cause too much of a problem in using a broad money definition as a target and as an indicator of monetary conditions. The post-Keynesian school, however, argues that monetary theory and control should emphasize *credit* money rather than 'deposit' money, as the latter is effectively brought about by the former (Moore 1988: 4).

Monetarists argue that the composition of those assets which are 'money' is an empirical matter. The ultra-monetarist view is that money is an indicator of nominal income, and that control of money will provide control of nominal income. The correct definition of money is then that aggregate of financial assets which most closely follows nominal income (Kaufman 1969; Friedman and Schwartz 1970).

The second empirical approach to defining money stems from the view that, if it is possible to identify a stable demand for money, effects of changes in the money supply on the economy may be predictable. Thus the appropriate definition of money is that which provides a stable aggregate demand for money function (Laidler 1969).

In terms of the first approach, Smith (1978) analysed the relationship between national income and five alternative definitions of the money supply for the UK. He found that both the best fitting function and the best forecasting performance were provided by what is called M5, consisting of conventional £M3 plus building society, Trustee Savings Bank and National Savings deposits, over the period 1924–77.

Mills (1983) also provided an empirical assessment of the monetary aggregates according to their ability to predict future movements in nominal income. He found that £M3 and Private Sector Liquidity 1 (PSL1) were the most informative aggregates.

Doubts have been cast, however, on the nature of empirical definitions that link the definition of money to the ability to track nominal income. Mason (1976) in particular gives a thorough critique of this methodology.

With reference to the demand for money, it has already been noted (Chapter 2) that the apparent existence of a stable demand function for £M3 persuaded the authorities to adopt it as a target. The adoption of a broad monetary target was also inspired by 'Radcliffian views' (Niehans 1982) of the importance of liquidity in the money supply proces, rather than a strict adherence to the transactions based quantity theory, with the Bank of England pointing out that the use of a broad money target relied as much on the importance of liquidity and credit as on the quantity theory (Bank of England 1983a: 201).

If the original reason for targeting a broad money definition was influenced by Radcliffian views, it can also be said that the decision to abandon the £M3 aggregate had a Radcliffian ring to it:

> Starting from a general concept such as broad money or narrow money, any precise definition involves drawing an arbitrary dividing line across a virtual continuum of financial assets. More-

> over, a particular measure chosen on the basis of past relationships is liable to be undermined over time by developments in the financial system. Given the recent fast pace of financial innovation and liberalisation, the problems of definition have arguably become more acute. There is now a vast array of slightly differentiated financial products available to the retail and wholesale depositor or investor, ranging from cash to long-maturity marketable securities. There is no obvious and appropriate criterion for discriminating unambiguously between those which are 'money' and those which are not.
>
> (Bank of England 1986b: 500)

Clearly, in one sense, we are all Radcliffians now. This appears greatly at odds with the monetarist proposition stated earlier that money is a 'unique' asset.

5.3 FINANCIAL INNOVATION AND RECLASSIFICATION OF THE MONETARY AGGREGATES

Financial innovations which represent close substitutes for money often necessitate a reclassification of the monetary aggregates. New financial instruments and improved terms on old ones by building societies has meant that those assets which perform the function of money are not immutable over time.

Increasing financial innovation by building societies, taking the form of changes in the terms of existing accounts and the new services introduced, meant that the monetary authorities had to undertake a reappraisal of such balances for the purposes of monetary control. Three-month notice accounts were originally treated as investment balances by the authorities in terms of monetary aggregation because of their fairly strict withdrawal terms. When some building societies reduced the terms to twenty-eight days' notice without further penalty, they were deemed to be better represented in the monetary measures as transaction balances. They were thus placed within the M2 aggregate of the end of the 1983.

Such innovation by building societies reduced the informational content of the M2 aggregate, and called into question the introduction of this 'transactions' aggregate.

Similarly, if term shares, which became increasingly liquid, were included in the old Private Sector Liquidity 2 (PSL2) definition, they would have affected its growth rate (Figure 5.1). Less stringent withdrawal facilities on term shares led to them growing rapidly between 1981 and 1984, and adding these term shares to PSL2 would have increased its growth rate during this period. By contrast, after 1984, growth of PSL2 would have been slower if term shares had been included, as a result of the decline in non-withdrawable term shares and slower growth in withdrawable term shares after the initial heavy increases.

A further problem affecting interpretation of the movement in the monetary aggregates was the competition for retail deposits between banks and building societies. Changes in interest rate differentials and non-price terms offered by building societies and banks meant that, at different times, short-term portfolio readjustments by the personal sector resulted in distortions of the growth rates of the broad measures of money. This tended to confuse interpretation of monetary conditions and reduced the value of monetary targets (Bank of England 1986c: 508–9).

The result was that the relationship between the various monetary aggregates, and between the aggregates and nominal income, became less stable. For example, the growth of term shares at building societies from £5.3 billion in 1981 to £15 billion in mid-1984 and the subsequent withdrawal (about £6 billion) in 1986 distorted the

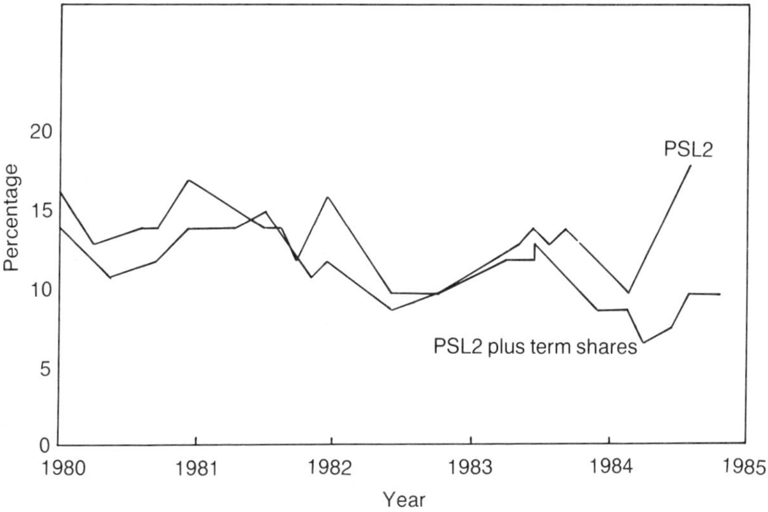

Figure 5.1 PSL2 and term shares

growth of £M3. It was estimated (Bank of England 1987a) that approximately half of the inflow in 1981 was drawn from other types of building society deposit, and the remainder represented 'new' money, most of it from £M3. The rate of growth of £M3 was thus reduced by between 2 and 4 per cent. On maturity in 1986, withdrawal from term shares and a subsequent portfolio reallocation was believed to have increased the rate of growth of £M3 by about 1 per cent.

It is in situations like this that policy can only be as good as the information that guides it (Hester 1982: 43).

In 1985 the monetary authorities admitted that the use of the broad aggregates as monetary indicators was somewhat limited (Budget Red Book 1985). Indeed, it was stipulated by the monetary authorities that a number of variables other than the monetary aggregate in question were being monitored:

> The £M3 rule has never operated in a purely mechanical way; we have always been prepared to over-ride its signals in the light of other, contrary, evidence on the state of monetary conditions.
>
> (Bank of England 1987c: 366)

In terms of the targets and instruments literature, it appears that the monetary authorities treated the money supply as *both* an intermediate target and one of several information variables (Lane 1985), although doubts have recently been voiced over the wisdom of the Medium Term Financial Strategy (MTFS) and the robustness of its theoretical foundation, given the likelihood that financial innovation would occur.

Currie (1987: 2) argues that the MTFS was seriously flawed in the way in which monetary targets were given a central role, given the impact of financial innovation.

The Bank of England appeared to favour the 'new' aggregate, M4 – which included building society and bank sterling deposit liabilities of the non-bank, non-building society private sector and that sector's holdings of notes and coin – largely because building society deposits and bank deposits were becoming increasingly homogeneous (Bank of England 1987a: 219).

The increasing substitutability of building society and bank deposits has been corroborated econometrically by Weale (1986) in an analysis of the demand for various types of deposit by the personal sector. Greater substitutability, he suggests, implies that emphasis upon £M3 may be inappropriate for the purposes of monetary control.

The problem, however, is not simply one of either a once-and-for-all classification of the monetary aggregates or a changing emphasis from £M3 to M4, but the recognition that financial innovation may require continual reclassification as new innovations emerge. This confuses the interpretation of monetary developments and hampers the operation of monetary control.

This means that even an aggregate such as M4 would still be vulnerable to switching of funds included in the aggregate and close substitutes excluded from the aggregate.

Traditionally, money has not borne a rate of interest. Indeed, the uniqueness of money and its very importance in monetary economies largely stems from the fact that the rate of interest on money is exogenously fixed at zero whilst non-money financial assets bear an endogenously determined rate of interest (Tobin 1969). (The exogeneity of the zero yield on money should perhaps be amended in the UK case, where there have been no specific controls on the payment of interest on money. It is rather that the banks have endogenously decided not to pay interest on money. Exogenous or endogenous, the importance of money bearing zero interest still remains.[4])

The fundamental issue which is raised relates to the *motives* for holding funds in the form of assets included within the various monetary aggregates. The receipt of a market-related rate of interest on funds which offer immediate or easy access, often with attached money transmission facilities, is likely to blur the distinction between pure transactions balances and pure investment balances. Moreover, from an opposite point of view, pure investment balances are likely to become more like transactions balances with a progressive reduction in illiquidity.

In other words, competition between banks and building societies means that wealth-holders have increasingly been offered the opportunity to hold attractive easy access investment assets which entail no explicit decision between the placing of funds in a transactions account with a financial intermediary and the use of funds to purchase additional non-money assets (which must be sold before a means of payment may be obtained).[5] Times have certainly changed since Keynes remarked, 'why should anyone outside a lunatic asylum wish to use money as a store of wealth?' (1936: 216).

5.4 THE EFFECT OF FINANCIAL INNOVATION ON THE MONETARY AGGREGATES

If monetary aggregates are to be used in a money supply targeting strategy, it is desirable that there is a reasonably stable relationship between the monetary aggregate(s) and the ultimate goal (but not necessarily close or systematic, according to Friedman, because of lags.[6] Moreover, the motives for holding money should remain consistent over time, such that the growth rates of the aggregates convey accurate information as to the level of expenditure. In monetary control terms, a reduction in the growth rate of the monetary aggregate(s) should thus imply a reduction in the amount of money available for carrying out expenditure decisions. There should therefore be a stable and close relationship between the monetary aggregates and nominal incomes. It appears that financial innovation may have altered the money–income relationship for the broad money aggregates, although a new stable relationship may now exist after the transitional period of financial innovation. The relationship between M3 and nominal income, and between M4 and nominal income, appears to have changed dramatically since 1980. After rising during 1974–9, the income velocity of circulation of M3 and M4 fell in the 1980s (Figure 5.2). Experience in the 1970s indicated that there was a lag of approximately two years between the growth of M3 and the subsequent growth of inflation (see Figure 5.3). A sharp increase in M3 in 1973 was followed by a rise in inflation in 1975. Similarly, a sharp rise in M3 in 1978 was followed by an increase in inflation in 1980. There was not such a relationship after 1980, however. Indeed, M3 grew sharply after 1983 and the rate of inflation fell. There appears to be no clear relationship between the broad monetary aggregates and inflation, as shown in Figure 5.3.

Given this 'great velocity decline' (Taylor 1987), to what extent was financial innovation and competition a factor in the rapid growth of the broad monetary aggregates, M3 and M4, relative to nominal income?[7] In particular, was the fast growth of M3 and M4 a consequence of the particular innovations (described in Chapter 4) introduced by the retail banks and building societies? It is argued here that the financial innovations examined in Chapter 4 which provide a market-related rate of interest on easy access accounts altered the money–income relationship as a result of offering both investment and transactions motives for holding money.

The Bank of England maintains that there were three broad factors

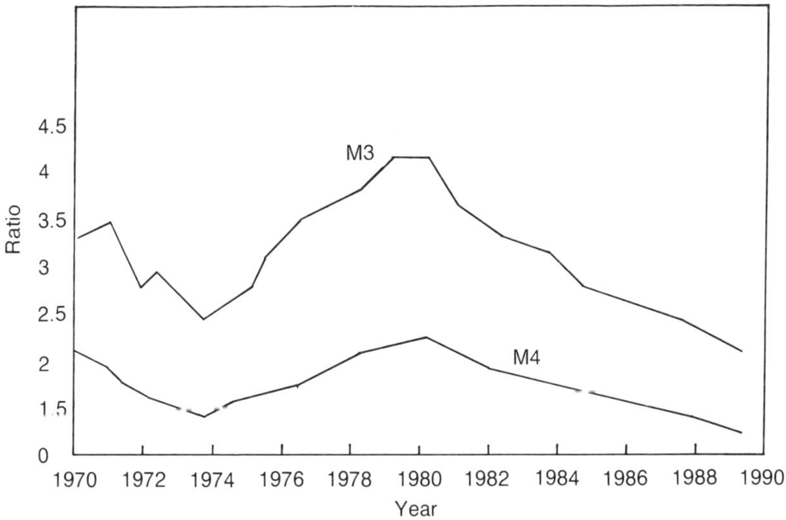

Figure 5.2 Velocity of M3 and M4 (M3 ceased in 1989)

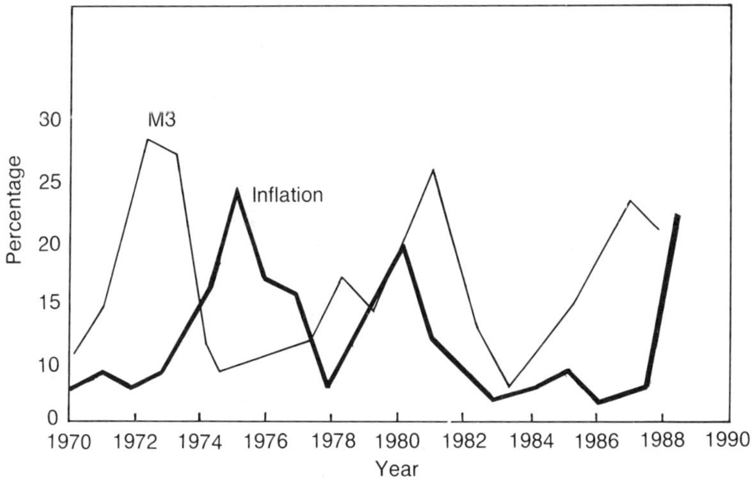

Figure 5.3 Growth of M3 and inflation (percentage change on previous year) (M3 ceased in 1989)

which caused the fall in the velocity of broad money (Bank of England 1985c – reported verbatim):

1 the removal of official restraints on the scale of banks' and building societies' business (i.e. the removal of monetary controls identified in Chapter 4);
2 the intensification of competition between and among banks and building societies, and the offering of more attractive returns and facilities to savers (see below);
3 the persistence of positive real interest rates (see below).

It is the second of these points to which attention is now turned.

Recall that 'money' now serves the purpose of both transactions and investment motives. The problem of financial innovations which combine transactions and investment rates is summed up by Johnson:

> The main difficulty for monetary control has been the conceptual one that so many bank liabilities now combine savings characteristics with transaction characteristics. There is an economy, in that the depositor does not have to have two separate kinds of account; one will fulfil his purpose. *This means that the velocity of many broad aggregates is tending to fall as people increase their savings with income.*
>
> (1986: 356)

It would thus appear worthwhile to analyse further the relationship between the growth of the broad monetary aggregates and financial innovation.

Starting with M3, it may be that the introduction of interest-bearing sight deposits and high interest cheque accounts (HICAs) at banks increased the growth rate of M3. The figures for HICAs are unfortunately not available. Quilter Goodison (in their market report in 1987) estimated that the total figure was £9 billion at the end of 1986. This, however, is a conservative estimate, as Midland Bank alone had £3 billion on its HICAs at this time (personal correspondence). The effect of the growth in interest-bearing sight accounts and HICAs on the growth rate of M3 depends ultimately upon where the assets have originated. If interest-bearing sight deposits and HICAs were so attractive that portfolio redistribution by wealth-holders took place from assets not included in M3 into new assets included in M3, then M3 growth will have increased. The growth rate of M3 will not be affected, however, under circumstances whereby portfolio allocation takes place solely between assets included in the M3 aggregate. It is possible, therefore, for there to be a large increase in holdings of the new innovative financial assets, interest-bearing sight accounts and HICAs without there being much effect on the growth rate of M3. The fall in the share of non-interest-bearing balances is shown in Figure 5.4 and appears to indicate that most of the growth in interest-bearing sight deposits was in fact from switching out of non-interest-bearing balances within M3, thus not affecting the growth rate of the aggregate.

That the fast growth rate of M3 was not directly due to the new bank innovations is further supported by the evidence from the velocity of sectoral M3 holdings. It is immediately obvious from Figures 5.5 and 5.6 that the decline of M3 income velocity was not due to the behaviour of the personal sector. The velocity of personal sector holdings of M3 has remained relatively constant over 1978–87 (see Figure 5.6). Relative to personal disposable income, the personal sector's holdings of M3 reached a peak in 1973–4, fell until 1979, and then remained relatively constant. In fact, the personal sector's share of M3 assets fell relative to that of industrial and commercial companies (ICCs) and other financial institutions (OFIs) (Figure 5.7). Moreover, from 1977 to 1987, the proportion of personal sector holdings of M3 in gross financial wealth declined from 15 per cent to only 10 per cent, with the greatest part of the fall happening since

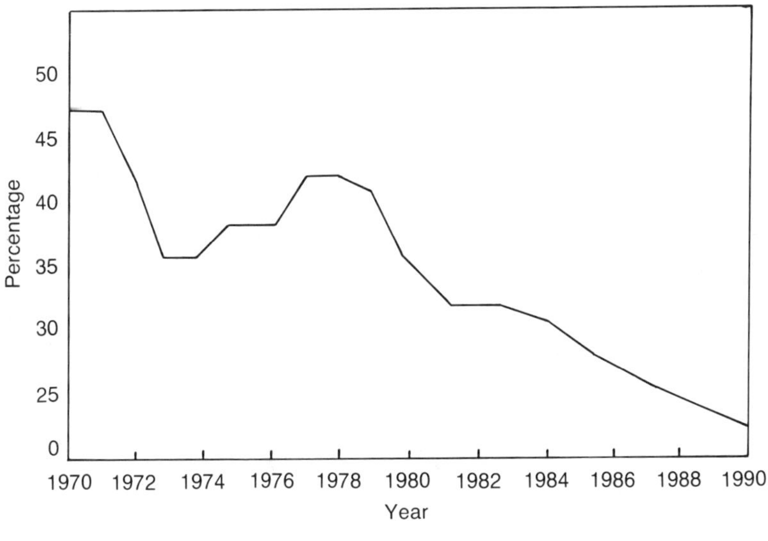

Figure 5.4 Share of non-interest-bearing M1 in M3

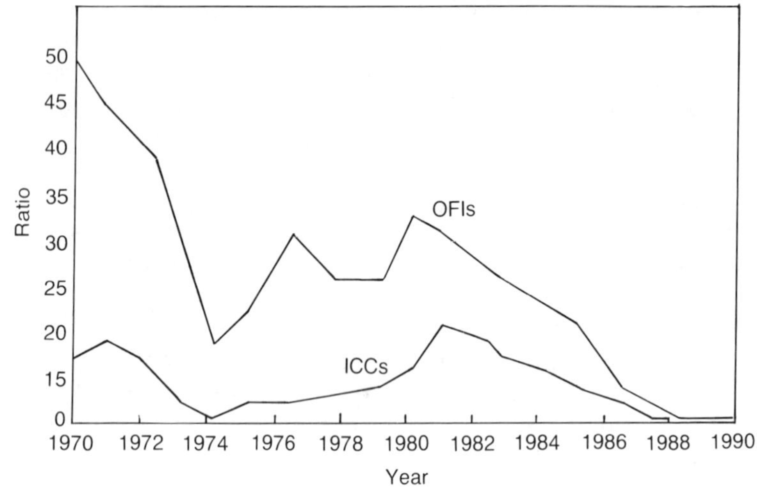

Figure 5.5 Velocity of ICCs and OFIs holdings of M3 (M3 ceased in 1989)

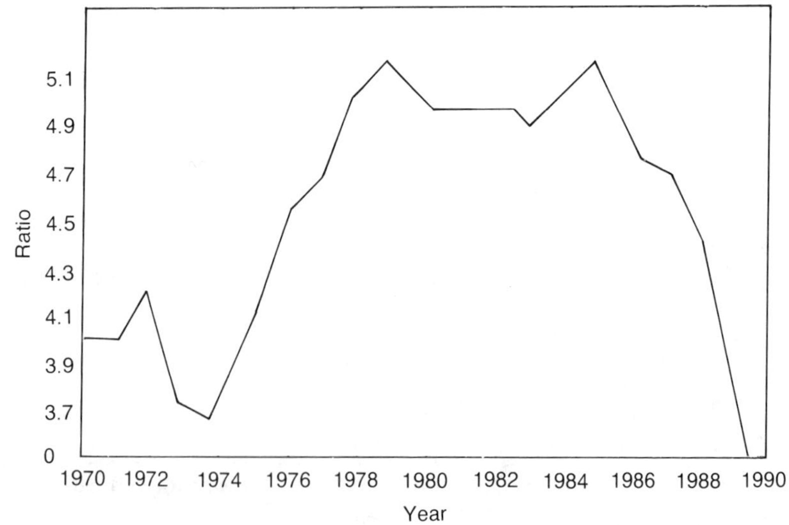

Figure 5.6 Velocity of personal sector M3 holdings

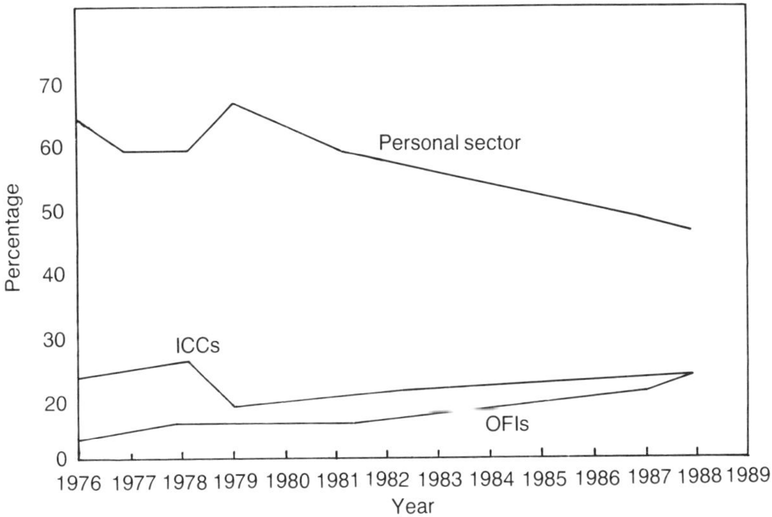

Figure 5.7 Sectoral share of M3 (M3 ceased in 1989)

1980 (Table 5.1), although previous levels were resumed by 1990. Given that the vast majority of HICAs would have been held by the personal sector, it appears that the fast growth of these accounts is not responsible for the rapid increase in M3. The majority of the growth in HICAs must have been due to an increase in the opportunity cost of holding non-interest-bearing deposits (and a decline in holdings of cash, which of course bears no interest), such that switching of balances by the personal sector occurred within M3. When holdings of balances within M3 are analysed, it is evident that the personal sector was not responsible for the fast growth of this aggregate.

From Figure 5.8 it seems that the behaviour of ICCs and OFIs was responsible for the fall in the income velocity of M3. OFIs' holdings of sterling with the monetary sector increased much faster than those of either the personal or the ICCs sectors.

The growth in holdings of £M3 by ICCs steadily increased relative to nominal income after 1980. This may have been the result of a higher average rate of return earned by companies on their liquid assets relative to interest rates on competing short-term assets during the 1980s compared with the 1970s. The share of the OFIs' holdings of M3 showed quite a dramatic increase over the 1980s. OFIs' holdings of M3 grew extremely quickly over 1972–3, fell marginally from

Table 5.1 Personal sector holdings of M3 as a percentage of gross financial wealth

Year	*Holdings of M3 (%)*
1977	15.1
1978	14.5
1979	14.7
1980	15.3
1981	14.8
1982	15.5
1983	14.0
1984	12.7
1985	11.5
1986	10.7
1987	10.7
1988	11.3
1989	13.6
1990	14.9

Source: *Financial Statistics*, various issues, Table 14.4

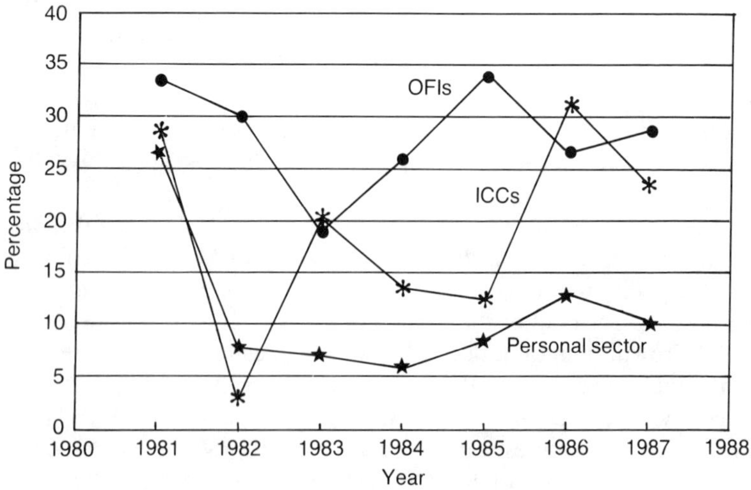

Figure 5.8 Growth of M3 holdings by sector (percentage change)

1974 to 1979 and then increased very rapidly from 1980 onwards (Figure 5.9). How can this growth in OFIs' holdings of M3 be rationalized? Furthermore, how are increased holdings of 'money' by financial institutions to be interpreted for the purposes of monetary control? A major reason for the build-up of OFIs' deposits at banks was regulation induced. Regulations relating to the taxation of building society transactions in gilts were changed in 1984. The change in regulations made bank deposits attractive relative to gilts, such that there was a portfolio reallocation decision by building societies leading to a significant movement away from holding public sector debt towards holding bank deposits. Building society holdings of bank deposits grew from 1980 onwards, and so this regulation-induced effect was obviously not the only factor involved. In fact, it is likely that the change in taxation regulations would have only led to a short-term portfolio readjustment, taking place particularly over 1985–6. As building society holdings of M3 grew almost ninefold during 1979–90, there must be other factors at work.

In explaining building societies' holdings of M3, it may be instructive to return to the financial innovations introduced by building societies, examined in Chapter 4.

It is clear that for the majority of the period 1980–90 building

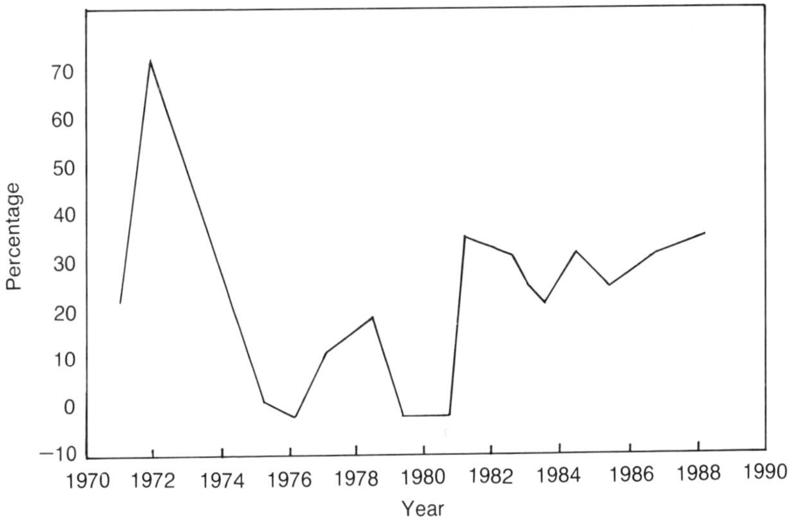

Figure 5.9 Holdings of M3 by OFIs (M3 ceased in 1989)

societies enjoyed a favourable competitive advantage over retail banks in terms of paying higher deposit rates of interest (see Chapter 4). These high rates of interest were largely paid on extremely liquid balances, with little or no withdrawal penalties. The competitive advantage of building societies over banks was exemplified in the growth of the building societies' share of personal sector liquid assets for most of the 1980s and the decline in the retail banks' share. The growth of building society liquid assets held by the personal sector was much faster than the growth in personal disposable income (Figure 5.10). Indeed, this growth was mainly responsible for the fall in income velocity of M4 (Figure 5.11). It appears that the effect of financial innovation may have been to induce the personal sector to hold more building society deposits relative to income. Financial innovation did not directly lead to a fast growth in persons' holdings of M3 relative to income, largely because of the superior interest rate at building societies. It could be argued, however, that financial innovation *indirectly* led to the fall in the income velocity of M3. The personal sector favoured building society deposits because of the relatively higher interest rates and the 'increased moneyness' of building society accounts (Bank of England 1987a: 219). These balances were in part recycled to banks, thus increasing M3 relative to nominal incomes.

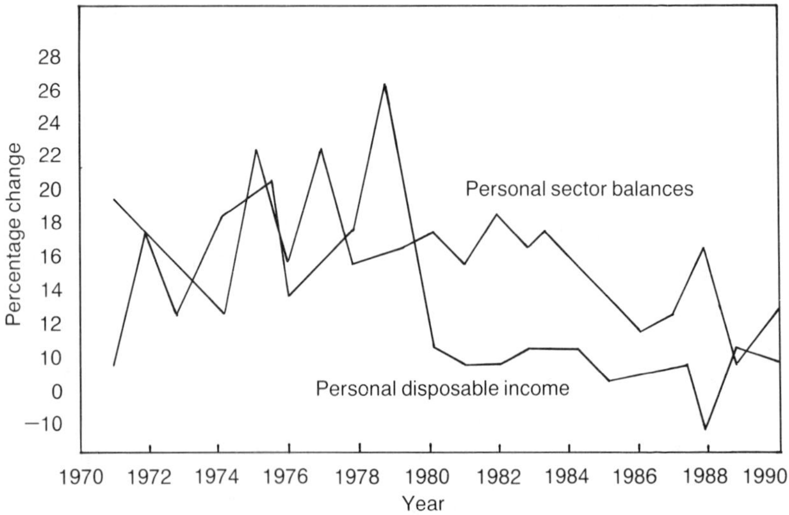

Figure 5.10 Personal sector balances at building societies (percentage change, year end)

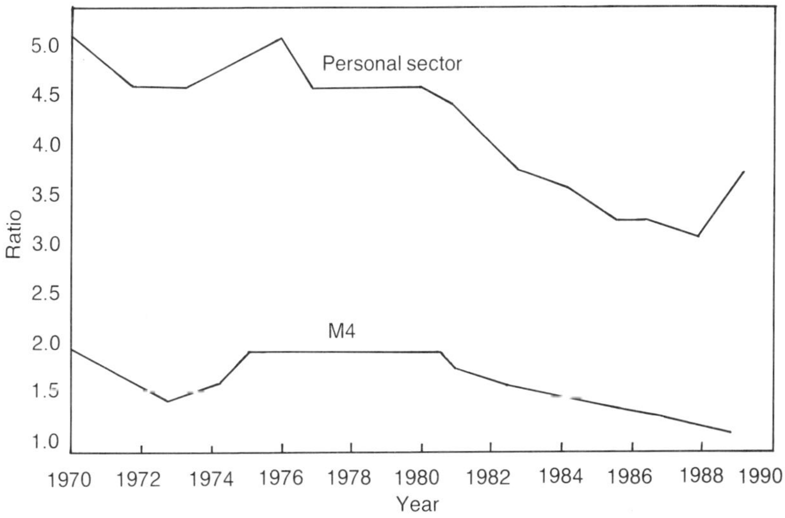

Figure 5.11 Velocity of personal sector deposits at building societies and M4

Financial innovation, therefore, *indirectly* led to an increase in M3 relative to income. This is because the innovation-induced fast growth of personal sector holdings of building society deposits had a counterpart in the fast build-up of building society holdings of bank deposits (Table 5.2), thus increasing the growth rate of M3.

It must be emphasized that whilst the decision to hold additional liquid investment assets is purely at the margin of financial portfolio selection, it may have crucial implications for the interpretation of movements in the UK's monetary aggregates, for the stability of money demand and for the implementation of monetary controls. First, individuals will no longer feel obliged to hold separate accounts for pure transactions funds and for funds held in readiness for making investments or as part of a financial investment portfolio. Second, changes in the general level of interest rates will have a much reduced effect on the opportunity cost of holding liquid transactions balances, and hence it could be expected that such changes would have a smaller and possibly less predictable impact on the growth of the aggregates. Third, there is the problem that even if a predictable relationship could be established between the growth of money and changes in the general level of interest rates, it would still not be possible to determine whether or not individuals had consciously

Table 5.2 Building society holdings of bank deposits

Year	*Holdings of bank deposits (£m)*
1980	2,168
1981	2,731
1982	4,104
1983	4,666
1984	5,115
1985	8,207
1986	9,349
1987	15,177
1988	19,768
1989	19,373
1990	23,084

Source: *Financial Statistics*, various issues, Table 7.7

altered the balance between the amount of funds held for transactions purposes and the amount held for investment purposes within their aggregate holdings of financial assets. Thus, it might still be quite possible for an increase in the general level of interest rates to dampen effective aggregate demand for goods and services without that increase having any discernible impact on the growth of the monetary aggregates. Indeed, as individuals would be able to alter the distribution of their financial assets portfolio (in terms of assets being ear-marked for specific functions) without having to take any explicit action (and hence without incurring related transactions costs and taking on the possible risks related to having to switch funds back into a spendable form at short notice), it is quite possible that official manipulation of the level of interest rates could have an enhanced influence on private expenditure decisions. This therefore raises the problem of the authorities' being in a position whereby they may be unaware of the effects of policy actions. The change in motives for holding liquid funds is likely to have broken the link between money and income. If transactions balances are being held for investment purposes rather than for expenditure purposes, an increase in the money supply may not necessarily lead to an increase in income. An increase in the money supply that is greater than the increase in nominal income may merely represent an increased desire to hold high interest money balances for investment purposes. The effect of high interest instant access balances on the break-up of the money–income relationship is tested econometrically in Chapter 9.

The problem of changing motives for holding money was recognized in policy statements:

> There have been significant changes in the relationship between broad money and spending over the years. Because it is used as a store of value as well as for transactions purposes, what matters so far as subsequent inflationary pressure is concerned is not its growth rate alone but the extent to which people are prepared to hold interest-bearing money balances rather than to spend them.
>
> (*Financial Statement and Budget Report* March 1989)

The problem for the monetary authorities was to decide whether 'excessive' growth of the monetary aggregates (relative to nominal incomes) was indicative of loose policy conditions or whether it was symptomatic of behavioural changes that were not foreseen and that did not necessarily augur future inflation.

It appears that, in the light of the increase in competition between banks and building societies and the financial innovations introduced, the build-up of liquidity and subsequent out-of-target growth of the broad monetary aggregates may merely have been a rational response by wealth-holders to the behaviour of financial institutions, and may have represented a once-and-for-all adjustment that only affected monetary control as the adjustment occurred.

If this were so, it may be that, rather than being representative of possible future inflation, it represented a rational portfolio redistribution on behalf of the non-bank private sector. As recognized by the Bank of England (Bank of England 1986b:503), it is important that the movements of the aggregates be interpreted rather than reacted to in a pavlovian manner. There are problems, of course, in exercising discretion:

> The difficulty is to know how much of the growth in personal sector liquidity one should explain in this way and how much reflects a build-up of money holdings for purely transactions purposes. For although one can make a qualitative assessment the separate influences cannot easily be quantitatively distinguished.
>
> (Bank of England 1986b: 503)

However, it should also be recognized that after almost a decade of negative real interest rates on retail financial assets, the 1980s witnessed a substantial shift back to positive real interest rates on retail assets.

If, as Lawson suggests, the 'increased amounts of broad money' were being willingly held, the continued willingness of the non-bank private sector to hold these balances may have depended crucially upon real interest rates being maintained at a high level.

If this were so, then unless it was the desire of the authorities that real interest rates should remain high indefinitely (or at least until domestic productive capacity could be raised sufficiently to allow for the absorption of the increased domestic spending power in a non-inflationary manner), the actual build-up of the money holdings could be neither condoned nor ignored if the control of inflation was to be seen as a long-run objective as well as a shorter-term objective of government policy. However, the shorter-term policy dilemma was always likely to be that whilst high real rates of interest may be necessary in order to induce holders of interest-bearing money assets to continue to hold the higher levels of liquidity, they were probably a primary cause of the build-up in these potentially destabilizing balances.

The official policy statements tended to utilize the developments in the financial institutions framework as a means of calming fears about the build-up of liquidity (in relation to nominal incomes) in the UK financial system and as a means of explaining the apparent breakdown in the relationship between money supply growth and inflation which had underpinned the government's approach to macroeconomic policy. As the Governor of the Bank of England pointed out in a lecture given on 22 October 1986:

> a good part of the increase in personal sector liquidity since 1980, *which is held largely with building societies rather than banks*, can be attributed to a redistribution of personal sector assets as a response to changes in the behaviour of financial intermediaries. To this extent it does not carry the same threatening message about future inflation as the same increase in liquidity would in the absence of the change in financial behaviour.
>
> (Bank of England 1986b: 503)

It was possible, however, that individuals might amass large amounts of assets for their (liquid) investment characteristics whilst real interest rates remained high, but then rapidly unload these balances through expenditure on goods, services and real assets once the real return on holding liquid assets began to fall. Thus, whilst a growth rate of the aggregates well in excess of the growth of domestic output might be legitimately rationalized as being of little concern for the short-term course of inflation and the current account of the balance of payments, so long as monetary policy remained restrictive with high real interest rates, any official action taken to ease monetary controls would have had a quite disproportionate effect on the growth of real spending power of the private sector. Not only would the return from holding liquid investment assets be reduced relative to the marginal utility to be gained from current consumption, but also inflationary expectations, stimulated by the recognition of the pent-up purchasing power within the economy, would have led to increased expenditures on real goods, services and assets.

This assumes, of course, that the adjustment of money balances involves expenditure on real goods and services. It may be that (and this is an empirical matter) portfolio readjustments take place largely through switching into other financial assets rather than through consumption expenditure.

The statement that 'increased amounts of broad money' were held relates, of course, to levels of broad money compared with nominal incomes. As stated earlier, the relationship between holdings of broad money and financial wealth remained fairly constant in the 1980s. The correct interpretation may be that the relationship between money and income was being restored to levels observed before the inflation shocks of the 1970s. It may be that velocity was returning to trend levels of the early 1970s such that, combined with a constant ratio of money to financial wealth, holdings of money were neither excessive, nor likely to flow into the pool of transactions, nor represented a build-up of potential purchasing power as perceived by the balance holders. Rather than being a breakdown of the money–income relationship, there may merely have been a stock effect followed by a new stable relationship.

However, when the monetary authorities attempted to constrain the growth of the monetary aggregates, the financial developments introduced by building societies and banks made a simplistic growth target inappropriate. Short-term movements of funds in response to interest rate differential changes, in addition to the apparent desire of individuals to hold liquid balances for investment purposes, made excessive dependence upon the monetary aggregates quite unrealistic. The monetary aggregates may still be part of a monetary *package*, however, as a guide to discretionary policy in a world of financial innovation:

> when the relationship between the money stock and the ultimate targets of policy is changing, due to deregulation or whatever reason, the case for utilizing additional information is *strengthened*. But this does not mean that there is no useful information in the monetary aggregates. Judgements about whether or not the

> monetary aggregates are growing too quickly will be harder than in a more stable regulatory framework but the information content of the aggregates will not be zero.
>
> (Jonson and Parkin 1986: 15)

The reliance of policy on a number of indicators necessitates a judgemental approach as to the relative significance of the various indicators.

Financial innovation meant that monetary policy had to be carried out in a discretionary interpretive manner:

> It is the counterbalance between the shifting structure of the financial system on the one hand, and the need for rules and pre-commitment on the part of the authorities on the other, that makes it so hard to select an optimal form of monetary targetry, one that could retain underlying discipline, while at the same time allowing a sensible and flexible response to the rapidly changing form of the financial system.
>
> (Goodhart 1986b: 325)

From the evidence of the 1980s, it seems that growth of the money stock in excess of the growth of nominal income did not always cause inflation when expected. This means that money may still be a *necessary* cause of inflation but not a *sufficient* cause. Essentially, a fast rate of growth of the money supply relative to nominal income *may* or *may not* cause an increase in inflation, depending on the *nature* of the monetary expansion.

A fast rate of growth of the money supply induced by financial innovation may have no effect on inflation. The problem for the monetary authorities is to *interpret* the nature of the monetary expansion and decide as to its possible effects (if any) and hence policy actions. The existence of financial innovation, or the *possibility* that it might occur, hinders the operation of monetary control.

5.5 CONCLUSION

Two broad effects of building societies' and banks' financial innovation on the relationship between money and income have been identified. First, there are those new financial assets that carry out what are termed the 'traditional' motives for holding money (transactions and precautionary) that at times make it necessary for the monetary authorities to reclassify the monetary aggregates (as in the case of building society innovations and M2/PSL2), and which may also lead to distortion in the growth rates of the monetary aggregates. Such innovation, it is argued, is not a new phenomenon, but merely the changing evolutionary development of the financial system. The institutionalist school has for many years pointed to the existence and emergence of close substitutes for money. The difference in the 1980s was the variety and pace of financial innovation and change.

Financial innovations which perform the traditional functions of money inhibit the short-term operation of monetary control. There will often be a time lag between the introduction of an innovation and the identification of that innovation by the monetary authorities. There may be a further time lag between analysing the innovation and deciding whether or not the monetary aggregates need to be re-classified. During this time, the growth of the new asset may lead to distortions in some of the targeted money supply figures, causing problems of interpretation of monetary conditions. Re-definition of the monetary aggregates to include a new asset may also invite scepticism as to the authorities' approach to monetary control in terms of accusations of manipulating the figures and/or 'moving the goalposts' (Johnson 1986: 3).

Second, there are those financial innovations that may be held for their investment properties. Highly liquid monetary assets (many of which are instantly accessible) have evolved which offer extremely competitive market-related rates of interest. 'Money' has not historically paid explicit interest. The payment of interest on instant access accounts means that these balances increasingly represent attractive repositories for investment balances. Moreover, these new assets *also* tend to fulfil the traditional functions of money. The important aspect of these assets is that they require no explicit action on the part of their holders to switch them from being investment balances to media of exchange and/or expenditure balances. These investment balances usually have the property of being instantly realizable. There tend to be few prohibitive transactions costs, investment and expenditure balances being kept in the same account and merely perceived as being separate in the mind of the holder.

These interest-bearing transactions balances may be relatively interest inelastic, and so may have more continuing effects on monetary control (see Chapter 7).

An analysis of the growth of the monetary aggregates in Section 5.4 suggests that the introduction of easy access high interest accounts that offer both transactions and investment characteristics may have been responsible for the breakdown of the money–income relationship. The fall in the income velocity of broad money since 1980, i.e.

the tendency for broad money aggregates to grow faster than nominal incomes, may be explained by the increasing emphasis placed on money balances as investment assets. The attraction of high real interest rates on money appears to have altered the money–income link. Thus, the money–income relationship appears to have changed because of the new role assigned to money by balance-holders. The specific contention that financial innovation in terms of high interest money balances has affected the money–income link through the demand for money function is tested econometrically in Chapter 9.

It may certainly be concluded from the evidence of this chapter that, at the very least, the operation of monetary policy should be carried out in an interpretive discretionary manner rather than through some pre-stated monetary rule. The usefulness of a discretionary policy will depend, moreover, on the ability of the authorities to control the money supply and on the stability of the demand for money, which are investigated in Chapters 9 and 10.

6 Competition, mortgage lending and the money–income relationship

6.1 INTRODUCTION

It is not simply money balances, of course, that are important for monetary control or that affect the growth rates of the monetary aggregates. The level of borrowing is also of importance for the analysis of monetary developments. In Section 6.2 the relationship between movements in the monetary aggregates and the growth of borrowing is examined. It is noted that there was a rapid expansion in both borrowing and monetary aggregates in the 1980s, particularly by the personal sector and largely for house purchase. This is a response to the factors outlined in Chapter 4, relating to the stock effects of the abolition of the building societies' cartel and the ending of the corset.

As personal sector borrowing was a major factor in the rapid growth of the broad monetary aggregates, it may be possible to rationalize the fast increase in the money supply figures in relation to nominal incomes by reference to lending to the personal sector. Indeed, it has been suggested by some authors that the personal sector 'mortgage leak' was responsible for the slow growth of nominal incomes compared with the broad monetary aggregates. This hypothesis is explained and fully examined in Section 6.2. An alternative argument as to the effect of personal sector borrowing on the fall in the income velocity of money is presented in Section 6.3. Specifically, the combined effect of an increased level of mortgage lending and greater financial innovation by building societies and banks upon the activities of 'last-time sellers' is analysed.

The idea outlined in Chapter 4 that finite stock adjustments following the abolition of the recommended rate system and the ending of the corset may have temporarily affected the stability of the demand for money and credit is examined in further detail.

The effects of deposit and credit shocks upon the operation of monetary control are examined in Section 6.4 in terms of the buffer stock model, and conclusions are drawn as to the applicability of this model both in theory and in reality. The debate as to whether the money supply is exogenous or endogenous in terms of the activities of building societies and banks as set out in Section 6.2 and in view of the effects of supply-side credit shocks to the economy is analysed in Section 6.5.

6.2 HOUSE PURCHASE, THE MORTGAGE 'LEAK' AND THE MONEY–INCOME RELATIONSHIP

It may be useful to examine the growth of the monetary aggregates in terms of the effects of bank and building society lending. Any analysis of the transmission mechanism between money and prices must include both the money and credit markets to get a full picture. Some would argue that this point has not always been expressly acknowledged:

> For many years, economists ignored the role of the credit markets. Recently there has been some change. The analysis of the transmission process is incomplete without both the money and credit markets and their interaction.
>
> (Brunner and Meltzer 1988: 446)

Indeed, the neglect of the credit market is exemplified in the IS–LM analysis introduced in Chapter 2, where money determines aggregate demand, all other financial instruments (including credit) being categorized under the amorphous heading of 'bonds'. Bernanke and Blinder (1988) and Brunner and Meltzer (1988) have extended the basic IS–LM framework to accommodate the roles of both money and credit.

The importance of the credit market to growth in the monetary aggregates can be seen in Figure 6.1, which shows the change in bank and building society lending to the non-bank private sector (NBPS) and the change in M4. It is clear that there is a close relationship between credit and growth in the money supply.

Figures 6.2 and 6.3 show that borrowing by industrial and commercial companies (ICCs), other financial institutions (OFIs) and the personal sector all grew extremely quickly in the last decade. As can be seen from Figures 6.4 and 6.5 there were marked trends in the growth of bank and building society sterling lending to the three categories that make up the NBPS. Much of the growth in bank and building society lending was to the personal sector.

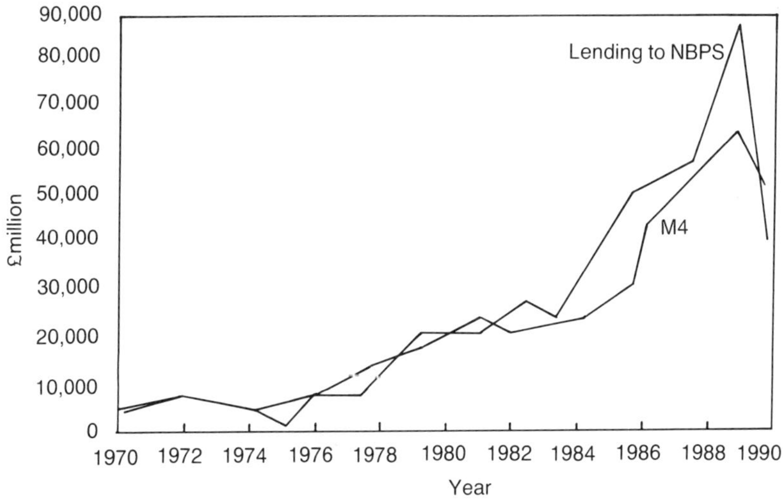

Figure 6.1 Change in M4 and bank and building society lending to the NBPS

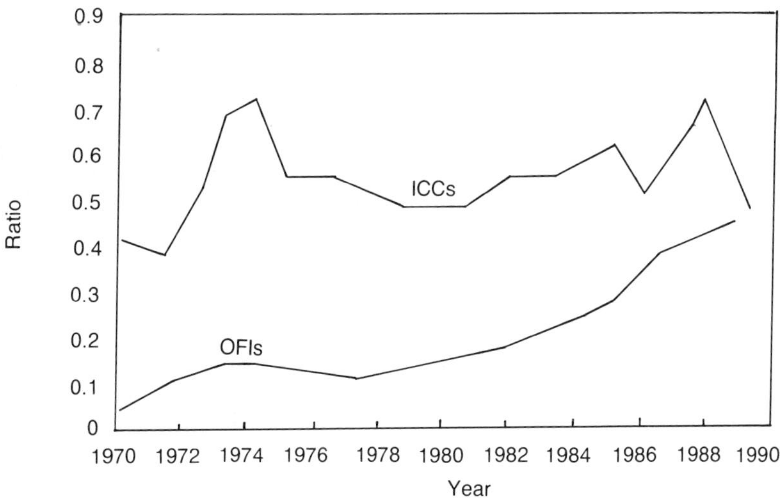

Figure 6.2 Bank borrowing by ICCs and OFIs (relative to nominal GDP)

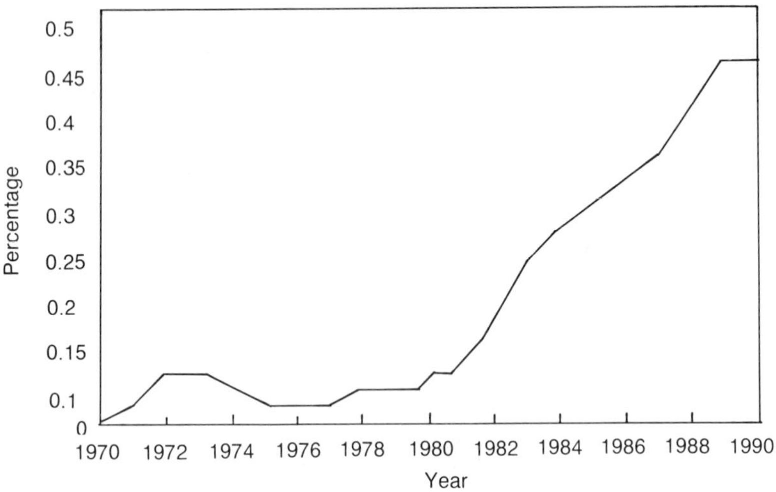

Figure 6.3 Personal sector bank borrowing (relative to personal disposable income, annualized)

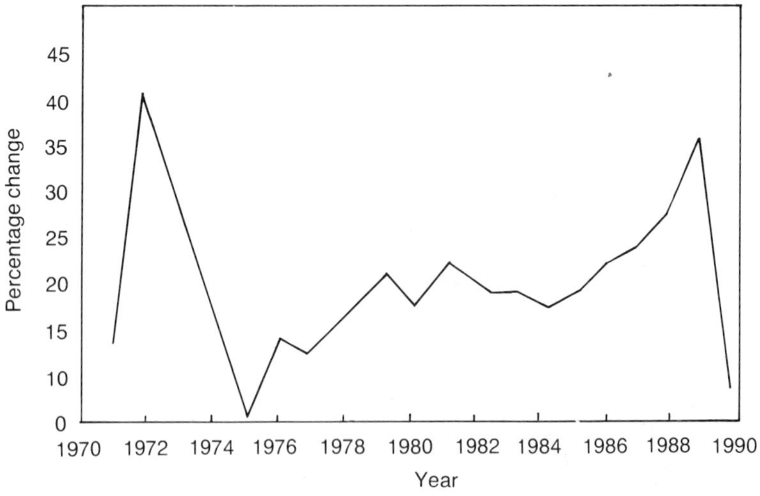

Figure 6.4 Bank and building society lending to the NBPS (percentage change, year end)

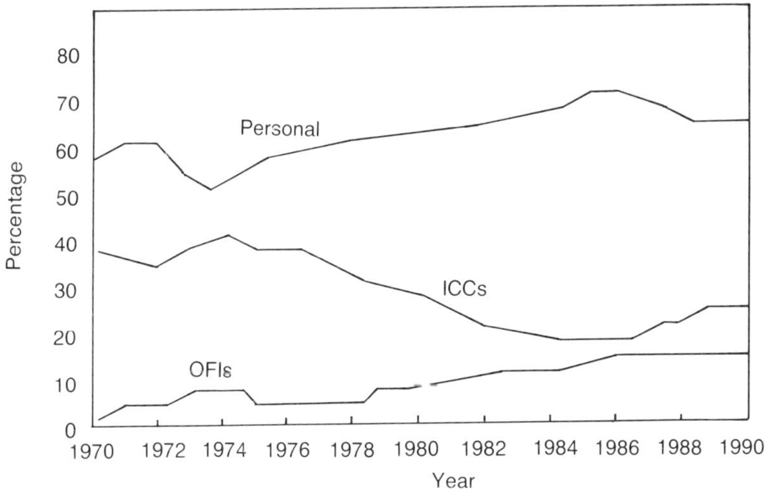

Figure 6.5 Sectoral shares of bank and building society lending to NBPS

The importance of personal sector borrowing from building societies and banks to the growth in M4 can be seen in Figure 6.6. The degree to which the growth in M4 is determined by personal sector borrowing from banks and building societies is seen by the close trend of the two series. Of total bank and building society lending to the personal sector, mortgage lending cannot be overemphasized, as Figure 6.7 shows. Indeed, when analysing the broad monetary aggregates, official comment centred upon the importance of lending for house purchase to the personal sector:

> In the United Kingdom at present, monetary growth is being driven to a considerable extent by the strength of lending to the personal sector in general, and by mortgage lending in particular.
>
> (Bank of England 1986d: 531)

That this upsurge in personal sector borrowing occurred should not be surprising, however.[1]

The increase in personal sector borrowing resulted from the stock adjustment of the increase in mortgages after the building societies' cartel and the removal of the corset on the banks. These changes entailed a greater supply of credit and a finite portfolio reallocation by the personal sector back towards its desired demand for credit function.

Wills (1982) argues that banks can be analysed as two-input, two-

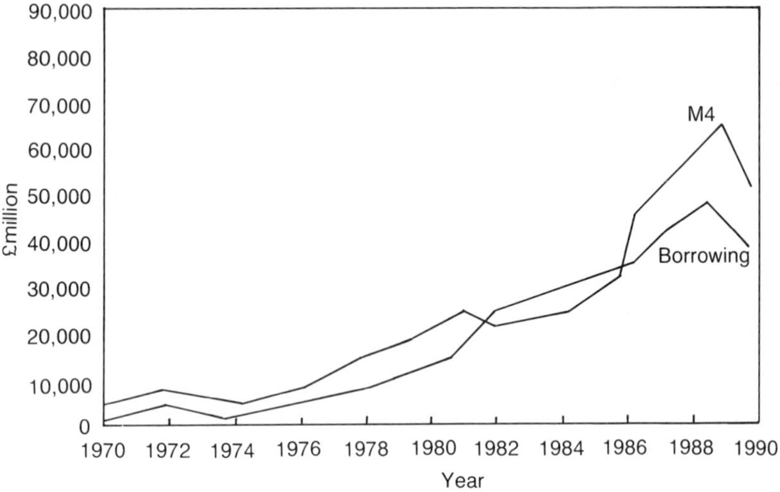

Figure 6.6 Change in M4 and personal sector borrowing from banks and societies

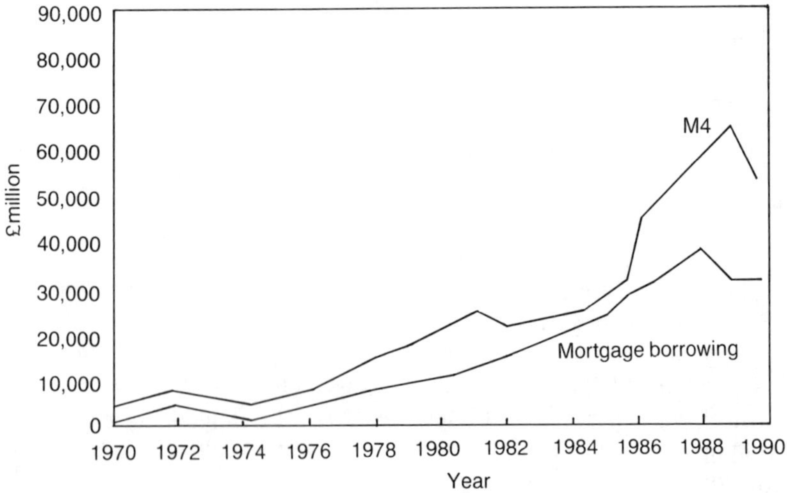

Figure 6.7 Change in M4 and personal sector mortgage borrowing

output firms. The two inputs are retail and wholesale deposits (liabilities) and the two outputs are retail and wholesale lending. If wholesale lending is ignored for the moment, this analysis can also be extended to building societies. Wills maintains that banks (and building societies) act as price setters and quantity takers in the retail deposit and loan markets, such that the supply curve for loans and/or credit is relatively flat. In Figure 6.8, as long as the market is competitive and unconstrained by restrictive monetary controls, we see that at price *P* banks and building societies will supply whatever credit is demanded (subject to the ability of the borrower to repay). At times in the period to 1980, however, the banks and building societies could not operate in this manner. The banks' ability to operate as price setters and quantity takers was circumscribed by the various monetary controls placed on them, as described in Chapter 3. Similarly, the building societies were constrained by the interest rate cartel agreement. For the majority of the 1970s, building societies

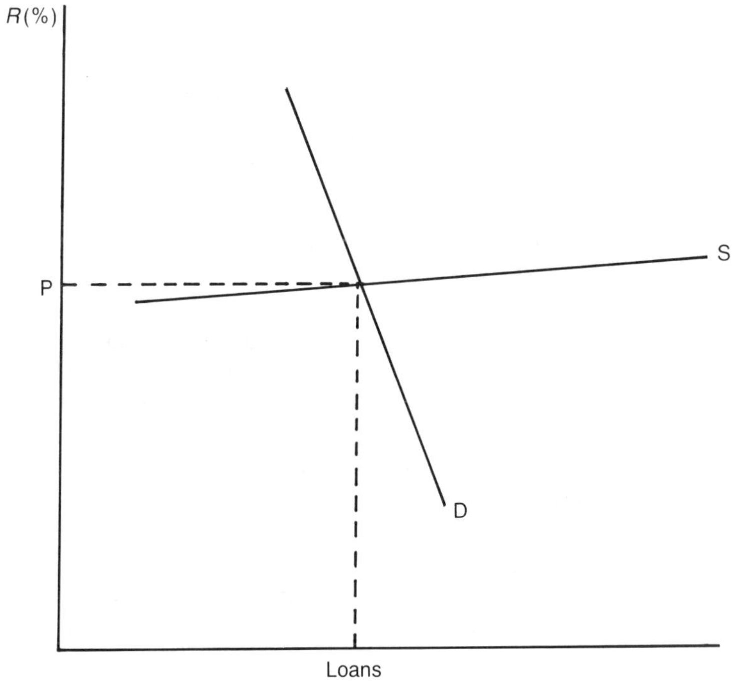

Figure 6.8 Supply/demand for loans

and banks effectively operated as *price takers* and *quantity setters.* The ending of direct monetary controls and the cartel meant that banks and building societies could return to being price setters and quantity takers as Wills suggests. This resulted in a considerable supply-side credit shock, with substantial reintermediation on the part of the personal sector, as evidenced by the rapid growth of the broad monetary aggregates.

The stock effect in terms of the reallocation of the personal sector credit portfolios would be expected to destabilize the demand for money and credit as the effect occurred but in the long term the relationships may become stable.

The fast growth of the broad monetary aggregates, and in particular the rapid increase in building society and bank lending to the personal sector in the 1980s, would be expected, under monetarist models, to lead to an increase in the rate of growth of inflation. An increase in the level of lending would be expected to lead to an increase in the level of expenditure, *ceteris paribus.* An increase in expenditure would be expected to push up prices. As is well known, inflation did not increase until after 1989. A comparison can be made with the 'Barber boom' years of increased monetary growth and, its counterpart, bank lending. The introduction of competition and credit control led to an upsurge in bank lending and a subsequent upturn in inflation, with a lag of about two years. Given the fast rate of growth of building society and bank lending in the 1980s, why did the UK economy not see any increase in the rate of inflation until the end of the decade?

One reason might be the mortgage 'leak' (or 'equity withdrawal'). Funds acquired through the mortgage leak, rather than being used to finance an increase in expenditure, may have been used to build up financial assets. This may be a rational response by personal sector borrowers, as in some years the rate of interest on mortgages has been below that available on deposit accounts at building societies, and this effect is enhanced when account is taken of tax relief on interest payments on mortgage borrowing for house purchase or improvement. The incentive to use mortgage loans is largely a reflection of the pattern of relative interest rates that has developed. With building societies paying a high rate of interest on easy access deposits, there was a reduction in the spread between the rate on mortgage loans and the rate on deposits of building societies. Indeed, there have been several occasions when the mortgage rate has been *lower* than the deposit rate, resulting in profitable arbitrage opportunities. In other words, if a person has, for example, £5,000 cash from a house he or she has sold, and wishes to buy a house for £30,000, it is profitable in some periods to take a mortgage of £30,000 and maintain the £5,000 cash in a high interest account. Of course, arbitrage opportunities are rare, but even when they are not present, it is still better to maintain portfolio allocation in this manner as mortgage rates are far cheaper than typical non-mortgage consumer credit rates.

As it appeared to be partly a stock readjustment following the abolition of monetary controls, it has led some commentators to minimize its economic significance:

> what we have seen is a change in the personal sectors' financial behaviour, resulting from the freer availability of credit, which may be of less economic significance than would have been implied by earlier relationships between borrowing and spending.
>
> (Bank of England 1988a: 49)

It is argued here that relationships between borrowing and expenditure may have changed but the reasoning about the importance of the 'mortgage leak' is both naive and flawed.

The effect of mortgage borrowers using their borrowings to add to liquid assets as in the 'mortgage leak' was too small to explain the divergence between the growth of personal sector money balances and the growth of incomes. Certainly this practice occurred, but it was not large enough to account for the discrepancy.

There is the theoretical possibility that bank and building society multiple deposit expansion through lending for mortgage may, in theory, have no effect whatsoever on the real economy. If *all* funds received by last-time sellers are placed in a building society, there will only be a constant market in second-hand houses, with no expenditure multiplier involved. Building society deposits and hence lending are increased, building societies lend more for house purchase and receive all the funds of the next last-time sellers, and so on. No expenditure is carried out by last-time sellers and hence there can be no expenditure multiplier. Of course, this assumes a perfect re-depository ratio for building societies, which will not occur. This theoretical case, however, may point to interesting possibilities and help to explain past monetary developments, as explained below.

Whilst not denying that this type of mortgage leak does have an effect in reducing the expected level of expenditure and hence nominal incomes, if it is used to purchase financial assets, it is argued here that the magnitude of such effects is not as strong as claimed by some.

6.3 HOUSE PURCHASE, LAST-TIME SELLERS AND THE MONEY–INCOME RELATIONSHIP

The majority of building society mortgage loans are extended for the purchase of *existing* housing, rather than new housing. The Stow Report (Stow 1979) estimates that 85 per cent of building societies' mortgage lending is for existing housing. Figures are not available for bank lending on mortgage, but it appears plausible to assume a similar proportion is for 'second-hand' housing. In buying an existing house, the purchaser will exchange a building society loan for the house, and the vendor becomes the recipient of the sale price for the house. There may then be a chain of further transactions (the vendor may wish to buy another house, for example), but at the end of the chain (if it involves *existing* housing stock) all of the funds apart from those for house purchase on the security of already existing housing stock *must* end up in the hands of those who are *'last-time sellers'* – i.e. those who are selling a house but not buying another house and therefore not requiring a further mortgage. There are several reasons why people become last-time sellers. Some may inherit the houses of their parents when they die, and subsequently sell the property. Some last-time sellers may be elderly people leaving their own house to move into rented rest-home accommodation. Furthermore, some houses which may formerly have been rented may be sold.

Every mortgage loan will therefore necessarily end up, after a (perhaps long) chain of transactions, as a receipt of funds by a last-time seller.

Let us assume that the last-time seller saves *all* the money received from selling a house. Further, let us assume all the money is saved at a building society. (The money may, of course, be used to acquire other financial assets, but here the case is limited to the funds being returned to a building society for reasons which should become clear). The building society will now have more funds which it will lend out by way of mortgage. Thus, it can be seen that building society lending may be in part self-financing. The degree to which funds do actually return to building societies from mortgage lending depends upon a variety of factors which are examined below.

The importance of these funds for the operation and interpretation of monetary control depends on what the recipient does with the money. Two possibilities can be isolated. The recipient can decide to spend the funds on real assets, or save the funds by way of a financial asset, or spend and save the funds in a desired proportion. The first case will lead to a greater level of expenditure and consumption, whilst the second will lead to greater saving. If the funds are spent on real assets, the extra expenditure will lead to an expenditure multiplier effect, whereby the receiver of the funds will spend some and save some, and so on, according to the marginal propensity to consume:

> the *flow* of loans granted and spent generates a significantly larger *flow* of income. (Or, if you prefer, an increment of loans generates a multiple increment of income).
>
> (McLeod 1984: 191)

The amount of funds received by last-time sellers and potentially available for re-lending is large. The categories below are reproduced from the Stow Report (1979) 'Mortgage finance into the 1980's'. As in the report, the total number of house sales is divided into two groups:

1 Sales where the funds realized are reinvested in housing or transferred overseas. This category can in turn be subdivided into the following four categories.

- (a) People moving where the proceeds are used as the deposit on the next house. Leakages are assumed to be used up in transactions costs.
- (b) Council house sales where the proceeds are used by councils.
- (c) New housing, where the proceeds cover the costs of labour, materials, profit and land.
- (d) Houses sold on emigration.

2 Sales where the funds are not reinvested in housing or transferred abroad, i.e. where they are retained for domestic investment or to finance consumption. These comprise the following.

- (a) People moving out of owner-occupation and into other tenures. The proceeds are assumed to be equal to the average house price less the average mortgage redemptions multiplied by the number of sales.
- (b) Household dissolution. This group consists principally of elderly households with little or no mortgage and the proceeds are assumed to be equal to the number of sales multiplied by the average house price.
- (c) The sales of formerly rented houses – adjusted to allow for company-owned rented property sales. The proceeds are assumed to be equal to the adjusted number of sales multiplied by the average house price.

According to the Stow Report, an estimated £4,500 million accrued to last-time sellers in 1979, the latest date of the report's calculations. Table 6.1 updates and recalculates the Stow data to show the amount of funds realized by last-time sellers (Holmans 1986). As can be seen, these estimates are somewhat higher than the Stow data and represent a large proportion of funds lent on mortgage.

It can be seen that in most years the moving owner-occupier's proportion of total equity withdrawal accounted for less than about 25 per cent, whereas equity withdrawal by last-time sellers was almost half the total. This considerably weakens any emphasis upon the importance of moving owner-occupiers affecting the income velocity of circulation of the broad money aggregates. The economic effects of these large holdings of money are dependent upon the proportion that is saved and the proportion that is consumed. The greater is the tendency to consume additional income, the larger will be the expenditure multiplier. The larger is the propensity to save additional income, the greater is the magnitude with which banks and building societies can expand deposits.

A change in the policy of rationing mortgage supply towards meeting mortgage demand will necessarily involve financing a greater number of loans for house purchase. A behavioural change by building societies from rationing mortgages to providing an excess supply of mortgages would be expected to increase both the equity withdrawal by 'owner-occupier movers' and the volume of money received by last-time sellers. It would be expected that, everything else being equal, such an increase in funds for owner-occupier movers

Table 6.1 Total equity withdrawal and withdrawal by last-time sellers and moving owner-occupiers

Year	*Total equity withdrawal (£m)*	*Last-time sellers (£m)*	*Moving owner-occupiers (£m)*
	£m	£m	£m
1977	4,115	2,255	1,050
1978	3,150	2,765	1,290
1979	6,205	3,395	1,415
1980	7,010	3,715	1,380
1981	8,810	4,390	1,960
1982	13,065	5,230	4,175
1983	12,720	5,830	3,520
1984	13,840	7,360	3,020

Source: Holmans 1986

and last-time sellers would lead to an increase in expenditure. Moreover, if the previously unsatisfied demand is met, it may lead to a rise in house prices. Home owners, with an appreciating asset, may adjust their expenditure plans in response to gains from house prices. If this is the case, personal sector expenditure may rise. This, in turn, may lead to a multiple expansion of incomes. If this scenario is correct, then increased building society lending for house purchase is likely to have had similar multiplier effects as those from an increase in bank lending for corporate investment. In fact this did not happen. Increased mortgage lending did not lead to a proportionate increase in expenditure.

It has already been noted (see Chapter 4) that competition between banks and building societies and the abolition of the cartel resulted in a higher average rate of interest paid on building society and bank deposits, coupled with enhanced liquidity. It appears reasonable to suggest (although difficult to quantify) that high real rates of interest on liquid deposits may have attracted a large number of last-time sellers to deposit a significant proportion of their funds in either building societies or banks (in view of the analysis of Chapter 5, mostly at building societies) rather than use the money for expenditure purposes.

High real interest rates on instant-access accounts means that an exogenous shock, such as an increase in building society and bank mortgage lending, *may not lead to holdings of 'unwanted' money.* Money, paying an attractive rate of interest (relative to other financial assets), may now be regarded as a portfolio investment asset rather than merely as a transaction medium (see Chapter 5). Financial innovation thus seems to have reduced the income-generating effects of building society and bank lending. Financial innovation means that money can at times be long-term buffer stocks after an exogenous shock to the system, and as such may be treated as investments rather than expenditure balances. Thus, income will not increase as much as might be expected. This may be part of the reason for the decline in the income velocity of the broad money aggregates in the 1980s. If a higher proportion of last-time sellers are being attracted to hold their funds as liquid balances at banks and building societies, the growth of the money stock will be distorted. The growth rate of the money supply would be expected to grow faster than the growth rate of nominal incomes because of a reduction in the expenditure multiplier.

At the extreme, if all funds of last-time sellers are redeposited with building societies and banks, and all these funds are subsequently lent for house purchase of existing housing stock, there will be absolutely no effect on the rate of growth of nominal incomes. Thus, this could be part of the explanation of the fall in the income velocity of money. Furthermore, as noted before, even that proportion of funds *spent* by last-time sellers may end up in banks and building societies, because of the desire of people to hold funds at these institutions after an unanticipated supply-side credit shock. The influence of relative interest rates on the inflow of 'large' sums of money to building societies is shown in Figure 6.9. It shows that there is a strong correlation between inflows of large sums of money and the interest rate differential.

Presumably the data for retail banks will exhibit a similar sensitivity of large balances to interest rate differentials (unfortunately, similar figures are not available for the monetary sector). These data confirm the suggestion that the high rates of interest due to an increase in the average rate of interest paid on deposits may have attracted investors (especially last-time sellers) to deposit with building societies. This evidence is analysed further in Chapter 10.

It is perhaps useful to recognize the effect that the increase in house prices may have on the credit multiplier for banks and building societies. It is likely that the demand for funds for house purchase will

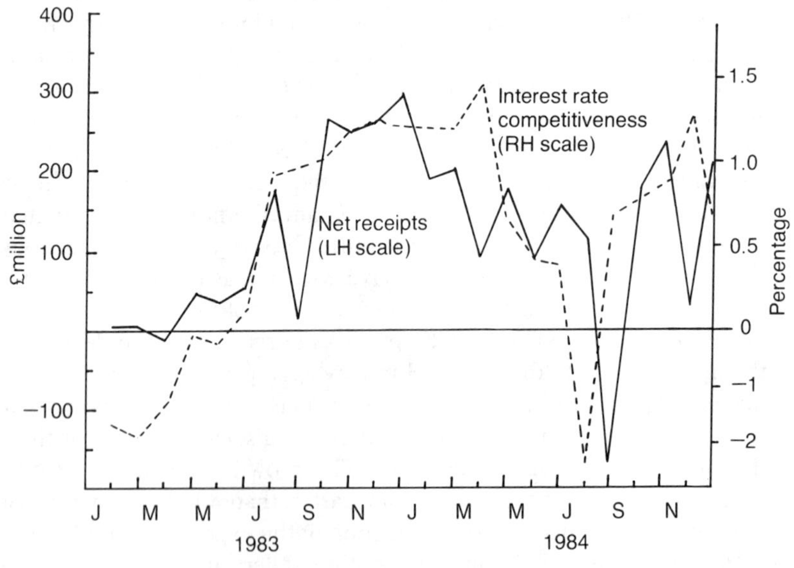

Figure 6.9 Building society interest rate competitiveness and net receipts (£2,001–£10,000 size band)

increase in line with the rise in house prices. It can be seen, however, that a rise in the house prices will also increase the volume of funds being received by last-time sellers.

It would appear plausible to suggest that, the larger the capital received by last-time sellers, the greater the proportion that will be saved rather than consumed. The rise in house prices which occurred in the 1980s and its corollary, a larger volume of capital being received by last-time sellers, would seem to imply a greater proportion of funds being attracted into banks and building societies than before the dramatic rise in house prices, given the tendency to consume less and save more as income increases. The rise in house prices may therefore have increased the banks' and building societies' ability to create credit.

6.4 BUFFER STOCK MODEL AND FINANCIAL INNOVATION

The buffer stock or disequilibrium model stems largely from the work of Artis and Lewis (1974, 1976). Artis and Lewis take exception to conventional specifications of the demand for money that implicitly assume that the actual stock of money being held must be equal to the amount demanded, usually explained by the assumption that the money supply is demand determined and that the demand for bank lending is interest insensitive (Artis and Lewis 1976: 156–7). On the contrary, Artis and Lewis maintain that:

> If the sources of new supply are augmenting the money stock fast enough it is plausible to suppose that individual transactors will find their money holdings are out of line with, and in excess of their expectations and desires. The dissipation of excess holdings of money through the rearrangement of portfolios, a generalised downward pressure on interest rates, and upward pressure on purchases, the level of prices and imports – a process which takes time – could therefore be overwhelmed by further unexpected increments in money holdings.
>
> (Artis and Lewis 1974: 244)

Disequilibrium between money supply and money demand came about in the early 1970s, according to Artis and Lewis, as a result of specific unique supply-side events at that time, in particular institutional change under competition and credit control, whereby controls were relaxed on bank advances and:

> Variations in reserve requirements and other institutional changes contributed initially to a disequilibrium between money supply and money demand. Further sources of new supply from government budget deficits and the Bank's abolition of controls upon bank advances perpetuated the cycle.
>
> (Artis and Lewis 1981: 31)[2]

Models of buffer stock money are frequently analysed in terms of inventory-theoretic models (Miller and Orr 1966). It is argued that money acts as a 'buffer' between variations in receipts and expenditures. The individual has a desired level of cash or sight deposit (money) holdings. This desired level of money holdings is allowed to fluctuate within upper and lower bands, owing to transactions costs of adjustment. When the upper or lower bands are reached the money balance is (instantaneously) returned to an intermediate level. The optimal rule (Miller and Orr 1966) is to have a lower band (0 in Figure 6.10) and a constant upper band (h). When these upper and lower limits are reached, money holdings are returned to the intermediate desired level z.

The buffer stock model suggests that an unanticipated increase in net receipts due to a supply-side shock (e.g. an increase in bank lending) will lead to an accumulation of holdings of buffer stock money (i.e. the recipients of the 'spent' bank credit will have an unexpected increase in their money holdings).

In terms of the Miller–Orr model, some money-holders will reach their upper threshold (h) and hence instantaneously reduce their money balances to the desired level (z). Other money-holders may not reach their upper threshold (despite having unanticipated

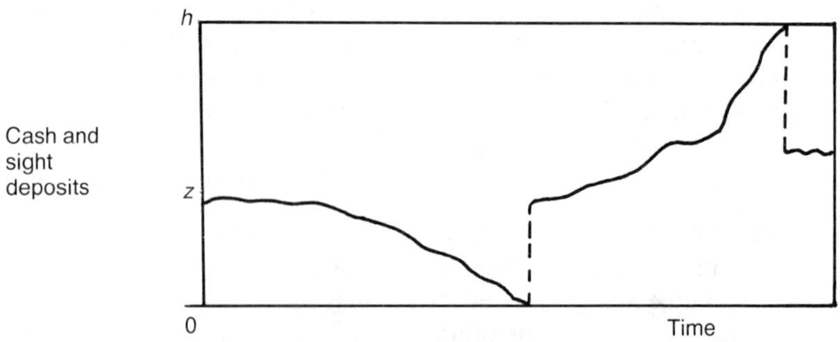

Figure 6.10 The Miller–Orr model

increases in money balances) and hence will willingly hold the 'buffer' money in the short run.

The net effect of an unanticipated increase in receipts depends upon the initial allocation of money balances amongst money-holders (Cuthbertson and Taylor 1987). Obviously, if all money-holders reach their upper threshold, then in aggregate there will be no increase in 'buffer money', as it will be instantaneously transferred to time deposits or other assets. Buffer stock proponents, however, argue that aggregate holdings of buffer money will be increased, especially if money-holders do not frequently check their money balances (Cuthbertson 1987: 107). Buffer stock money will be willingly held in the short run, but holders of buffer stock money are assumed to have been forced off their long-run desired function for money balances because interest rates, the price level and income adjust only slowly (Artis and Lewis 1976; Laidler 1980; Goodhart 1984). This 'disequilibrium' notion, that the long-run demand for money is not always equal to the supply of money, has been widely quoted as the rationale for instability in econometric short-run money demand functions, which assume that money-holders are always on their desired short-run money demand functions (Laidler 1982, 1984).

Laidler (1984) and Milbourne (1986a) provide recent surveys of the fast expanding literature on buffer stock money. Laidler (1982, 1984), in particular, argues that the buffer stock hypothesis may provide an explanation of the problem of instability of the demand for money. Milbourne (1986a), however, is sceptical of the (limited) empirical evidence so far produced on the buffer stock model.

The Miller–Orr model analyses cash and sight deposits. This model can be extended to a situation whereby economic agents have an upper and lower target threshold for broader money balances other than cash or sight deposits.[3] Indeed, with recent financial innovation it is difficult to distinguish between pure transactions and investment balances. There is often little difference in liquidity or return characteristics between sight deposits and so-called 'time' deposits at banks and building societies. It is likely that, given the combination of increased return, increased liquidity and high real interest rates, the upper threshold for holdings of broad money balances will have increased (as a result of the increased attractiveness of money relative to other assets). The upper return point at which money balances would normally be reduced may therefore now exist at a higher level (h_1 in Figure 6.11).

At first sight an increase in the upper threshold may appear to

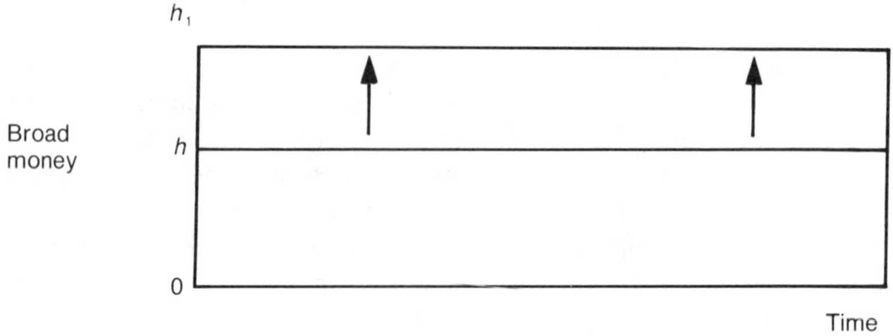

Figure 6.11 The Miller–Orr model with financial innovation

enhance the applicability of the buffer stock model. If the upper return threshold is increased, fewer economic agents will reach the upper band after a given supply-side shock. Hence more money will be held initially as a buffer stock, and slowly spent.

The evidence suggests, however, that this scenario has not occurred. It is argued that the fast growth of M3 and M4 (i.e. the fall in income velocity of the broad aggregates in the 1980s) was the result of a combination of supply-side stocks emanating from the abandonment of the corset and subsequent increased mortgage lending, and the attractiveness of market-determined high real rates of interest at building societies and banks. It appears that 'excess' money balances in evidence since 1980 as a result of credit shocks were willingly held as investment balances in wealth-holders' portfolios. Not only were these balances willingly held in the short-run, as the buffer stock model would suggest, but they appear also to have been held willingly in the medium term, contrary to the buffer stock model. The upper threshold level may have increased to such an extent that most money-holders take some time to reach their upper level, despite increased holdings of money.

It was impossible to determine when or if these money balances emanating from supply-side shocks would be 'unwillingly' held and hence spent.

It may be, therefore, that financial innovation has *delayed* the point at which money becomes a buffer stock. In this scenario supply-side shocks which create unanticipated receipts will be willingly held for long periods of time but may become buffer stocks if there is a fall in the rate of interest.

The 'higher' upper threshold (h_1) may not be immutable over time. It is possible that, if interest rates fall, the upper threshold may return to *h*. In this case, some money-holders will find that they are above their threshold levels and will have unwanted money, which will be instantaneously transferred. Many balance-holders, however, will still be below their threshold levels (depending on the initial distribution of money across economic agents), so that, in aggregate, there are excess money balances. Initially, these money balances will be willingly held, but in the long run they will be spent. It thus appears that money willingly held as a result of a supply-side shock may become a buffer stock some time after the original supply-side shock.

Alternatively, and this may be a crucial point for the operation of monetary control, it is possible that when the monetary authorities attempt to control the money supply (e.g. the increase in interest rates in the second half of 1988) wealth-holders may run down the large holdings of buffer stocks that have been amassed rather than cut down on spending. There may thus be a substantial period of time before interest rates affect the rate of spending and hence the price level.

Chapter 5 maintained that money may indeed be a *necessary* determinant of inflation but at certain times (e.g. when financial innovation occurs) it is not a *sufficient* cause of inflation. Likewise with credit. It is possible that an increase in the growth rate of credit over and above the growth rate of income may not lead to an increase in inflation. Therefore, credit may indeed be a necessary cause of inflation but not always a *sufficient* cause of inflation.

6.5 CREDIT SHOCKS AND ENDOGENEITY

It must be recognized that post-Keynesians have for a long time argued that it is the growth of credit that determines the growth rate of the money stock. Increases in the quantity of money are seen as the result of increases in the quantity of credit created, and it is credit that plays the dominant role in the economy (see *inter alia* Kaldor 1970; Tobin 1970; Blinder and Stiglitz 1983; Davidson and Weintraub 1983; Godley and Cripps 1983; Lavoie 1984).

Dow (1987) points out that it has been a long held Keynesian belief that the fundamental cause of monetary growth is expenditure decisions which lead to a greater supply of credit being made available, such that monetary growth is only the proximate cause of inflation. Credit is the engine of monetary growth, stimulated by changes in demand. This does not mean, however, that the monetary authorities cannot control the money supply, nor that such a policy will be ineffective.

A credit-induced money stock is rationalized by post-Keynesians through reference to the actions of financial intermediaries in an unconstrained competitive system, and by the traditional role of the Bank of England. Returning to the microtheoretic model of banks and building societies as price setters and quantity takers, it should be noted that the use of liability management in the wholesale markets leads to 'liability-side liquidity'. Banks and building societies will lend whatever is demanded (within prudential limits and the ability of the borrower to repay) at a given rate of interest, so that according to post-Keynesians the volume of credit granted is demand determined. The role of the Bank of England as lender of last resort is important in this respect:

> the central rationale for the creation of central banks, and still by far their most important function, was to provide an elastic currency supply. To ensure the ultimate liquidity of financial assets and so the viability of the financial system, central banks must stand ready to perform the role of lender of last resort.
>
> (Moore 1983: 543)

In other words, the Bank of England appears to allow the money supply to increase to accommodate rises in the demand for credit, as a result of its role of supporting the banking systems. Post-Keynesians argue that the money supply process should be examined as part of the interaction between financial institutions and firms in an income-generating process (Davidson 1972). An increase in wage rates which increases production costs will require extra working capital. Extra working capital is gained by borrowing from the banking system. It appears that in the 1980s, however, re-regulation and competition has been the dominant factor in influencing supply-side credit shocks, rather than increases in wages. With re-regulation and competition, it is plausible to assume that the money supply may be endogenous. Endogeneity, as opposed to Friedman's assertion of an exogenous money supply, appears to be strongly grounded in intuitively plausible real-world terms.

The analysis that the money supply is essentially demand determined with the quantity demanded depending on a host of real-world factors at least has the distinction of providing an explanation of how and/or why excessive money growth may come about, instead of the Friedmanian helicopter that increases the money supply. Increases in the money supply have to originate *somewhere* (Davidson 1972: 107).

According to Cobham (1988), a 'disequilibrium monetarist' school is emerging which agrees that the money supply appears at various times to exhibit both endogeneity and exogeneity, so that there is a convergence of opinion amongst monetarists and Keynesians. The above analysis would tend to concur with the suggestion that the money supply can be either endogenous or exogenous. An endogenous money stock is particularly likely in a competitive financial system, with banks and building societies operating as price setters and quantity takers, but not in a constrained system, as in the 1970s.

The origin of any supply-side credit shock is likely to have important repercussions for any subsequent link between the money supply and the price level. A wage-induced credit shock is likely to involve an increase in the money supply and the price level, whereas a credit shock emanating from re-regulation and portfolio restructuring as has occurred in the 1980s may not necessarily lead to an increase in prices.

In terms of monetary control, the debate is to an extent superfluous. If the money supply is endogenous because credit is the prime motivator behind the monetary aggregates, as suggested by post-Keynesians, it does not mean that the aggregates cannot be controlled. If monetary growth is a necessary feature of inflation, and if credit which leads to monetary growth can be controlled, then there is still a place for monetary control.

The Bank of England may still be able to control the money supply if interest rates are a determinant of the demand for money and the demand for credit; the potency of its control will depend on the interest elasticity of the demand for credit and the demand for money.

The emphasis of the monetary authorities on the supply-side counterparts to the monetary aggregates exemplifies this control mechanism. Control of the credit counterparts implicitly presupposes endogeneity, but of course does not imply uncontrollability.

As has been seen from the evidence of Chapter 5 and this chapter, the money supply appears to show signs of both endogeneity and exogeneity. It is emphasized in this book that the importance lies in the identification of money and credit shocks and the analysis of effects on nominal income. If shocks occur through financial innovation and change, they may have no effect on nominal income and inflation. Money may be a necessary cause of inflation but not a sufficient cause. The money supply may increase for endogenous reasons (i.e. be demand determined) but at the same time may or may not have effects on inflation.

6.6 CONCLUSION

Monetarist theory has in the past largely neglected lending when examining monetary developments and has emphasized the liabilities side of financial institutions' balance sheets, in contrast with the practical approach which relies on the control of bank lending.

It was argued in Chapter 4 that financial innovation and financial change, in the form of high interest easy-access accounts and liberalization of the mortgage credit market, have been major stock adjustment factors in altering the relationship between money and nominal income and credit and nominal income.

It has been noted that borrowing from building societies and banks by the personal sector for the purpose of house purchase has grown far faster than the growth in personal incomes since 1980. This led to speculation that the owner-occupier 'mortgage leak' was in large part responsible for the fall in the income velocity of circulation of broad money. This proposition has been examined in Section 6.2 and found to be unsatisfactory.

This proposition does emphasize, however, the importance of examining the monetary aggregates in terms of *both* money holdings and the level of lending. Section 6.3 retained this outlook in an alternative idea about the effect of the personal sector on the growth of broad money.

The monetary aggregates can be both deposit driven (see Chapter 5) and credit driven. Growth in the money supply is thus the outcome of the combination of deposit-side and credit-side interaction.

The stock adjustment induced by the ending of the cartel and the corset and increased competition between building societies and banks may have resulted in 'unwanted' excess money balances held by last-time sellers. If these balances are 'neutralized' by financial innovation and high real interest rates, there may be no concomitant increase in nominal income for some time – the money may be held as long-term investment balances rather than transactions balances. The greater the number of last-time sellers who hold the proceeds of the sale of their house as investment money balances, the smaller will be the expenditure multiplier of any given level of building society and bank lending. The relationship between lending and nominal income is likely to change. Increased levels of lending may result in smaller increases in nominal income than previously experienced. The fall in the income velocity of circulation of the broad money aggregates appears in large part to be explainable by the interaction of re-regulation, competition, increased mortgage lending and financial innovation.

Section 6.4 analysed the implications of the combined effects of credit shocks and financial innovation upon the buffer stock model. It was argued that the buffer stock mechanism, whereby excess money balances are dissipated and eventually lead to an increase in prices, may not be applicable in the face of financial innovation. If money is held as a buffer stock, then it is held as an extremely long-term buffer, the consequences of which may be vital for monetary control. If these balances are induced by high real interest rates, then they will be spent when interest rates fall, with consequent inflationary effects. Conversely, at times of monetary restraint (e.g. as in 1988 with the authorities trying to cut off the credit boom via high interest rates), balances that have been amassed for their investment characteristics may be used to sustain inflationary levels of spending.

The opposing views of the money supply being either endogenous or exogenous was examined in Section 6.5. It was concluded that the money supply can at times be demand led from the credit side and hence can at times be endogenous. This endogeneity does not suggest, however, that there is no role for monetary policy, as argued by Keynesians. The money supply may not be a sufficient cause for inflation, but as long as it is a necessary cause (and many Keynesians accept this) and as long as the authorities are *able* to control the money supply, there may be a role for a policy of controlling the money supply. It is the ability of the authorities to control the money supply that Chapter 7 turns to.

7 Financial innovation and the effectiveness of monetary control

7.1 INTRODUCTION

When monetary policy is aimed at maintaining a target rate of growth of the money supply in order to achieve a desired rate of growth of nominal income, it is necessary that the monetary authorities have the *ability* to influence the monetary aggregate(s) being targeted. As Hester (1982: 42) points out, there is no point in trying to guide monetary policy by using targets over which there is no control.

In Chapter 2 the preliminary general argument was established that financial change involving building societies and banks has hampered the ability of the monetary authorities to control the money supply. The evidence examined in Chapter 5 suggests that high market-related real rates of interest paid on building society and bank easy-access accounts have been responsible for the fast growth of the broad monetary aggregates (M4 directly and M3 indirectly) relative to nominal income.

It is suggested that 'money' assets have increasingly been held as investment balances, as a result of the combination of liquidity and high real rates of return.

Given these developments, it is of some interest to establish whether they have any bearing on the general contention that financial change by building societies and banks has proscribed the ability of the monetary authorities to control the money supply.

Section 7.2 outlines the monetary control techniques envisaged under the competition and credit control (CCC) system, and stresses the deficiencies and distortion that occurred, as a counterpoint to the monetary control tools used under the Medium Term Financial Strategy (MTFS). Section 7.3 examines the broad approach of monetary control under the MTFS, and leads on to an analysis of the efficacy of the authorities' main monetary control instrument, the manipulation of interest rates.

Controlling the money supply through interest rates is evaluated in terms of the financial innovations and financial change that have occurred in the building society and bank sectors. Particular attention is paid to the effects of financial innovation on the interest elasticity of the demand for money and the demand for credit. The effect of credit liberalization of the mortgage market, as a result of the abolition of the corset and abandonment of the cartel, is examined in terms of the increased mortgage debt of the personal sector and possible effects on the interest elasticity of expenditure. The ability of the monetary authorities to control the money supply is considered with respect to the likely effects that increasing rates may have on the personal sector's expenditure function.

7.2 THE ABANDONMENT OF PORTFOLIO CONTROLS

The original emphasis of CCC was the control of monetary growth through the manipulation of interest rates and an abandonment of the previous distorting portfolio controls. The intention was to move towards a system which had free operation of the price mechanism and free competition in the financial system, with the level of credit to be determined by cost. The re-intermediation effect that occurred and the effect on the monetary aggregates has been documented in Chapters 3 and 5. It was also noted that the major problem of this system was the aggressive liability management policies of the banks, for which the corset was devised and which heralded the end of the monetary authorities' policy of controlling the money supply through its price and a move towards more direct portfolio controls.

The use of portfolio controls upon the banking system produced a number of distortions in the financial system. A major problem that occurred intermittently throughout the 1970s was the phenomenon of 'round-tripping' or 'hard arbitrage'. Wholesale rates tended to be more fluid than bank-based rates, so that prime borrowers profited by taking up unused overdraft facilities at a base-related rate and re-lending the funds at the wholesale deposit rate.

This practice tended to have a perverse effect on the rate of growth of the broad monetary aggregates as bank assets were cosmetically increased. The particular monetary controls in force – special deposits – acted to increase the tendency for round-tripping to occur. Calls for special deposits, rather than having the intended effect of a reduction in lending, resulted in the banking system competing even more fiercely for deposits. In effect, the banks were engaging in liability management rather than asset management, increasing the level of deposits in order to finance greater levels of reserve assets. This has the effect of reducing the yield on reserve assets relative to non-reserve assets.

The subsequent monetary control mechanism, the supplementary special deposits scheme, was also undermined by the activities of the banking system. Wide-scale disintermediation occurred when the corset was in operation, particularly in the parallel money markets. Indeed, the very existence of these markets is in large part a result of the frustration of credit-worthy corporate borrowers who were unable to raise bank finance because of various monetary controls. When the banking system is restricted from lending by a control mechanism such as the corset, it is unsurprising that companies should seek greater recourse to the money markets. Of special relevance in the 1970s was the use of acceptances by companies. Here, companies with surplus funds would lend to deficit companies through the agency of a broker in the form of an acceptance rather than through the banking system as in the traditional financial intermediation process. The banking system is involved, of course, in guaranteeing (i.e. accepting) bills issued by corporate customers. These 'bank bills' are effectively underwritten by the banks and are therefore extremely low risk and marketable, and as such may be sold for fine prices. For the banking system, fees are earned, but the acceptances are only contingent liabilities, and hence are counted as off-balance-sheet items and not included in the interest-bearing eligible liabilities definition. It was thus possible for borrowing and lending to take place, but outside the traditional financial intermediation channels.

The existence of disintermediation placed in doubt the effectiveness of portfolio monetary controls. Borrowing and spending were still able to occur, despite the strict operation of the supplementary special deposits scheme. Moreover, the increase in bank bills held as off-balance-sheet items (often called the 'bill leak') made it difficult to analyse monetary developments as they were not part of the M3 money supply definition. Thus, M3 was at this time a poor indicator of monetary conditions. To the extent that M3 was growing more slowly than if bank bills were included in the definition, the money supply figures indicated relatively tighter monetary restraint than in fact was the case. In practice the bill leak was widely known about (Bank of England 1982b: 82) and figures for the bill leak were even included in the private sector liquidity series of the *Bank of England Quarterly Bulletin Statistical Annex*. Recognition of disintermediation does not, of course, eliminate the problem of avoidance of direct monetary controls. With hindsight, the Bank of England points out that although direct controls are inefficient in terms of disintermediation activities, the bill leak was possibly a less problematical form of avoidance as it was directly measurable, and, indeed, if the bill leak did not occur, then it is likely that other (possibly hidden) forms of disintermediation would occur (Bank of England 1982b: 82).

The use of portfolio controls really only attacked the symptoms of monetary growth, rather than the underlying root cause, and led to distortions in competitive neutrality and ultimately to disintermediation, a problem which has become more acute with re-regulation and financial innovation:

> Money is the most fungible of commodities and our experience over a long period is that the effect of direct controls is largely to direct financial flows, typically into less efficient channels, rather than to achieve any deeper purpose. These difficulties can only be greater now with the disappearance of traditional barriers between different financial functions and of distinctions between different financial activities, and with the merging of financial markets into a global whole. Controls in one area would either be ineffective or spread rapidly as further and further controls were introduced to head off successive leakages from those already in place.
>
> (Bank of England 1987c: 366)

The previous use of portfolio controls could be rationalized because of the relative lack of alternative sources of finance. It was possible for the non-bank private sector (NBPS) to circumvent credit controls in a variety of ways given the number of credit channels that became available, and policy has had to move towards the *price* of credit rather than its availability. Of course, with the abolition of exchange controls in 1979, direct controls on the banking system could be circumscribed by offshore disintermediation and thus were abandoned in 1980 (Bingham 1985; Vaciago 1985).

7.3 FINANCIAL INNOVATION AND THE EFFECTIVENESS OF MONETARY CONTROL UNDER THE MEDIUM TERM FINANCIAL STRATEGY

A major tenet of the MTFS involved a strong relationship between the money supply, interest rates and the public sector borrowing requirement (PSBR).

The MTFS paid particular attention to the consequences of a 'high' PSBR on the money supply and interest rates. Too high a PSBR, it was argued, would lead to either higher interest rates or an increase in the rate of growth of the money supply. The former was based on the premise that if the monetary authorities attempted to restrict the growth of the money supply *without* cutting the PSBR at the same time, interest rates would have to be maintained at a high level to sell government debt and to cut the demand for bank borrowing. High interest rates, it was argued, would 'crowd out' private sector investment (conversely, high rates on corporate debt instruments may in fact lead to companies borrowing *more* from the banking system, with attendant inflationary consequences). The latter is based on the view that, again, if the money supply is cut *without* reducing the PSBR and if the PSBR is not being financed through selling government debt to the NBPS, then the government will have to borrow from the banking system, thus increasing the money supply.

Thus, if the monetary authorities wished to control the money supply without concurrently maintaining interest rates at an unacceptably high level, the PSBR would have to be reduced (Treasury and Civil Service Committee 1980: 2).

Thus, the role of fiscal policy was that of support for monetary policy, as evidenced at the outset of the MTFS when it was stated that the PSBR would be reduced as a proportion of gross domestic product (GDP) over a period of time in order to bring down interest rates (*Financial Statement and Budget Report* 1980–1: part II, paragraph 4). In the late 1980s the Chancellor stressed the target for a balanced budget, a PSBR of zero (*Financial Statement and Budget Report* 1988–9: paragraph 2.13).

The target path of the PSBR changed somewhat over the time of the MTFS. Originally it was expected that the PSBR would be reduced, unless it appeared likely that a future recession was possible, in which case the PSBR could be maintained at its previous level. Subsequently, the aim was to maintain the PSBR at 1 per cent of GDP (Budget speech, 17 March 1987) in the hope of achieving zero inflation and a stable debt–income ratio, a policy advocated by Budd and Dicks (1980).

Currie (1987) does point out, however, that under this type of policy, if GDP is rising quickly and government spending is set as a target of GDP, then it too can rise rapidly. Conversely, in a downturn, a government spending target as a proportion of GDP will require a reduction in government spending which may be difficult to implement.

PSBR targeting may, however, have bolstered the intention to reduce inflation by including an automatic contractionary response to inflation (Begg 1987; Currie 1987).

The evidence of the relationship between the PSBR, the money supply and interest rates does not appear to be robust, however. Simulations by Kearney and MacDonald (1985) show that a tight fiscal policy which reduces the growth of the PSBR causes only *some* interest rates to rise, and *others* to fall (see Llewellyn and Kearney (1984) for further analysis).

Moreover, Artis (1988) points out that there can be large errors in PSBR forecasting, leading to the conclusion that PSBR targeting is not a viable policy in view of the mistakes that could be made.

Kaldor (1980) disputes the assertion that the PSBR and the growth of the money supply are closely linked. His figures show that the 'unfunded' PSBR (i.e. that financed by bank credit rather than by the sales of government securities to the NBPS) could have contributed only a 'negligible' 2.1 per cent to the increase in the money supply over the period 1977–80. By contrast, the 'unfunded' element of the PSBR in the previous three years was twenty-six times as large, yet the increase in the money supply was only half as large. According to Kaldor, it is the growth of bank lending which is the main determinant of money supply growth.

A useful distinction to make is that of controlling the monetary aggregates from either the demand side or the supply side (Lewis 1980b; Artis and Lewis 1981; Davis and Lewis 1982). In the demand-side approach, the authorities influence the general level of interest rates in order to influence the demand for bank liabilities. In terms of the demand-side approach, two effects of financial innovation by building societies and banks may be isolated:

1 The average rate of interest on building society and bank deposits has increased.
2 The rates of interest at these institutions have become less sticky, and now closely follow the general movement of interest rates.

The monetary authorities have a limited number of instruments with which to control the money supply. Indeed, it was recognized by the Bank of England that it is ultimately constrained to using only one instrument. Given the emphasis upon control of the money supply through manipulating interest rates, it is of some interest to examine in detail the effectiveness of the demand-side approach with respect to the above effects of financial innovation on bank and building society interest rates.

In the demand-side approach, an increase in general rates of interest engineered by the monetary authorities was intended to induce money-holders to switch into alternative interest-bearing assets. However, when money balances at building societies and banks paid a high real rate of interest, a given policy-induced increase in the general level of interest rates was likely to have a reduced effect on the opportunity cost of holding money, in contrast with the traditional situation where money did not bear interest.

As more deposits pay market-related rates of interest, the effect of a change in interest rates on the money supply would be expected to get smaller, making it necessary to use higher and higher interest rates to affect demand (Bingham 1985: 7).

The increase in the average rate paid on building society and bank deposits was of itself likely to reduce the opportunity cost of holding money when general interest rates rose, and hence to restrict the ability of the authorities to induce a movement out of money holdings. Moreover, the second impact of the increased competition upon interest rates was likely to enhance this effect. Not only did competition increase the average rate of interest paid on bank and building society deposits, but it also altered the speed with which these financial institutions altered their deposit rates in response to a policy-induced rise in interest rates. In an extremely competitive market situation, as existed between building societies and banks for money deposits, movements in the general level of interest rates tended to be quickly paralleled by movements in the deposit rates offered by the two sets of financial intermediaries. This is not to imply that deposit rates were at the same numerical level as other rates but that they moved in line with other rates, so that *interest rate differentials* between the financial intermediaries and other non-money assets remained unchanged. In other words, as interest rates in general rise, so too do the rates on the assets within the broad monetary aggregates, so that there is little incentive to move out of money balances. When operating from the demand side, it is unlikely that interest rate differentials will be substantially changed and unlikely that the level of broad money holdings will be reduced (abstracting from supply-side considerations) when interest rates are raised (Bank of England 1983b: 375).

It is argued here, however, that, as high market-related rates of interest on building society and bank easy-access accounts move so closely in line with general rates of interest, interest differentials do not often change, and the interest elasticity of the demand for money is likely to have fallen. If interest differentials between money and other assets change only rarely and for a short period of time, profitable portfolio switching opportunities are not likely to be frequent. Monitoring of the rates between building society, bank accounts and other assets is likely to be downgraded given the consistently high real rates of return on building society and bank accounts in the 1980s and the lack of profitable portfolio switching chances. It is likely that there was a stable pool of balances at banks and building societies that became increasingly desensitized to interest rate differentials.

Some authors argue, however, that asset-holders may be becoming *more* sensitive to changes in interest rate relativities between different financial assets (Goodhart 1986a: 84). The problem, in terms of monetary control, is that the monetary authorities can only influence the *general* level of market rates. When money bears explicit market-related rates of interest the authorities cannot exert any control over the interest rate relativities between different financial assets. This result tends to modify the monetarist contention (set out in Chapter 2) that the greater the interest inelasticity of the demand for money is, the more potent will monetary policy be. The effect of the shift towards interest-bearing balances is to raise the 'own' rate on the broad monetary aggregates.

In IS–LM terms, the LM curve will become progressively steeper. In theory, it could become completely vertical and completely inelastic.

This effect, whereby increasing competition for deposits tends to offset the effects on the demand for money of changes in market rates of interest, was foreseen by Laidler (1973). He argued that a reduced interest elasticity of the demand for money would lead to a *more effective* monetary policy (Laidler 1973: 62).

On the face of it, the more responsive are the rates paid on building society and bank deposits to changes in market rates of interest, and the larger the proportion of deposits which attract such interest payments, the greater the force with which Laidlers' argument may be applied (also see Cagan 1979). However, this neglects the question of *how* the money supply is influenced. When the *method* of control of the money supply is taken into account it can be shown that, because of a situation of financial innovation and competition, a relatively inelastic demand for money is not *sufficient* evidence as to the relative merit of a policy of controlling the money supply. Referring back to the IS–LM apparatus, it can be seen that increased interest inelasticity (i.e. a steeper LM curve) may lead to problems of monetary control:

> If the differential [between bank deposit rates and other assets] becomes a constant, the demand for deposits will be independent

> of the level of interest rates. A rise in market interest rates will not reduce the demand for deposits as it does in the old regime and in the standard model, because the rate paid on deposits will rise too. The old monetarist assumption of interest-inelastic money demand will apply, though for a reason quite different from its original motivation.
>
> (Tobin 1983a: 164)

If the demand for money is becoming less elastic with respect to the general level of interest rates, then in terms of IS–LM analysis it implies that the LM curve is becoming steeper. It may also mean, however, that it is shifting unpredictably to the right or left (Akhtar 1983: 37).

If interest elasticities of final demand rise, then the IS curve is likely to become flatter and possibly also to shift unpredictably. Akhtar (1983: 44) suggests that the combination of a steeper LM schedule and a flatter IS schedule implies that economic activity may become more responsive to monetary policy, *assuming that monetary policy is still able to move the LM curve in an identifiable manner.*

Indeed, it may be the case that an attempt to reduce the growth rate of a broad monetary aggregate from the demand side may lead to an *increase* in the growth rates of the monetary aggregates. Looking at the demand for money balances, it has been noted that as far back as the period 1963–78 the overall effect of policy-induced interest rate changes on the money supply have in fact been perverse. A rise in interest rates has often increased the money supply (Kaldor 1980: 289).

This effect is also corroborated by Lewis (1980a) and Artis and Lewis (1981) who found that when the authorities attempted to reduce the growth of the monetary aggregates by raising short rates through the discount market in 1973, 1976 and 1979, the rate on time deposits increased relative to long-term rates. Thus, an attempt to reduce the rate of growth of the money supply had the opposite effect of *increasing* the money supply, through the increased demand for time deposits. Of course, these perverse effects occurred *before* the onset of financial innovation in the early 1980s, which has raised the own rate on money. It is possible to hypothesize, then, that the impact of financial innovation may have enhanced this perverse effect of movements in the monetary aggregates in response to changes in the general level of interest rates.

In the supply-side approach, the authorities attempted to influence the general level of interest rates in order to influence the demand for building society and bank assets, i.e. the demand for loans. Of course, changes in the rate of interest may have effects upon *both* the demand for money and the demand for loans (credit); it is useful, however, to separate the effects for expository purposes.

The stated intention of the monetary authorities was to influence the growth of the broad monetary aggregates from the supply side. The Green Paper (1980) on monetary control stated that the main way of controlling the growth rate of the money supply was through interest rates and fiscal policy (p. 17).

The main instrument was that of influencing interest rates by the Bank of England's intervention at the short end of the bill market. In broad terms the aim was to maintain short-term interest rates within an unpublished band. Ultimately, the force of a supply-side policy rests on the effect of interest rates upon building society and bank lending. Early empirical studies, however, show a poor relationship between the level of bank lending and interest rates (Hotson 1979) and experience has shown that, in practice, the effectiveness of this instrument is open to question. The Bank of England has pointed out that for the whole post-war period there has been a weak link between interest rates and the demand for credit (and it has also acknowledged Kaldor's point that the demand for credit and interest rates have sometimes had an inverse relationship (Bank of England 1987c: 368)).

Furthermore, with the overwhelming majority of credit being financed on a floating rate basis, it may be that increases in interest rates had little impact on the demand for credit. There may be little incentive in waiting for lower rates as the borrower does not face the risk of being 'locked in' at high interest rates if they should fall in the future (Hall 1983).

Given that past empirical evidence appears to show that there is a poor response of bank lending to increases in interest rates, it is difficult to see how the monetary authorities could have hoped to control the growth of the monetary aggregates through influencing interest rates. Indeed the effects of financial innovation upon the demand for credit, if shown to be empirically valid, appear to reinforce Friedman's criticisms of attempting to control the money supply through interest rates (Friedman 1980: 58; Treasury and Civil Service Committee 1980).

Friedman has pointed out that trying to control the money supply through interest rates in fact confuses money and credit. He argues that interest rates may have a (limited) effect on the demand for credit, but will have an unpredictable influence on the demand for money.

The fact that the monetary authorities chose to control the money supply through the instrument of interest rates appears to be an implicit acceptance that the money supply is demand-determined, if it is to be controlled by altering its price and hence altering its demand.

The problems of switching monetary control away from a system of portfolio controls which impinge directly upon bank profitability towards controlling the money supply through interest rates, and hence profitability indirectly, are summed up by Bingham, who maintains that bank interest rates have become the main mechanism of monetary control (whereas with direct controls there was an effect on the quantity of credit) and interest rates do not seem to dampen demand (Bingham 1985: 42).

This statement is, perhaps, too strong inasmuch as the MTFS was in effect an attempt to return to the original underlying ethos of CCC, that of determining credit through its price, and as such the CCC period represented a useful model of the likely effects of attempting such a policy. Reintermediation that occurred originally under CCC was surely to be expected under the MTFS when portfolio controls were dismantled, as examined in Chapters 5 and 6.

Similarly, the effectiveness of the manipulation of interest rates to control the money supply could perhaps have been derived from the earlier policy.

The impact of financial innovation, however, may be to reinforce the applicability of the argument that control of the monetary aggregates through manipulation of interest rates is an inefficient method of controlling the growth of the money supply. In a situation where 'money' bears interest, the effect of increasing the general level of interest rates may have limited effects on the demand for credit, especially if credit liberalization has led to substantial portfolio reallocations by the personal sector.

As bank and building society lending is seen as a major determinant in the growth of the money supply, it may be possible to control the money supply by inducing borrowers to switch from bank loans to other forms of debt. This would involve manipulating relative rates of return to facilitate funding of bank loans. The ability of the authorities to affect relative rates is likely to be limited, however. A rise in the central bank rate which raises bank lending rates will also increase interest rate expectations and rates on substitute forms of finance (Dow and Saville 1988: 138). Raising the intervention rate is unlikely to have any effect on interest differentials amongst financial institutions.

Moreover, it is noticeable that, with the large increase in personal sector borrowing from banks and building societies in the 1980s, lending by banks and building societies to the personal sector was greater than lending to ICCs. This is important because the ability of the personal sector to 'fund' bank and building society lending, i.e. to switch to alternative finance, is always likely to be limited.

One possible avenue of monetary control is the link which may exist between mortgage interest rates and consumers' expenditure. The elasticity of personal sector spending with respect to mortgage interest rates is ultimately an empirical matter. If, however, there is a strong link between personal sector expenditure and mortgage interest rates, this relationship may be amenable to control. Forcing up interest rates on mortgage loans may effectively choke off consumer spending as mortgage holders face increased repayments and cut back on expenditure plans. If this is the case, then this could be a powerful if perhaps politically unpalatable method of monetary control.

Turnbull has argued that the housing and mortgage credit markets are the main factors in the transmission of monetary control (1984: 6). The possible importance of this transmission mechanism has been pointed out by Artis:

> Simply by reason of its relative scale, consumption rather than investment may well be the component of expenditure through which monetary policy has its greatest impact on aggregate demand. General considerations suggest three main ways in which monetary factors might bear upon consumers' demand. Firstly, in several popular forms of the consumption function wealth has an important role and short-run fluctuations in the value of measured wealth are usually dominated by changes in stock and bond prices; secondly, changes in the rate of interest may exercise a general influence apart from their wealth effects upon the decision to save or consume; finally, credit rationing by financial institutions and its formal reinforcement by official controls also affect consumer spending.
>
> (1978: 293)

If there is a strong link between mortgage interest rates and the propensity to consume, then it is likely that the effects of financial innovation and financial change may have *increased* the interest elasticity of the consumption function. The liberalization of the mortgage market and the rapid increase in house prices in the 1980s tend to suggest that real mortgage repayments in the 1980s were far higher than in the 1970s. It would then seem that an increase in general interest rates would have had a relatively harsher impact on mortgage holders. An increase in interest rates may have had substantial effects on consumer spending as higher interest repayments forced mortgage holders to cut back on expenditures. Indeed, there was much official speculation that such effects may have occurred.

People would have had any previous liquidity constraints removed through financial liberalization, and could move closer to desired levels of expenditure and hence at the same time become less sensitive to changes in interest rates on their expenditure patterns (Dicks 1988: 2).

It is thus possible that mortgage liberalization, which importantly gave rise to market clearing mortgage rates (see Chapter 4) and higher house prices, may have increased the interest elasticity of consumption. Market clearing mortgage rates in the 1980s are likely to mean that mortgage holders were hit harder during periods of rising interest rates as mortgage rates became far more market related than in the 1970s. Combined with the increase in the mortgage debt-to-income ratio in the 1980s, it is plausible that there may have been considerable increases in the interest sensitivity of consumption.

7.4 FINANCIAL INNOVATION AND THE EFFECTIVENESS OF MONETARY BASE CONTROL

Monetary base control (MBC) operates through the monetary authorities' controlling the size of the monetary base in accordance with a monetary target and leaving interest rates to move freely in order to mop up any excess supply or demand for base money that the banks require.[1] The demand for base money is determined by the banks' need for reserves to back their total liabilities.[2] Interest rates are thus the equilibrating mechanism (Llewellyn *et al.* 1982) under MBC rather than the instrument of money control. (The argument is that the link between the money supply and the monetary base is more stable than the link between interest rates and the money supply.)

If a fall in reserves is brought about by the Bank of England the banks may reduce lending, bid for deposits and exchange them for reserves, borrow from the Bank of England, reduce any excess reserves or reduce non-reserve assets. In order to maintain lending, banks may bid for reserves if the demand for credit is greater than the banks can supply with a given volume of base money. This will tend to bid up interest rates on deposits and loans until the demand for credit has fallen in line with what the banks can supply with the restricted level of base money.

The effectiveness of MBC thus rests on the interest elasticity of the demand for credit. Given that the interest sensitivity of credit has tended to be relatively weak (Hotson 1979) and that there is no reason to suggest that this will change with financial innovation, then it can be argued that the technical capacity of MBC is unlikely to be altered. Indeed, one of the benefits of MBC, it has been argued by some proponents, is that it is not likely to be adversely affected by financial innovation and credit liberalization. The monetary base certainly would be subject to the stock effects of financial innovation noted in Chapters 5 and 6.

It is possible that MBC became *more* effective as a result of financial innovation. The banks' endowment effect has tended to be eroded by the increasing proportion of accounts that bear interest and, purely on a profitability basis, it will be less attractive to bid for retail deposits in the face of excess demand for credit at given volumes of base money.

With the large proportion of zero interest balances that the banks previously enjoyed, it would have been more profitable to bid for deposits and exchange them for reserves to maintain lending than when more balances bear interest. The marginal cost of retail funds has risen and may to some extent deter banks from competing for deposits. It may become more attractive to reduce lending or borrow from the central bank.

7.5 CONCLUSION

It is widely acknowledged that portfolio controls placed on the banking sector are inequitable and cause distortions in the financial system. Section 7.2 briefly outlined some of the problems of using portfolio monetary controls, particularly in the form of disintermediation, as a counterpoint to the recognition that the manipulation of interest rates is the only feasible method of monetary control recognized by the monetary authorities.

This chapter has concentrated on what are expected to be the continuing effects of financial innovation, credit liberalization and the abolition of the cartel on the effectiveness of monetary control.

For expository purposes, the manner in which monetary control is expected to work was divided into the demand-side and supply-side approaches in Section 7.2, although it is acknowledged that there are objections to such a classification. With respect to the demand-side approach, it is argued that as a result of money bearing a market-related rate of interest there is likely to be a reduced effect on the opportunity cost of holding money when the monetary authorities increase interest rates. Quite simply, interest rate differentials between money and non-money assets may remain relatively unchanged. It is hypothesized that an increase in general rates of interest is therefore unlikely to induce money-holders to switch into alternative (non-money) interest-bearing assets. It is unlikely that control from the demand side will have marked effects on the growth rates of the broad monetary aggregates (abstracting for the moment from supply-side considerations) when general interest rates are raised, and hence there may be a reduction in the potency of monetary control.

Conversely, the abolition of the cartel may have *increased* the potency of monetary control. The greater flexibility of mortgage interest rates, and the increased importance of the price of mortgages after the abolition of the cartel, may have increased the interest elasticity of expenditure. A plausible monetary control mechanism is the link which may exist between mortgage interest rates and consumers' expenditure. If there is a strong link between mortgage interest rates and consumer spending, then this relationship may be a fulcrum of control. If the monetary authorities increase interest rates and the cost of mortgage loans rises, there may be a dual effect of both a reduction in new mortgage loans demanded and a decrease in consumer spending as mortgage holders facing increased repayments are forced to cut back on expenditures. If such a mechanism works, then the effect of liberalization of the mortgage market, which has increased the level of personal sector mortgage debt, and more market-related mortgage rates after the abolition of the cartel may have increased the ability of the monetary authorities to affect consumer spending through an increase in general interest rates. Mortgage liberalization and the increase in house prices mean that the size of real mortgage repayments are far higher in the 1980s than in the 1970s, and consequently the debt burden of an increase in interest rates should be far more harsh.

It was suggested that developments in the building society industry would not alter the technical capacity of MBC, but may in fact improve the effectiveness of this mode of operation. MBC would still work in the same manner, but would possibly be more effective as a result of financial innovation.

8 Financial innovation, the demand for money, the demand for credit and the consumption function

8.1 INTRODUCTION

Given the above conjectures as to the possible effects of building society and bank intermediation activities on the efficacy of monetary control, in terms of both stock and more continuing effects, it is desirable to analyse previously published empirical evidence in this area, to determine whether research has provided answers to the above contentions. It is important to point out that the following critique of the econometric research is not intended to be an exhaustive examination of the vast literature on demand for money functions, demand for credit functions and consumption functions. Such a task is an enormous undertaking, which has been more than adequately covered elsewhere (Laidler 1985a; Cuthbertson 1987). Rather, particular econometric studies which impinge upon the ideas raised above will be examined.

The number of econometric studies that have examined the effects of financial innovation on the demand for money, the demand for credit or the consumption function is limited. Those studies that directly or indirectly consider the effects of financial change when modelling demand for money and credit functions are considered in Section 8.2. There have been a number of other (partly interrelated) broad areas of research into the demand for money, mainly aimed at attempting to explain the problems of instability; these are briefly reviewed. There is recognition in Section 8.3 of the fact that different sectors in the economy may have specific demand functions for assets (money and near money) such that a disaggregated sectoral approach may be appropriate. Section 8.4 examines the evidence as to the effects of financial innovation and financial change on the consumption function.

8.2 FINANCIAL INNOVATION AND THE DEMAND FOR MONEY FUNCTION

Instability of the demand for money function is well documented.[1] Grice and Bennett (1981) categorize the empirical work on the demand for money function as 'the years of hope' (1966–71), the 'years of despair' (1972–8) and the period of 'Hendrification' (post-1978). To this classification Taylor (1987) has added a fourth period, 'the years of uncertainty' (1980 to date).[2]

Most of the above models of the demand for money function do not take account, or attempt to take account, of the effects of financial innovation, despite a growing consensus that financial innovation may have an important role to play:

> It is clear that the real world is more complicated than the models in question, and that in fact money-holding agents treat a rather wide variety of assets as alternatives to money in their portfolios. There is nothing surprising about this; indeed it would be startling had things turned out otherwise. However, it does mean that as the menu of assets available to money holders changes over time, we might expect their behaviour *vis-à-vis* money holding also to change as a result. This is a *potentially important* point when recent stability problems with the demand for money function are analysed.
>
> (Laidler 1985a: 133)

Moreover, official publications tended to emphasize the rapid changes that took place in the financial institutional framework when explaining the difficulties of implementation of monetary policy in the 1980s. The view that was consistently propounded suggested that the impact of increased competition between building societies and banks, and financial innovation by these institutions, may have been a major determinant of the observed change in the relationship between the various monetary aggregates and nominal incomes as shown by the fall in the velocity of broad money (Bank of England 1982d, 1983b, c, 1984d, 1985a).

The importance of using the correct own rate variable and of taking account of financial innovation is exemplified by Budd and Holly (1986). Their equation is affected by an inadequate proxy for the rate of interest on money. In particular, their function appears to have been inadequately specified as a result of exclusion of the rate of interest on high interest accounts. They estimate an equation for M3 over the period 1878–1970.[3] The function appears to be stable (according to the test statistics reported), although when it is estimated up to 1984 it exhibits instability, largely, according to Budd and Holly, because of the competition and credit control (CCC) reforms. They re-estimate their equation up to 1984, include a dummy variable for 1972–4 and argue that the resultant formulation is stable. It is noticeable, of course, that stability is dependent upon the elimination of the CCC period by the inclusion of a dummy variable.

Their claim of stability is rather undermined, however, by the inability of their equation to predict M3 (they do not apply any specific forecast tests. Actual growth in M3 in 1983 and 1984 is about 2 per cent *slower* than their model predicts whilst actual monetary growth in 1985 and 1986 is about 2½–3½ per cent *faster* than predicted. They argue that the increase in *high interest accounts* may be responsible for the inability of their equations to forecast accurately monetary growth. It is unclear how they can claim that they have identified a stable demand for money function whilst at the same time noting that their equation cannot explain monetary growth because of 'changes in banking practice; such as the introduction of high interest accounts' (1986: 18). A rise in the average rate of interest paid on building society and bank retail deposits is a rise in the 'own' rate on money.

The effect on the demand for money equation of a *higher own rate* on money depends, however, on whether or not the own rate was previously included in the function. If it is included in the empirical demand function, a higher own rate may merely be represented as a change in the own rate parameter of the demand for money function and as such should not affect parameter constancy (Johnston 1984). This is dependent, of course, on applied researchers' recognizing that the own rate has in fact increased and subsequently including the higher rates in the function (see Chapter 9). If the own rate was not previously included, the demand function will appear to be unstable. The equation should then be respecified to take account of the (higher) own rate of the demand for money.

It is argued here that for a stable demand for money function to be identified, and for the purposes of gaining knowledge as to past monetary developments, such institutional behaviour should be explicitly modelled. A further factor affecting Budd and Holly's equation is the changing competitive positions of building societies and banks. It is noticeable that when their equation over-predicted the demand for M3 in 1983 and 1984 the building societies were successful in attracting retail deposits relative to the retail banks. Thus Private Sector Liquidity 2 (PSL2) would have grown at the expense of M3 (see Chapter 5). On the other hand, over 1985–6, when the retail banks competed aggressively for deposits, the Budd–Holly model under-predicted. Budd and Holly's equation may have been unable to model this behaviour because of the inadequate variable used to measure the opportunity cost of money. The use of the differential between the rate on money and a long rate as the proxy for the opportunity cost of money may have understated the opportunity cost in 1983–4 whilst overstating it in 1985–6. It is reasonable to suggest that the relevant opportunity cost variable for M3 would be the differential between the return on (bank) money and that on a near-money liquid asset, in this case the rate on building society shares and deposits, in view of the 'switching' that occurred during this period (see Chapter 5). It is possible that, if this opportunity cost variable were used and allowance was made for high interest accounts, a stable demand for M3 might be found.

Taylor (1987) estimated a demand function for M3 over the period 1964/2–1985/4 and attempted to model some of the effects of financial innovation. A proxy was used to model the specific innovation of high interest cheque accounts at banks. This he measured as the maximum of the seven-day deposit rate and the rate available on high interest chequing accounts. Furthermore, the three-month Treasury bill rate was used in an attempt to capture the effects of switching out of M3 assets into short-term negotiable assets. The final equation is stable and the out-of-sample forecasts are good. Moreover, there is no evidence of a structural shift after the introduction of CCC. The own rate on money is significant, leading to the conclusion that the effects of financial innovation can be captured through the differential between high interest cheque accounts and the Treasury bill rate.

Taylor emphasized the importance of the own rate variable, and hence financial innovation, by dropping the term from the equation and re-estimating the model over the same time period. The equation breaks down, showing, according to Taylor, the necessity of including financial innovation variables in the equation.

This test of the importance of financial innovation in an equation for the demand for money is not particularly stringent, however. If *any* significant variable in an equation is omitted, it is likely that the equation will suffer in terms of insignificant parameters and test statistics. In the case of financial innovation, a more reliable test would be to replace the own rate – which contains interest on the new, innovatory, high interest access accounts – with a rate of interest that is unaffected by such financial innovation. A useful test would be to substitute the own rate for the net rate on ordinary shares at building societies. This would provide a far more stringent test of the effect of financial innovation on the demand for M3. Of course, it may be argued that the rate of interest paid on ordinary shares was, in general, higher in the 1980s owing to increased competition with the retail banks and that the liquidity of these accounts increased, both of which represent a form of financial innovation. It is important to know, however, the extent to which the specific innovation of high interest instant-access accounts was responsible for the rapid growth in M3.

Johnston (1985) attempted an interesting quantification of the effects of financial innovation on the personal sector's demand for liquidity aggregates (both money and credit). These liquidity aggregates do not correspond to any of the official monetary aggregates as sectoral holdings are not available, and hence it may be argued that this research is of limited value for direct policy purposes. Although it is of use in terms of exploration of the effects of financial innovation on demand for money and credit functions, the author would argue that knowledge of the effect of financial innovation upon official published money supply series is of greater relevance than knowledge of the effects upon some 'hybrid' money supply data. However, Johnston's liquidity aggregates z_1 and z_2 are respectively defined as personal sector holdings of currency, bank deposits, building society deposits, all National Savings instruments, 'other' money market instruments and certificates of deposit (CDs) and z_1 less National Savings instruments and other money market instruments and CDs.

Both financial wealth and income are included in the equation[4] on the grounds that the demand for liquid assets will be dependent upon the transactions and precautionary characteristics of liquid assets (see Chapter 2). Of course, if a narrow non-interest-bearing money aggregate is being estimated, only income is usually included, as a measure of transactions demand. The own rate on money was constructed as the average rate of return on the various assets included in the aggregate. The average rate on building society deposits was also tested as a measure of the own rate. Competing interest rates included were the three-month inter-bank rate and the gross redemption yield on twenty-year gilts.

The results for holdings of liquid assets are disappointing, however. The equations pass the out-of-sample Hendry forecast test and the Chow test for stability over the period 1980/1–1982/4, but there is evidence of forecast instability when the forecast is extended to 1983. Johnston suggested that instability in the equations may be the result of factors not included in the function. He suggested that the rise in the stock market may be a factor, although including the

FT All Share Index made no difference. There are a number of points which may be relevant to instability in Johnston's equations, given the arguments of Chapters 4 and 5. In particular, Johnston does not explicitly allow for the effects of inflation on the demand for liquid assets. This may be the reason for the continuous under-prediction in the out-of-sample dynamic simulation over the period 1980/1–1983/4. Furthermore, the introduction of high-interest chequing accounts and high interest easy-access accounts may have increased the demand for liquid assets, yet Johnston's equations do not contain a proxy for such innovative financial assets. However, Johnston does provide an interesting dynamic simulation in an attempt to quantify the effects of what he terms 'financial liberalization' (which may be taken to mean the increased competitive pressures in the market for retail deposits) over the period 1980–3. His results suggest that financial liberalization may have added about 6 per cent to personal sector holdings of liquid assets over the period, about 1½ per cent per annum. Johnston argued that the adjustment process due to liberalization may have come to an end by 1984.

Johnston also attempted to estimate a function for total debt of the personal sector, which included bank lending, building society lending, other lending for house purchase, trade credit, hire-purchase and instalment debt.[5] The function is a reduced form model containing elements of the demand and supply of debt to the personal sector. It was found that total personal sector real debt is positively related to personal sector net real financial wealth, house prices and the return on building society deposits, and negatively related to the mortgage rate, the general level of short interest rates, real personal disposable income and inflation. There is also a variable for excess mortgage demand, which has a significant negative impact on persons' holdings of total debt. The equation appears to be relatively stable. The variable for excess mortgage demand (XSMD) is used to provide an estimate of the effect of financial liberalization on the personal sector's holdings of total financial debt. The XSMD variable is from Meen (1983), and shows continuous excess mortgage demand up to the emergence of excess mortgage supply after the removal of the corset. Johnston made the assumption that the shift in the supply of mortgages was the result of liberalization in the personal sector financial market. Estimates were then made of the effect of removing the corset by running two simulations for 1980/3–1983/4 of the debt equation. For one simulation XSMD was set at the level estimated by Meen, and for the other XSMD was set at a pre-corset-removal level which was taken to be the average level of excess mortgage demand estimated by Meen over the period 1978–80.

The simulations suggest that financial liberalization (or removal of the corset) may have added an extra 20 per cent to the stock of personal sector debt by the end of 1983. The fact that the percentage difference between the simulations remains relatively stable after 1982/4 suggests to Johnston that the adjustment as a result of financial liberalization may have finished by mid-1982. However, these results must be treated with some caution. Although Johnston's work in this paper is innovative, the conclusions he draws are in fact considerably weakened by the use of Meen's *early* estimate of excess mortgage demand. Meen has since (1985) amended and corrected his data series, which will considerably alter Johnston's results and conclusions, based as they are on an inadequate proxy or measure for mortgage rationing. The two data series, Meen (1983) and Meen (1985), are included in Appendix 8A for comparison.

Although not aimed at investigating financial innovation, the work of Grice and Bennett (1981, 1984) is of interest given the hypothesis stated earlier that through financial innovation wealth has become an increasingly important variable in the demand for money function.

Grice and Bennett examined the possible importance of wealth in the demand for money function for M3.[6] They estimated an equation for the non-bank private sector (NBPS) over the period 1963–78, utilizing gross financial wealth, a transactions variable and an own rate on money consisting of the rate of money minus the return on gilts. Grice and Bennett found that wealth is a major determinant of money demand, more important than an income/transactions variable. Their estimated equation appears to be relatively stable, although concern over the length of the adjustment process leads to a Monte Carlo test of the function.[7] In particular, Grice and Bennett concluded that the wealth data may have been collated with a certain degree of measurement error, possibly resulting in biased results.[8] Indeed, subsequent official data series have shown that Grice and Bennett's wealth data were in fact measured with a considerable degree of error (see Appendix 8B where the two series are shown for comparison). The conclusion must be that the equation is not entirely satisfactory. Given this measurement error, and the pre-1980 period of estimate (1963–78), further research is needed to establish whether or not wealth became a more important variable in the demand for money function in the face of the breakdown in the money–income relationship and to confirm the argument that money became an investment asset in the NBPS's overall portfolio.

Hall *et al.* (1989) used cointegration to estimate equations for the demand for M3 and M4. The M4 equation includes income, inflation, wealth, change in the FT Ordinary Share Index and a dummy for CCC.[9] The FT Ordinary Share Index was used to reflect changes in liquid asset holdings after the fall in the stock market index in the early 1970s.

Somewhat surprisingly, Hall *et al.* found no interest rate effects in either the demand for M3 or the demand for M4. They suggested that this may be due to difficulties in accurately measuring interest rates when financial innovations are taking place. It should also be noted that both equations have an exceptionally low R^2 (0.3 for M4 and 0.32 for M3) which must cast some doubt on the specification.

8.3 THE SECTORAL APPROACH

The different rates of growth of holdings of M3 by other financial institutions (OFIs), industrial and commercial companies (ICCs) and the personal sector identified in Chapter 5 emphasize the fact that it is possible that demand for money equations may be unable to forecast accurately if they have to take into account diverse behaviour patterns by different agents in the economy. It is perhaps more useful to carry out research on sectoral demand for money equations.

The sectoral approach provided plausible long-run equations for Weale,[10] who analysed the demand for a variety of assets by the personal sector over the period 1967/2–1981/3 in terms of the allocation of short-term assets among money and near money. Interestingly it was found that

> the results do not suggest a sharp distinction, in terms of substitution properties, between money and near money (building society and local authority deposits); this suggests that the usual emphasis on monetary aggregates may be unhelpful, and also indicates that an analysis of the demand for money which nets out the building societies by aggregating the non-bank private sector is unlikely to yield satisfactory results.
>
> (1986: 158)

Currie and Kennally (1985) modelled liquid assets and liabilities by disaggregating those that act as buffer stocks and those that do not on the assumption that some assets have a low cost of adjustment for some agents and a high cost of adjustment for others (i.e. the same assets may be more or less liquid to different holders).[11] The estimated buffer stock consists of building society deposits and time and sight bank deposits of the personal sector over the period 1968/1–1983/1. They found a stable function for this 'liquidity' aggregate.

Of special relevance is the finding that the liquidity demand equation is stable across the period 1971–4 when most demand equations show instability. There are problems in the short-run dynamic behaviour of the equation, however (long-run elasticities exceed short-run elasticities), which tends to cast doubt upon the buffer stock nature of the model.

8.4 INTEREST ELASTICITY OF EXPENDITURE

The perceived wisdom of the 1970s, according to a survey of the consumption function by Ferber (1973), was that interest rate effects on consumption were likely to be relatively weak. In the 1980s, however, Cuthbertson (1980) and Davis (1984) found significant interest rate effects on durables expenditure. Dicks (1988) estimated a durables consumption function which consisted of terms representing real household disposable income, the clearing banks base rate, the minimum deposit rate on durables, the flow of mortgage lending and personal sector real liquid assets.[12] The model passes a variety of tests and has a good forecast performance. The absolute interest elasticity of −0.84 during 1963/3–1985/4 was compared with two subperiods derived from splitting the sample in 1974.

The interest rate is positive in the sample ending in the early 1970s, but negative later. The interest rate on durables has risen closer to zero over time and that on real net liquid assets has fallen. Dicks interpreted these findings as suggesting that interest rates became a more important factor in determining when households buy durables.

Interestingly, Dicks found that splitting lending for house purchase between that used for housing investment and that for net cash withdrawal and using these as variables in the equation did not lead to significant coefficients. Either equity withdrawal did not have a large effect on consumption (as suggested in Chapter 6) or the simple proxies used for equity withdrawal were not adequate for modelling how much lending leaked into consumption.

Dicks also investigated the interest elasticity of non-durables consumption.[13] The final equation consisted of terms representing the lagged dependent variable (real consumer's expenditure on non-durable goods and services), real household disposable income, real personal sector net financial wealth and the clearing banks' base rate.

Again, interest elasticity effects were examined by splitting the sample, this time at the end of 1974, and re-estimating the model for the subperiods. In the first period, the interest rate term was small and insignificant. Conversely, the interest rate term in the second subperiod was significant and about as twice as large as that estimated for the sample as a whole. Dicks concluded that:

> Clearly this result implies that further work is needed if we are to understand why interest rate effects appear to be becoming more important, particularly given that we found much the same story was true of durables expenditure. One possible reason, suggested in Dicks (1987), is the greater competition in the markets for personal sector saving and borrowing has resulted in a reduction in liquidity constraints, which may be correlated with changes in interest rates. (1988: 26)

Despite this, proxies for mortgage rationing and net cash withdrawal were not found to be significant in Dicks' work, nor were the house price–earnings ratio or the flow of real mortgage lending.

Dicks' work suggests that the effect of monetary control through the interest elasticity of the consumption function has increased over time, with the interest elasticity of consumption rising. It is by no means clear, however, whether this is the direct result of financial innovation, market clearing mortgage rates and increasing house prices. A further avenue of research would be to analyse the interest elasticity of consumption according to the mortgage interest rate. As noted above, Dicks used the clearing banks' base rate for interest rate effects, but this is not necessarily the same as utilizing mortgage rates. Base rates change at different times from mortgage rates, particularly given the widespread practice of changing interest rates for existing mortgage borrowers only once or twice yearly.

If the interest elasticity of consumption with respect to mortgage interest rates also rose, there would be a greater case for maintaining that the ending of the cartel, market clearing mortgage rates and higher mortgage-to-income ratios were responsible for greater interest sensitivity of consumption, and hence more effective monetary control.

8.5 CONCLUSION

The problems noted by Johnston, Budd and Holly, and Grice and Bennett in terms of instability of the demand for broad money may be the result of taking inadequate account of the effects of financial innovation on the own rate on money, as Taylor's work shows. The notion that wealth became a more important variable in the demand for money as a result of money becoming an increasingly attractive form of holding wealth has not been fully corroborated by past research, although the work of Grice and Bennett may provide a useful base to build upon.

None of the published work on the demand for money or consumers' expenditure examines the interest elasticity of these functions over time. Given the importance of these elasticities for the purposes of monetary control, and the expected effects on these elasticities, this appears to be a fruitful area for research (see Chapters 9 and 10).

Dicks provided evidence as to the effects of financial innovation upon the interest elasticity of consumers' expenditure, but did not examine whether the ending of the cartel and more fluid mortgage interest rates increased the interest elasticity of expenditure. Given that this is likely to increase the ability of the monetary authorities to control the growth of the money supply, this again seems a useful avenue for further research (see Chapter 10).

APPENDIX 8A

Table 8.A1 Mortgage rationing (MRAT), Meen 1983

Year		*Year*		*Year*	*Percentage*
1967/1	34.56	1974/1	30.05	1981/1	−5.1
1967/2	27.89	1974/2	33.15	1981/2	−9.95
1967/3	30.51	1974/3	27.28	1981/3	−0.91
1967/4	24.18	1974/4	26.66	1981/4	−5.62
1968/1	20.56	1975/1	21.79	1982/1	5.55
1968/2	25.33	1975/2	15.52	1982/2	−5.82
1968/3	33.69	1975/3	8.91	1982/3	−1.04
1968/4	39.40	1975/4	6.46	1982/4	0.52
1969/1	37.97	1976/1	5.880	1983/1	0.51
1969/2	29.79	1976/2	2.160	1983/2	−0.62
1969/3	34.30	1976/3	5.40	1983/3	2.09
1969/4	36.40	1976/4	3.12	1983/4	2.90
1970/1	32.95	1977/1	10.01		
1970/2	26.35	1977/2	9.16		
1970/3	27.79	1977/3	4.60		
1970/4	27.79	1977/4	12.86		
1971/1	23.04	1978/1	13.28		
1971/2	16.65	1978/2	10.48		
1971/3	21.89	1978/3	18.12		
1971/4	23.39	1978/4	24.49		
1972/1	20.50	1979/1	10.84		
1972/2	20.57	1979/2	17.01		
1972/3	28.31	1979/3	14.41		
1972/4	33.03	1979/4	18.79		
1973/1	28.12	1980/1	8.16		
1973/2	19.26	1980/2	3.76		
1973/3	32.03	1980/3	2.72		
1973/4	26.73	1980/4	−7.18		

Table 8.A2 Mortgage rationing, Meen 1985

Year	*Percentage*	*Year*	*Percentage*	*Year*	*Percentage*
1963/1	4.76	1970/1	3.37	1977/1	0.98
1963/2	3.75	1970/2	2.71	1977/2	0.90
1963/3	4.05	1970/3	2.81	1977/3	0.47
1963/4	3.45	1970/4	2.69	1977/4	1.28
1964/1	3.52	1971/1	2.28	1978/1	1.40
1964/2	3.16	1971/2	1.68	1978/2	1.18
1964/3	3.84	1971/3	2.15	1978/3	1.78
1964/4	4.19	1971/4	2.29	1978/4	2.40
1965/1	3.82	1972/1	2.22	1979/1	1.21
1965/2	4.83	1972/2	2.24	1979/2	0.82
1965/3	5.09	1972/3	2.81	1979/3	1.61
1965/4	3.84	1972/4	3.24	1979/4	3.03
1966/1	3.71	1973/1	2.85	1980/1	0.93
1966/2	2.23	1973/2	2.11	1980/2	0.49
1966/3	2.49	1973/3	3.19	1980/3	0.22
1966/4	4.14	1973/4	2.50	1980/4	−0.78
1967/1	3.46	1974/1	2.85	1981/1	−0.43
1967/2	2.79	1974/2	3.24	1981/2	−0.90
1967/3	3.03	1974/3	2.68	1981/3	−0.17
1967/4	2.40	1974/4	2.18	1981/4	−0.76
1968/1	2.05	1975/1	2.21	1982/1	0.28
1968/2	2.55	1975/2	1.93	1982/2	−0.75
1968/3	3.35	1975/3	0.91	1982/3	−0.50
1968/4	3.87	1975/4	0.58	1982/4	−0.67
1969/1	3.82	1976/1	0.46	1983/1	−0.40
1969/2	3.02	1976/2	0.22	1983/2	−0.10
1969/3	3.40	1976/3	0.53	1983/3	0.16
1969/4	3.67	1976/4	0.30	1983/4	0.35
				1984/1	−0.61
				1984/2	−0.89

APPENDIX 8B

Table 8.B1 Grice and Bennett's gross financial wealth figures

Year	*Amount (£)*	*Year*	*Amount (£)*
1967/4	48,163	1974/1	79,315
1968/1	48,455	1974/2	81,199
1968/2	49,032	1974/3	82,653
1968/3	50,138	1974/4	83,554
1968/4	50,880	1975/1	86,281
1969/1	50,161	1975/2	88,422
1969/2	50,111	1975/3	91,111
1969/3	50,481	1975/4	93,946
1969/4	51,744	1976/1	97,468
1970/1	52,059	1976/2	101,406
1970/2	52,621	1976/3	105,703
1970/3	53,473	1976/4	109,596
1970/4	54,296	1977/1	114,405
1971/1	55,897	1977/2	116,482
1971/2	56,916	1977/3	122,133
1971/3	58,756	1977/4	126,083
1971/4	61,387	1978/1	128,731
1972/1	62,766	1978/2	132,521
1972/2	66,506	1978/3	137,045
1972/3	68,032	1978/4	141,576
1972/4	71,133		
1973/1	72,439		
1973/2	74,909		
1973/3	76,665		
1973/4	79,565		

Table 8.B2 Updated gross financial wealth

Year	*Amount (£)*	*Year*	*Amount (£)*
1967/4	53,142	1974/1	87,665
1968/1	53,385	1974/2	89,967
1968/2	53,903	1974/3	91,449
1968/3	54,884	1974/4	92,824
1968/4	56,161	1975/1	98,004
1969/1	55,989	1975/2	100,301
1969/2	56,144	1975/3	104,749
1969/3	56,527	1975/4	109,480
1969/4	57,590	1976/1	114,390
1970/1	57,166	1976/2	118,504
1970/2	58,006	1976/3	121,095
1970/3	58,578	1976/4	126,859
1970/4	59,727	1977/1	130,267
1971/1	61,636	1977/2	133,494
1971/2	63,098	1977/3	142,356
1971/3	65,897	1977/4	146,732
1971/4	68,845	1978/1	146,678
1972/1	70,827	1978/2	151,322
1972/2	74,017	1978/3	155,921
1972/3	76,270	1978/4	159,877
1972/4	79,775		
1973/1	79,833		
1973/2	82,504		
1973/3	84,446		
1973/4	87,469		

Source: *Financial statistics*, various issues, Table 14.4

9 Econometric evaluation

9.1 INTRODUCTION

Few studies of the demand for money function have taken into account, or attempted to take into account, the effects of financial innovation, as the scarcity of empirical work surveyed in Chapter 8 shows, despite the growing consensus that financial innovation may have had an important role to play:

> It is clear that the real world is more complicated than the models in question, and that in fact money-holding agents treat a rather wide variety of assets as alternatives to money in their portfolios. There is nothing surprising about this; indeed it would be startling had things turned out otherwise. However, it does mean that as the menu of assets available to money holders changes over time, we might expect their behaviour *vis-à-vis* money holding also to change as a result. This is a *potentially important* point when recent stability problems with the demand for money function are analysed.
>
> (Laidler 1985a: 133)

Given the analysis of Chapter 5 as to the changing definition of money as a result of building society innovations, the monetary authorities' own comments as to the increasing convergence of the deposit liabilities of banks and building societies, and the problems of money-holders switching their balances between building societies and banks and hence distorting the growth rate of M3, the broad monetary aggregate M4 is used when estimating the demand for money function.

Sections 9.2–9.5 analyse the broad econometric modelling strategies and methodologies in the empirical literature and provide critiques of the main functions estimated under these strategies: the partial adjustment mechanism, the error-correction model and cointegration.

A theoretical model of the demand for broad money is specified in Section 9.6 with due regard to the likely relevant variables as outlined in Chapter 8. This theoretical model is used as the basis for the econometric specification of the demand for broad money. The final equation is then used to evaluate the various arguments as set out in earlier chapters. Specifically, Section 9.6 attempts to specify a stable demand for money function by taking account of interest on building society accounts, and the interest elasticity of the demand for money over time is investigated. The final section concludes with an overview of the econometric results and their implications.

9.2 ECONOMETRIC METHODOLOGY

The breakdown of an econometric model may occur for a variety of reasons, functional form misspecification, inadequate econometric modelling techniques or exogenous 'structural breaks' to the system under study. The latter phenomenon has been widely blamed for instability in demand for money equations (Hendry 1979, 1985).

The existence of external shocks, such as competition and credit control (CCC) or the abandonment of the corset, necessitates, it is argued, a revision of econometric equations to take into account the altered system. It is far from obvious, however, *when* a structural break has occurred in previously stable relationships, or even if it has occurred. The very breakdown of an econometric model is often used as evidence that a structural break must have happened, because of the sudden breakdown of the model; it is by no means clear, however, whether the model was correctly specified at the outset. A change in exogenous variables which forces a model to break down may be evidence of misspecification of that model, rather than evidence of a structural break. Indeed, a correctly specified equation may have been able to model a change in the behaviour of exogenous variables and hence not exhibit any signs of instability or structural breaks (Hendry 1979).

For example, the fast rate of growth of inflation in the 1970s, which represented a change in the behaviour of an exogenous variable, may have appeared to produce structural breaks or shifts in those estimated models that did not include an inflation variable, if the underlying true economic relationship did indeed depend upon the behaviour of the inflation variable (see Hendry 1979: 220). Thus it is extremely difficult to ascertain whether model breakdown or a reduction in model forecast accuracy is a result of a structural break in the system *or* because of model misspecification.

The econometric methodology undertaken when estimating *any* economic relationship can be of vital importance to the stability and robustness of the model. Moreover, it can be argued that if an inappropriate methodology is pursued it is likely that at some point in time the equation may suffer from instability merely as a result of an inadequate modelling strategy rather than because of any change in the economic relationship under observation. If an equation becomes unstable during a period when there are changes in the economic system, for example during a policy regime change (e.g. CCC), it may appear that the change in the economic system has forced the equation to break down, whereas in fact it may be that the inadequate modelling methodology could not emulate the regime change whilst a more robust modelling strategy may have been able to cope with such a situation without exhibiting signs of instability.

It is thus difficult to distinguish between a 'true' structural break that even a correctly specified equation using sound econometric modelling methodology would break down under, and a change in exogenous variables that appears to be a structural break when using a misspecified model based on inappropriate or inadequate modelling strategy. The choice of econometric methodology is therefore of paramount importance. The adoption of a particular methodology is, as might be expected, a contentious issue.

Certain commentators have argued that econometric models have been constructed according to *ad hoc* procedures (Blaug 1980: 257). Some would argue that the standard textbook approach has led to a situation where research is concerned with confirming theories rather than evaluating alternative theories (Pagan 1984). With different techniques leading to different conclusions there are often no methods for deciding which theories command the most credible support, and as a result contradictory hypotheses are maintained side by side for many years. Whilst there are opposing and sometimes rather extreme views, it is clear that there is a certain amount of dissatisfaction with standard methods. This has resulted in attempts to re-evaluate econometric methodology, leading to a variety of alternative routes for the applied researcher.[1]

The well-known policy critique of Lucas (1976) argues that model breakdown occurs as a result of ignoring the role of expectations in modelling, so that structural instability may be unknowingly built into empirical models. The Lucas critique is theory oriented and has led to rational expectations playing a major role in this approach to the modelling of time-series data (Lucas and Sargent 1981), although little work has been carried out on rational expectations and the demand for money (see Cuthbertson and Taylor (1987) for a rare exception, but note the reservations of Hendry (1988)).

For purposes of illustration it is possible to distinguish between two broad categories of empirical econometric modelling methods: the 'specific-to-general' and the 'general-to-specific'. The former has been branded by Hendry (1979: 222) as 'excessive presimplification with inadequate diagnostic checking'. It is worth repeating here in full Hendry's caricature of 'specific-to-general' modelling, whereby researchers (see also Hendry and Mizon 1978; Hendry and Ericsson 1983; Hendry and Richard 1982, 1983)

1 commence from theories that are drastic abstractions of reality (usually of a long-run steady-state world subject to stringent *ceteris paribus* assumptions concerning all but a very small number of variables);
2 formulate highly parsimonious relationships to represent their theories;
3 estimate their equations from the available data using techniques which are 'optimal' only on the assumption that the highly restricted model is correctly specified;
4 test a few of the assumptions explicitly or implicitly underlying the exercise;
5 revise the specification in the light of the evidence acquired; and
6 re-estimate accordingly.

The dangers of starting with a model that is too restrictive are examined in Hendry and Mizon (1978) and Hendry (1979).

The general-to-specific methodology is characterized by initial over-parameterization followed by further simplification (Hendry 1979: 228).

There are severe critics of the general-to-specific approach, however. In particular, it has been argued that the method relies too heavily on a statistical basis rather than on economic theory *per se* (Lawson 1983: 80; Laidler 1986). The general-to-specific approach maintains that economic theory cannot be used to model long-run demand for money functions as the data generation process is essentially a disequilibrium phenomenon (Hendry 1985). Lags, either dependent or independent variables in the long-run relationship, are therefore used to model the adjustment process. Thus, the general-to-specific method is open to the criticism of *ad hoc* modelling.

Moreover, it is argued that the search for *stable* functions in the general-to-specific methodology precludes the researcher from admitting that the function is unstable: it just has not yet been found. Some would go so far as to say that the general-to-specific approach finds stability when none is evident, largely as a result of the assumption that stability is there to be found (Darnell 1987: 4).

Given the emphasis placed on the rigorous testing of econometric models in the general-to-specific approach this is probably an over-harsh characterization, although the problem should be acknowledged by applied researchers.

This research programme argues that the temporal structure of the data should be allowed to play a more important role in model specification (Sargan 1964). This has been extended by Hendry and Anderson (1977) and Davidson *et al.* (1978). The methodology combines a constructionist approach along with a destructive strategy. In other words, if the worst models are eliminated the less bad ones are left (Hendry 1979).

One of the main prerequisites for accepting a model is its ability to explain previous models, including the reason for their breakdown. Use of this 'encompassing principle' (Mizon 1984) provides a progressive sequence of models which at worst are summaries of previous research but at best are robust and stable characterizations of economic phenomena (Hendry and Richard 1983). Of course, a general model will always be able to explain models that are special cases of it, and would lead to the adoption of an over-general model. A further requirement, therefore, is that parsimony is upheld. This is characterized as a 'general-to-specific' modelling strategy, where the researcher starts from a general dynamic specification and tests downwards for a more parsimonious and theoretically meaningful relationship (Gilbert 1986).

A vital aspect of the approach is the rigorous testing of models both against the data and against each other. This accords with a Popperian methodology (Popper 1972) where a falsificationist approach is adopted in place of the positivist methodology. Thus, model tests are *necessary* conditions for models not to be invalid. Philosophically, there are no *sufficient* conditions under which models can be validated. Failure to reject one of the *necessary* conditions does not establish that the model is valid, but only that the model is not demonstrably invalid (Hendry 1985). This destructive approach can be defended on the grounds that it is better to recognize uncertainties in models through vigorous testing than to use invalid models as a basis for policy decisions. This general-to-specific methodology argues that much of traditional econometric analysis suffers from excessive pre-simplification and inadequate diagnostic checking (Hendry 1985). General-to-specific, on the other hand, is characterized by intended over-parameterization with data-based simplification. Starting from the most general model which it seems reasonable to specify, sequential testing procedures are used to select a data-coherent specification.

It is worth emphasizing that exponents of this form of modelling do in fact recognize that it does have its limitations. Again, it is worth repeating Hendry in full:

1 the chosen (ostensibly general) model could actually comprise a very special case of the data generation process, so that diagnostic testing remains important;
2 data limitations – sample size or the information content of the data may be inadequate;
3 there is no uniquely 'best' sequence for simplifying the model – different approximations which have similar sample likelihoods may forecast very differently.

Exponents of the general-to-specific approach maintain that these problems are outweighed by the uncertainty of lag responses in any relationship under consideration and hence the desirability of starting from a general unrestricted maximum lag length (constrained by degrees of freedom limitations). Moreover, this methodology appears to have produced more robust (but by no means problem-free) models, which can be used as a useful starting point for applied researchers (Hendry and Mizon 1978; Hendry 1979; Grice and Bennett 1981, 1984; Johnston 1984, 1985; Taylor 1987).

9.3 PARTIAL ADJUSTMENT MODELS

Many demand for money models pre-1975 were based on partial adjustment principles. These models have been heavily criticized (Courakis 1978; Hendry and Mizon 1978) for their *ad hoc* nature and over-restrictive assumptions. It is argued by some (e.g. Hendry 1979) that it is not surprising that such models exhibit instability, given their underlying theoretical basis and the method by which they are developed. Although the emphasis of this book remains the effects of building society and bank developments on monetary control, it is obviously of importance to examine alternative econometric techniques to evaluate their appropriateness for the econometric work to follow.

The long-run demand for money function is typically derived thus:

$$\frac{M^*}{P} = f(X) \tag{9.1}$$

i.e. desired real money balances M^*/P are a function of a set of explanatory variables X. In the long run it is assumed that *observed* real money balances M/P equal *desired* real money balances M^*/P:

$$\frac{M}{P} = \frac{M^*}{P} \tag{9.2}$$

This is rationalized on the grounds that the demand for money is for a target level of money balances that holders attempt to meet on average over time. In the long run, it is therefore a useful approximation that observed balances equal desired money balances. The long-run demand for money can then be represented by

$$\frac{M}{P} = f(X) \tag{9.3}$$

However, it is unlikely that observed money holdings will be at their desired level in the short run, because of costs of adjustment in achieving long-run desired levels of money balances. Therefore,

$$\frac{M}{P} \neq \frac{M^*}{P} \tag{9.4}$$

It is assumed that money-holders take a two-stage decision process. First, the long-run desired level of money balances is decided and, second, the optimum speed of adjustment towards some desired level is calculated.

The speed of adjustment, however, is affected by adjustment costs, of which there are assumed to be two forms:

1. the costs of being out of the long-run desired equilibrium of money holding, e.g. the opportunity cost of interest income on alternative assets, or an inability to buy goods when needed, represented by

   $$a\left(\frac{M}{P} - \frac{M^*}{P}\right)^2$$

   where a is the cost of being out of equilibrium;
2. the costs of *changing* the observed level of assets in order to move *towards* the long-run desired equilibrium level of money holding, e.g. the 'shoe-leather' costs of inconvenience and the opportunity cost of time, represented by

   $$b\left[\frac{M}{P} - \left(\frac{M}{P}\right)_{t-1}\right]$$

   where b is the cost of changing towards equilibrium.

Costs of adjustment are represented by the first-order partial adjustment mechanism which is derived as follows (Cuthbertson 1985: 64). Money holders choose actual balances M to minimize costs C:

$$\min C = a\left(\frac{M}{P} - \frac{M^*}{P}\right)^2 + b\left[\frac{M}{P} - \left(\frac{M}{P}\right)_{t-1}\right]^2 \tag{9.7}$$

$$\frac{\partial C}{\partial M} = 2a\left(\frac{M}{P} - \frac{M^*}{P}\right) + 2b\left[\frac{M}{P} - \left(\frac{M}{P}\right)_{t-1}\right] = 0 \tag{9.8}$$

$$\frac{M}{P} = \frac{a}{a+b}\frac{M^*}{P} + \frac{b}{a+b}\left(\frac{M}{P}\right)_{t-1} \tag{9.9}$$

$$\frac{M}{P} = \frac{M^*}{P} + (1-\lambda)\frac{M}{P}_{t-1} \tag{9.10}$$

which is the partial adjustment model,

and $\lambda = \dfrac{a}{a+b}$. If costs of adjustment are zero, $b = 0$, $a = 1$ and $\dfrac{M}{P} = \dfrac{M^*}{P}$. If costs of being out of equilibrium are zero, $a = 0$, $b = 0$ and $\dfrac{M}{P} = \dfrac{M^*}{P}_{t-1}$. The partial adjustment mechanism is thus used to link observed values of money balances with desired levels.

Combining (9.1) and (9.10) gives the short-run estimating equation:

$$\frac{M}{P} = f(X) + (1-\lambda)\frac{M}{P}_{t-l} \tag{9.11}$$

where X is a set of explanatory variables.

Partial adjustment assumes that short-run desired money holdings are a weighted average of desired long-run money holdings and lagged values of money holdings. The parameters of interest from the short-run function can be used to obtain those of the long-run function by dividing the short-run by one minus the coefficient of the lagged dependent variable.

The lagged dependent variables represent the slow adjustment of observed money holdings to desired levels and hence the lags in price adjustment.

Partial adjustment models that performed well in the 1960s (Dow 1958; Paish 1958; Kavanagh and Walters 1966; Laidler and Parkin 1970; Laidler 1971) were found to be unstable in the 1970s (Hacche 1974; Artis and Lewis 1974, 1976).

Criticism of these partial adjustment models of the demand for money function has tended to emphasize the constraints involved in the short-run dynamics of adjustment. Detailed critiques are put forward in Courakis (1978) and Hendry and Mizon (1978). Of vital importance is the method of modelling lags in the adjustment process in the partial adjustment model. The coefficient λ is used to model the lag response in the short-run demand for money function (equation (9.11)). This means that the dependent variable (observed real money balances) will adjust to changes in any one of the independent variables X with the same parameter λ. So, the partial adjustment model constrains the lag length to be the same, despite the fact that the initial disturbance may derive from either income or interest rates. *A priori*, it would be expected that the lag length of adjustment would be different according to where the disturbance arose. Early partial adjustment models were thus extremely restrictive in their specified portfolio adjustment mechanisms, in the manner in which lag lengths of variables determining the demand for money were assumed to be the same.

Further criticisms of the partial adjustment model also relate to the restrictiveness of some of the assumptions. Many partial adjustment models have employed the following.

1 The true errors of the model are assumed to be correlated.
2 The price elasticity of the demand for money is assumed to be unity.
3 Equations are estimated in first difference form.

It is not obvious *a priori* that these assumptions hold true, and a crucial part of the general-to-specific methodology is that the restrictions should be *tested*. A particular criticism is the practice of imposing non-linear restrictions on the equation by the assumption of autocorrelation, usually through employing the Cochrane–Orcutt (1949) transformation (e.g. Hacche 1974). Sargan (1980) and Hendry and Mizon (1978) show that autoregressive errors entail a variety of restrictions on the general dynamic model which should be tested for. Residual autocorrelation is normally a symptom of model misspecification rather than autoregressive errors (Mizon and Hendry 1980; McAleer *et al.* 1985; Baba *et al.* 1987).

From examination of the underlying assumptions of the partial adjustment model of the demand for money function, it is clear why numerous authors have argued that instability in these models may have arisen as a result of inadequately specified relationships. In particular, misspecification may have arisen from inappropriate restrictions on the econometric model. If so, a structural change such as financial innovation may appear as a breakdown in the relationships under study, whereas it may be that the model cannot adequately take account of such changes because of misspecification and omission of relevant variables. Perhaps a model which allows for more flexible lags in the adjustment process is more appropriate to the money demand function. Flexible lags can be allowed for in the general-to-specific modelling strategy, examined in the next section. Use of the encompassing principle (see earlier), that acceptance of a model is dependent on its ability to explain previous models and the reason for their breakdown, provides a stringent test of the general-to-specific strategy.

9.4 ERROR-CORRECTION AND AUTOREGRESSIVE DISTRIBUTED LAG MODELS

In the general-to-specific modelling strategy, the temporal structure of the data is allowed to play a much more important role than in previous partial adjustment models (Davidson *et al.* 1978; Hendry and Richard 1982, 1983, 1987) although, as mentioned earlier, there is still the criticism that the lags are represented in a rather *ad hoc* manner. The general-to-specific methodology takes the standpoint that much of 'traditional' econometric analysis suffers from excessive pre-simplification and inadequate diagnostic checking (Hendry 1985). General-to-specific, on the other hand, is characterized by intended initial over-parameterization combined with subsequent data-based simplification. Starting from the most general model which it seems reasonable to specify, sequential testing procedures are used to select a data-coherent specification.

This approach is flexible in the manner in which lag responses adjust to changes in different independent variables. Typically, a general unrestricted autoregressive distributed lag (ADL) model is initially specified. This set of models may be written in general terms as

$$\frac{M}{P} = a(L)X_t + b(L)\left(\frac{M}{P}\right)_{t-1} \tag{9.12}$$

where $a(L)$ is an arbitrary lag polynomial, $L^n X_t = X_{t-n}$ and X is a set of explanatory variables.

Nested within this general ADL model is the error-correction mechanism (ECM), which modifies the partial adjustment model by allowing the adjustment process to be modelled by a dynamic reaction function rather than restricting the lag structure at the outset. In the ECM, money-holders adjust balances in response to deviations between current and target money holdings. The ECM is of the form

$$\frac{M}{P} = a(L)e_t \tag{9.13}$$

where $a(L)$ is an arbitrary polynomial in the lag operator L and e_t is the error between current and target money holdings (Salmon 1982: 3):

$$e_t = \frac{M}{P} - \frac{M^*}{P} \tag{9.14}$$

The ECM–ADL equation thus allows for an unrestricted flexible lag pattern at the outset of the modelling process. The initial general unrestricted equation is simplified by eliminating insignificant variables and by introducing restrictions into the equation such as differencing and common factor restrictions. The restrictions placed on the parameters are tested at each stage so that a parsimonious data-coherent model is estimated (Spanos 1986).

Engle and Granger (1987) have shown that ECMs generate cointegrated series and vice versa. Moreover, a cointegrated error-correction representation is not susceptible to problems of spurious regression (Granger and Newbold 1974). The basic approach is to use a two-step estimator by first carrying out a static levels regression and using the residuals from this in a dynamic model. The estimator is shown to be consistent and convergence on the true parameter values tends to be faster than normal ordinary least squares (OLS).

It is necessary to find the order of integration of the separate time series under investigation, i.e. how often the individual time series need to be differenced in order to become I(0). A time series that has a finite non-zero spectrum is said to be I(0) – integrated of order zero. If a time series has to be differenced once, it is integrated of order one. More generally, differencing a time series d times to induce I(0) reflects integration of order I(d).

If two time series X_t and Y_t are integrated of order I(1) then X_t and Y_t will be cointegrated through a linear combination:

$$Z_t = Y_t - \lambda X_t = \mathrm{I}(0)$$

An estimation of λ can be found through the regression of Y_t on X_t, and the ECM is

$$Z_t = Y_t - \hat{\lambda} X_t$$

The ECM can then be used in a dynamic model as all variables are I(0).

9.5 THEORETICAL AND EMPIRICAL CONSIDERATIONS OF THE DEMAND FOR M4

The demand for money function may be written as:

$$M = f(W, Y, P, r)$$

where W is gross financial wealth, Y is income, P is the price level, r is a vector of own and competing interest rates and M is M4 Full definitions of the variables and data sources are provided in Appendix 9A.

It is expected *a priori* that the demand for a broad aggregate such as M4 is likely to be influenced by transactions, precautionary and speculative considerations for liquid balances.

Some researchers have used income as a measure of transactions. Grice and Bennett (1981, 1984) note, however, that other studies utilize permanent income as an explanatory variable on the grounds that it is a proxy for wealth. There is thus some ambiguity as to the role of the income variable. A preferable method is to include an explicit wealth measure combined with income as a transactions variable. This provides plausible results for Grice and Bennett. Speculative motives may be allowed for by including expected capital gains to gilts in the equation (Spencer 1981).[2]

The general model was specified in terms of the real demand for money

$$\Delta\left(\frac{M}{P}\right) = a + \sum_{i=0}^{4} \text{GFW}_{-i} + \sum_{i=0}^{4} \left(\frac{M}{PY}\right)_{-i} + \sum_{i=0}^{4} \Delta\left(\frac{M}{P}\right)_{-i}$$
$$+ \sum_{i=0}^{4} (\text{RT}_{-1} - \text{RS})_{-i} + \sum_{i=0}^{4} \Delta P_{-1} + \sum_{i=0}^{4} Y_{-i}$$
$$+ \sum_{i=0}^{4} \text{RG}_{-i} + \text{seasonals} \qquad (9.15)$$

where M is M4 (unadjusted), GFW is the gross financial wealth of the non-bank private sector, Y is the real gross domestic product (GDP) at factor cost, P is the implicit GDP deflator, RT is the rate of interest on three-month Treasury bills, RG is the rate of interest on twenty-year gilts and RS is the rate of interest (net) on building society high interest instant-access accounts.

Initially the model was estimated by OLS with four lags on each variable in accordance with previous demand for money studies (Hendry 1979; Spanos 1986). In view of the strictures of Wallis

(1974) on the use of seasonally adjusted data, unadjusted data are used here throughout. The general model was reparameterized according to a sequential testing down procedure (see Cuthbertson 1985). This involves removing insignificant variables, differencing variables and setting parameters equal to each other when data permissible. These restrictions are tested at each stage against the general model for data acceptability using *F* tests.[3]

Proceeding in this manner, the following model was derived:

$$\Delta\left(\frac{M}{P}\right) = \underset{(0.021)}{0.048} + \underset{(0.035)}{0.123}\text{GFW}_t - \underset{(0.036)}{0.126}\text{GFW}_{t-3}$$

$$+ \underset{(0.06)}{0.133}\,\Delta\left(\frac{M}{P}\right)_{t-2} - \underset{(0.048)}{0.254}\left(\frac{M}{PY}\right)_{t-1}$$

$$- \underset{(0.08)}{0.204}(\text{RT}_{-1} - \text{RS})_t - \underset{(0.09)}{0.622}\,\Delta P_t$$

$$+ \text{seasonals} \tag{9.16}$$

$R^2 = 0.85$ SER $= 0.01$

AR $F[4, 64] = 1.40$ Normality $[2] = 3.43$

Reset $F[2, 66] = 0.22$ Arch $F[4, 60] = 0.47$

Heteroscedasticity $[15, 52] = 0.98$

where AR is the Lagrange multiplier (LM) test for fourth-order residual autocorrelation, ARCH (autoregressive conditional heteroscedasticity, see Engle 1982) is the LM test for autocorrelated squared residuals, Normality is the Jarque and Bera (1980) statistic for normality, Heteroscedasticity is White's (1984) test for heteroscedasticity, Reset is the Ramsey (1969) test for omitted variables (for adding two other basic variables), SER is the standard error of the regression and Δ represents the first-difference operator.

Single figures, e.g. Normality[2], are degrees of freedom for an asymptotic χ^2 distribution; double figures, e.g. AR $F[4, 64]$, are degrees of freedom for *F* statistics (Kiviet 1986). Figures in parentheses under the coefficient estimates are *standard errors*. All variables except interest rates are in log form.

The equation consists of variables representing wealth, interest rates and inflation and a lagged dependent variable. Although income is not explicitly included in the function, it is present in the form of the error-correction term M/PY (see Hendry 1979; Salmon 1982; and Chapter 8).

The own interest rate term $(RT_{-1} - RS)_{-i}$ is after Taylor (1987). The rate on competing assets (RT_t) is entered lagged one period to reflect information costs or perception lags (Taylor points out that it is easier for a wealth-holder to monitor the return on his or her money than the returns on alternative assets). The term $RT_{-1} - RS$ thus represents the differential between holding money and a short-term asset.

All the estimated coefficients are significant and the R^2 is reasonably high (0.85, against 0.76 for Taylor's equation). The equation passes a wide variety of tests. The model tracks well (Figure 9.1) and when the model is estimated up to 1981/4 the out-of-sample forecast is reasonable (Figure 9.2). Although the equation has a tendency to over-predict, in only two quarters are the forecasts insignificant at the 5 per cent level (1982/2 and 1983/2). The actual and fitted values of quarterly growth in real M4 are shown in Figure 9.3. The equation passes a Chow test for parameter constancy over the period 1982/1–1986/4.

Incidentally, the equation also passes a test for residual auto-

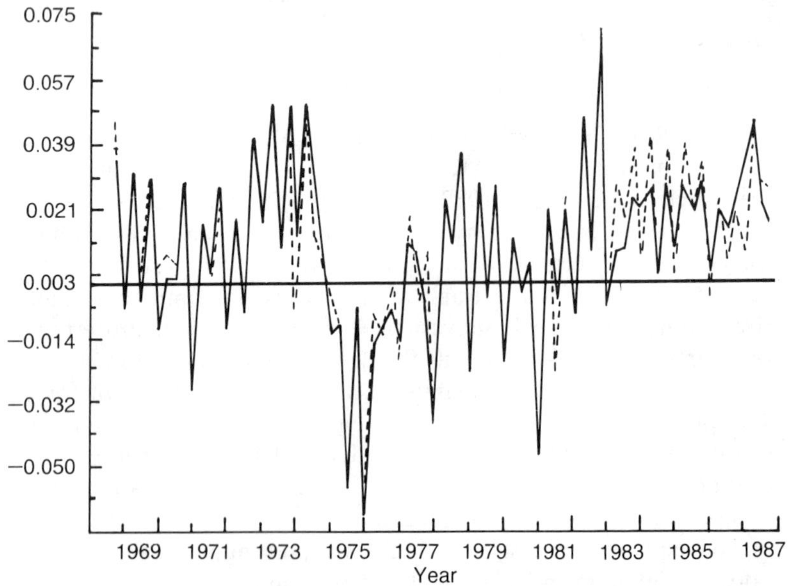

Figure 9.1 Tracking of the ECM–ADL model: ——, $\Delta(M/P)$; ------, fitted

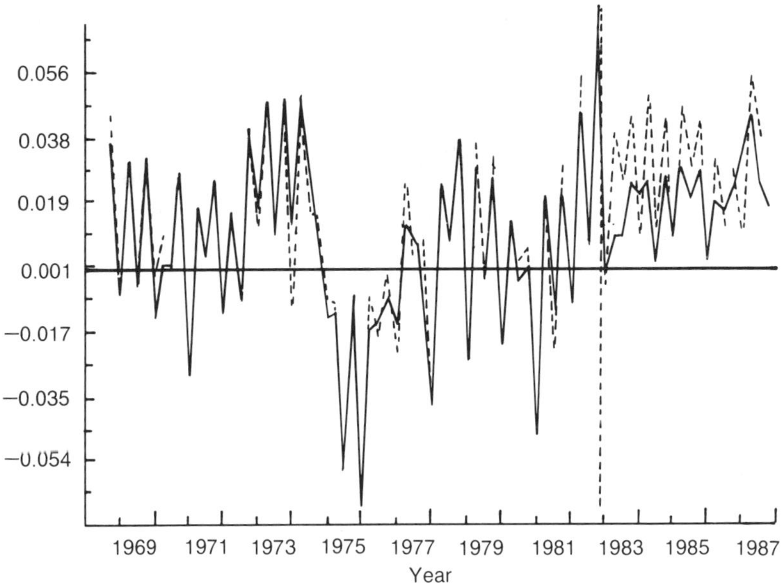

Figure 9.2 Out-of-sample forecast: ——, $\Delta(M/P)$; ------, fitted

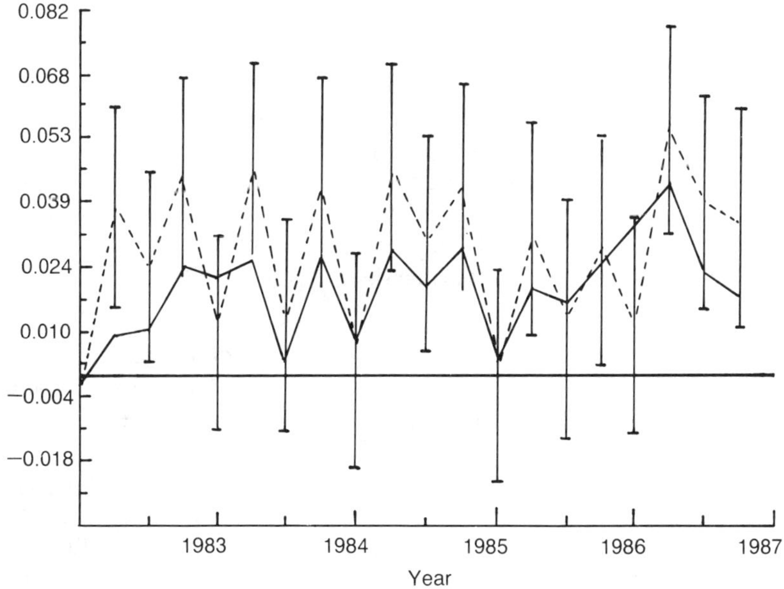

Figure 9.3 Actual and fitted values of quarterly growth in real M4: ——, $\Delta(M/P)$; ------, forecast

correlation, and so avoids Gordon's (1984) criticism that demand for money equations suffer excessively from this problem.

It is immediately noticeable that there is no explicit income variable in the final equation, consistent with the view that some balances are being used for investment purposes rather than as transactions balances. As such, wealth is becoming more relevant in the demand for money function as a result of financial innovation, which reflects the view that

> money is also used as a store of wealth, and an increasing proportion of it, although perhaps slightly less liquid, carries its own real rate of interest. This suggests that gross financial wealth may have an increasingly important role to play in determining the demand for money, since money is becoming a more attractive form of holding wealth.
>
> (Bank of England 1987b: 230)

Thus, although the money–income relationship has not totally broken down, the lack of an explicit income variable may reflect the reduced importance of the income variable relative to wealth.

The increasing importance of wealth in the demand for money function as a result of financial innovation has also been emphasized by Thygesen:

> Because of the rise in the share of monetary assets, even within a narrow definition of money, yielding a market-related return, the transactions and investment purposes for holding money have become less easily separable. This has a consequence not unfamiliar to economists from Cambridge: whatever measure of the money stock chosen, from M1 to private sector liquidity in a broad sense, the role of wealth has increased relative to that of income as a determinant of money demand.
>
> (1986: 23)

The coefficients on the own rate on money and on the inflation term are significant, implying that the effects of financial innovation and inflation are significant determinants of the demand for money (M4). The negative terms on the differential interest rate term and on the inflation variable suggest that, *ceteris paribus*, an increase in the differential between interest-bearing non-money assets and money will reduce the demand for money, as will an increase in inflation. These results appear to confirm Taylor's observation that financial innovation is an important factor in demand for money equations. Taylor emphasizes the importance of the own rate variable, and hence financial innovation, by dropping the term from the equation and re-estimating the model over the same time period. The equation breaks down, showing, according to Taylor, the necessity of including financial innovation variables in the equation.

Dropping the interest rate term from the equation above also has significant detrimental effects. The R^2 drops to 0.7 and the error-correction term becomes barely significant.

This test of the importance of financial innovation in an equation for the demand for money is not, however, particularly stringent. If *any* significant variable in an equation is omitted it is likely that the equation will suffer in terms of insignificant parameters and test statistics. In the case of financial innovation, a more reliable test would be to replace the own rate $(RT_{-1} - RS)_t$, which contains interest on the new, innovatory, high interest instant-access accounts, with a rate of interest that has been unaffected by such financial innovation. A useful rate to substitute would be the net rate on ordinary shares at building societies. This would provide a far more stringent test of the effect of financial innovation on the demand for M4. Of course, it may be argued that the rate of interest paid on ordinary shares has, in general, been higher in the 1980s as a result of increased competition with the retail banks, and that liquidity of these accounts has increased, both of which represent a form of financial innovation. It is important to know, however, the extent to which the specific innovation of high interest access accounts is responsible for the rapid growth in M4.

The previous model is used again, merely substituting RT_{-1} − ORD, the differential between Treasury bills lagged one period and the net rate on ordinary accounts at building societies, for RT_{-1} − RS.

It was found that there was no discernible change in the parameters of the equation. There was also no change in the test statistics. Moreover, the equation was stable when used for a twenty-period out-of-sample forecast. Interestingly, the equation still over-predicted the growth rate of M4. This suggests that it is not necessarily the specific financial innovation of high interest instant-access accounts which has been responsible for the fast rate of growth of M4 (relative to nominal income), as the net rate of interest on ordinary shares can also be used to explain the demand for M4. As mentioned earlier, ordinary shares have in fact become increasingly liquid and have paid, on average, a higher rate of interest in the 1980s than in the 1970s, but they are still much less attractive than high interest instant-access accounts, upon which most of the informed comment has placed the blame for the relatively fast growth of M4 (see Chapter 5).

An equation which included the differential between Treasury bills and the maximum rate at banks was not significant. Although the test statistics changed little, the lagged dependent variable M/P_{t-2} became insignificant and the own rate term $RT_{-1} - RB$ was only just significant. It thus appears that the differential between Treasury bills and building society instant-access accounts is a better measure of the own rate of the demand for M4 than is the differential between Treasury bills and the maximum rate on instant-access accounts at banks. It may be that this is because building society interest rates were in general above those of the retail banks in the 1980s, and hence more accurately reflected the return on broad money and thus the demand for broad money as measured by M4.

9.6 FINANCIAL INNOVATION AND THE INTEREST ELASTICITY OF THE DEMAND FOR MONEY

It has been suggested by some commentators (e.g. Goodhart 1984) that, with the impact of financial innovation and high real rates of return, it is the interest differential between 'money' and competing assets which is relevant for the demand for money function, rather than the general level of interest rates. Indeed, this is the reasoning behind using the differential between the own rate on money and that on Treasury bills in the models above:

> with the availability of market-related interest rates on deposits, and low spreads, the volume of deposits will increasingly prove an elastic function of *relative* interest rates, i.e. the spread between market rates and deposit rates and the spread between loan and deposit rates.
>
> (Goodhart 1986a: 92)

If the hypothesis that the demand for money has become insensitive to the general rate of interest is to be fully tested, it will be necessary to take into account not only the rate of return on gilts, but also any expected capital gains on gilts. Grice and Bennett (1981) suggest the following four methods of estimating capital gains on gilt holdings.

1 Direct information – survey information as to expected interest rates and capital gains could be transformed into time-series data for econometric usage. In practice, this would be likely to produce inaccurate information and be extremely time consuming.

2 Indirect information – the differential between the rate of inflation and the nominal interest rate may provide a forecast for future

changes in interest rates. For example, if the rate of inflation is relatively high compared with nominal interest rates, capital losses on gilts would be expected. On the other hand, if the *ex post* real rate of interest is relatively high, capital gains may be made on gilts as the nominal interest rate falls. In practice, however, the equilibrium real rate of interest will tend to be determined by the rate of inflation and may fluctuate in the short term.

3 It may be possible to include the *ex post* capital gains to gilts as a proxy for *ex ante* expectations of capital gains. This is attempted below, using the change in the FT index of gilt prices, although reservations as to the applicability of this proxy indicated in point (4) below should be taken into consideration.

4 Grice and Bennett (1981) point out that the approach in (3) above cannot be vindicated as *ex post* capital gains will only equal *ex ante* capital gains if investors have perfect foresight. As they do not have this capacity, *ex post* capital gains are equivalent to the correct variable measured with error. The traditional solution to such a problem is to search for instrumental variables that are correlated with the variables that exhibit measurement error although not correlated with the measurement error or the true disturbances. Grice and Bennett follow Durbin's (1954) proposal of using the rank of the badly measured variable as the instrument.

5 Alternatively, it may be possible to use economic theory to choose the instrument of the badly measured variable (McCallum 1976). This approach is also tried by Grice and Bennett and by Spencer (1981) and Johnston (1985) with some degree of success. The basic rationale is that expected capital gains will be formed by investors in terms of the expected value of an equation explaining *ex post* capital gains. Data for expected capital gains can therefore legitimately be obtained as the estimated values from the equation explaining *ex post* capital gains. This approach is also attempted below.

Using approach (5) above, the initial general specification of the gilts equation is of the form:

$$G + CG + r = a + \sum_{i=0}^{4} ED_{-i} + \sum_{i=0}^{4} P_{-i} + \sum_{i=0}^{4} \left(\frac{TFE}{P}\right)_{-i}$$

$$+ \sum_{i=0}^{4} \left(\frac{NFW}{P}\right)_{-i} + \sum_{i=0}^{4} G_{-i} + \sum_{i=0}^{4} r_{-i}$$

where G is gilts, ED is the interest rate on three-month Eurodollars, TFE is total final expenditure, NFW is the net financial wealth of the non-bank private sector, P is the implicit consumers' deflator, R is the yield on 2½ per cent consols, CG is the capital gains on gilts and r is the short rate.

The idea is to attempt to specify a model that explains *ex post* capital gains to gilts. Data from this model can then be used as expected capital gains on gilts in the demand for money equation. This is dependent, of course, on the assumption that expected capital gains are formed by investors in terms of the expected value of this equation which explains *ex post* capital gains.

The variables were chosen largely as a result of the work of Spencer (1981) on the demand for gilts. The final equation was of the form:

$$\begin{aligned} R + CG + r = & \underset{(0.21)}{-0.9ED_{-1}} + \underset{(0.073)}{0.43ED_{-4}} \underset{(0.3)}{-0.62P_{-1}} + \underset{(0.02)}{0.14P_{-2}} \\ & \underset{(0.2)}{-0.66}\frac{TFE}{P} + \underset{(0.37)}{0.92}\frac{NFW}{P} + \text{constant} \\ & + \text{seasonals} \\ & R^2 = 0.55 \end{aligned}$$

Surprisingly, utilizing the total return to gilts (i.e. the interest yield and capital gains) in the form of the data provided by the expected capital gains equation also proved to be insignificant in the demand for broad money equation:

$$\begin{aligned} \Delta\left(\frac{M}{P}\right) = & \underset{(0.18)}{-0.14} + \underset{(0.052)}{0.055}GFW_t - \underset{(0.052)}{0.042}GFW_{t-3} \\ & + \underset{(0.12)}{0.005}\,\Delta\left(\frac{M}{P}\right)_{t-2} - \underset{(0.1)}{0.59}\left(\frac{M}{PY}\right)_{t-1} \end{aligned}$$

$$+ \underset{(0.24)}{0.2} (RT_{-1} - RS)_t + \underset{(0.51)}{0.47}\, CG_{t-1}$$

$R^2 = 0.89$

AR	$F[4, 63] = 1.22$	Normality	$[2] = 3.6$
Reset	$F[2, 65] = 0.35$	Arch	$F[4, 59] = 0.31$
Heteroscedasticity	$[15, 51] = 2.55$		

The differential return between gilts and building society interest rates $(CG_{t-1} - RS)_t$ was also insignificant.

This result is surprising as it contradicts that of Grice and Bennett (1981), Spencer (1981) and Johnston (1985), all of whom find the total return on gilts to be an important factor in the demand for money. It is feasible, of course, that financial innovation has made the demand for money completely inelastic with respect to a long rate of interest, in terms of both a differential return and the general level of return on gilts.

Alternatively, there may be misspecification in the above equation explaining the expected capital gains to gilts. Concern must be expressed as to the nature of this equation, particularly in view of the possibility of omitted variables.

Spencer (1981) and Johnston (1985) included in their capital gains equations a measure of the structural balance of payments consisting of the current account and non-market-clearing capital flows. The data used were from Treasury estimates, which are unfortunately not available.

Thus the capital gains equation may suffer from omitted variables, which seems possible given the low R^2. The evidence as to the hypothesis that the demand for money has become less sensitive to the general rate of long interest rates is therefore inconclusive, although it does not appear to support the strong assertions of Akhtar:

> Over the past few years, the demand for money, especially at the broader level, has become less sensitive to the general level of interest rates. The share of financial instruments with market-related rates in monetary aggregates has risen over time, and the trend is continuing. The yield or return on those instruments tends to rise or fall with the rise or fall in market rates, leaving the differential unchanged. Consequently, there is no incentive to shift into or out of instruments the return on which moves in line with the general level of interest rates. This view is fairly broadly accepted,

> *although at this stage there is very little evidence on the quantitative significance of the shift in interest elasticity of money demand.*
> (Akhtar 1983: 37; italics added)

It is also of interest to test the effect of *levels* of interest rates on the demand for money function, to ascertain the relative importance of interest differentials *vis-à-vis* interest rate levels. Separating the differential term $(RT_{-1} - RS)_t$ from equation (9.15) to see whether the levels of interest rates are significant yielded similar results to those found earlier. It was immediately noticeable that the own 'level' rate of interest is insignificant when used for a twenty-period out-of-sample forecast. Furthermore, the competing rate of interest (RT_{-1}) was barely significant. This may be interpreted as an indication of the reduced importance of 'levels' of interest rates compared with differentials.

Chapter 7 set out the argument that financial innovation led to a decrease in the interest elasticity of the differential between the own rate on money and competing rates in the demand for broad money function. This was tested by successively re-estimating equation (9.16) over different subsample periods from 1967/3 to 1977/4 and then adding an extra year on each estimation up to 1986/4. The equations and test statistics are shown in Table 9.1 and the long-run interest elasticities of the differential are given in Table 9.2.

An examination of the coefficient on the interest differential $(RT_{-1} - RS)_t$ shows that it has halved in the period 1977/4–1986/4. It thus appears that the interest differential between an interest-bearing asset (Treasury bills) and interest-bearing money (building society high interest accounts) has become a *less* important determinant of the demand for money over time. Within these results, however, it should be noted that the size of the coefficient reached a low in 1982/4 of −0.180 and grew marginally in each year from 1982/4 to 1986/4 to reach −0.204.

The interest elasticity in Table 9.2 fell from −2.13 for the period 1967/3–1977/4 to a low of −0.71 for the period 1967/3–1983/4. The interest elasticity then appears to level off and, indeed, to rise marginally. Clearly this does support the hypothesis that the interest elasticity of the differential has become less elastic over time. A possible explanation of the finding is that as the interest differential has tended to fall steadily over time (see Chapter 4) the attractions of shifting out of money and into interest-earning assets have become less. In other words, the interest rate on money has closely followed other general rates of interest (as shown in Chapter 4), so that the interest differential is small and changes only infrequently.

Table 9.1 Demand for M4 equations

Period	*Constant*	GFW.	GFW_{t-3}	$\Delta(\frac{M}{P})_{t-2}$	$(\frac{M}{PY})_{t-1}$	$(RT_{-1} - RS)_t$	ΔP_t
1967/3– 1986/4	+0.048 (0.021)	+0.123 (0.035)	−0.126 (0.036)	+0.133 (0.067)	+0.248 (0.045)	−0.204 (0.08)	−0.622 (0.09)
1967/3– 1985/4	+0.054 (0.023)	+0.132 (0.035)	−0.135 (0.036)	+0.145 (0.067)	+0.233 (0.046)	−0.199 (0.08)	−0.622 (0.092)
1967/3– 1984/4	+0.071 (0.029)	+0.153 (0.041)	−0.158 (0.043)	+0.142 (0.069)	+0.236 (0.047)	−0.177 (0.084)	−0.626 (0.094)
1967/3– 1983/4	+0.070 (0.036)	+0.152 (0.045)	−0.156 (0.048)	+0.145 (0.071)	+0.241 (0.050)	−0.183 (0.093)	−0.622 (0.098)
1967/3– 1982/4	+0.047 (0.043)	+0.121 (0.049)	−0.123 (0.052)	+0.141 (0.071)	+0.262 (0.052)	0.212 (0.097)	0.621 (0.098)
1967/3– 1981/4	+0.014 (0.043)	+0.141 (0.047)	−0.140 (0.049)	+0.196 (0.074)	+0.249 (0.051)	0.212 (0.094)	−0.618 (0.100)
1967/3– 1980/4	+0.036 (0.047)	+0.150 (0.044)	−0.151 (0.047)	+0.162 (0.071)	+0.230 (0.051)	−0.255 (0.09)	−0.599 (0.10)
1967/3– 1978/4	+0.049 (0.055)	+0.154 (0.053)	−0.157 (0.055)	+0.175 (0.076)	+0.202 (0.062)	−0.327 (0.110)	−0.608 (0.12)
1967/3– 1977/4	+0.036 (0.096)	+0.105 (0.071)	−0.099 (0.077)	+0.188 (0.081)	+0.197 (0.064)	−0.419 (0.150)	−0.630 (0.118)

Note: R^2 ranged from 0.8 to 0.85.

Table 9.2 Interest elasticity of the demand for M4

Subperiod	*Interest elasticity*
1967/3–1986/4	−0.82
1967/3–1985/4	−0.85
1967/3–1984/4	−0.75
1967/3–1983/4	−0.71
1967/3–1982/4	−0.68
1967/3–1981/4	−0.85
1967/3–1980/4	−1.11
1967/3–1979/4	−1.63
1967/3–1978/4	−1.62
1967/3–1977/4	−2.13

The opportunity cost of holding money balances when general interest rates rise is thus likely to be minimal, and the (largely unchanged) differential will have little effect on the demand for money. Given that money has tended to become increasingly market related over time, there has been a reduction in the interest sensitivity of the demand for money with respect to interest differentials.

In monetary control terms, this appears to show that the ability of the monetary authorities to control the money supply by inducing money-holders to switch into alternative interest-bearing assets has become weaker. An increase in short-term interest rates will have had less effect on the interest differential between money and short rates in the 1980s than in the 1970s, largely, it is argued, because of the influence of high interest instant access accounts.

The warnings of Cooley and LeRoy should perhaps be noted here:

> The data are such that a modestly energetic specification search will give back almost whatever interest elasticity one wishes to extract, particularly if more than one interest rate is included and if the specification search involves extensive tinkering with dynamic effects.... The preponderance of empirical studies of the demand for money which show significant negative interest elasticities reflects the acknowledged prior beliefs of the researcher and not the information content of the data.
>
> (1981: 836)

Given that the original model was specified with due regard to stability and robust testing and that the initial focus was on the importance of financial innovation to the demand for money, estimating the (unchanged) model over successive time periods appears justified. No 'experiments' have been made with different model formulations to bring out any particular elasticity that may accord with prior beliefs.

Although significant interest rate effects have been found in the standard ECM model above it is recognized that for an ECM to exist the variables in the model must cointegrate (Engle and Grander 1987). Conversely, if the variables in an equation are cointegrated then there is always an ECM formulation of that model. Table 9.3 shows the number of times the individual time series need differencing in order to induce stationarity, and hence the order of integration.

It appears that the interest rate terms and income are all I(1) and M4, prices and gross financial wealth are all I(2). This accords closely with the results of Hall *et al.* (1989), who also note that money and prices are I(2) and combine to be I(1) so that real money will co-integrate with the other variables.

An OLS regression of the demand for M4 was run on the levels of each variable in order to find a stationary linear combination of the individual time series (see Hall *et al.* 1989):

$$\frac{M}{PY} = -0.153\text{RS} - 0.0082P + 0.88\frac{GFW}{PY} + 0.094\text{DCCC}$$

$$\text{DF} = -5.96 \qquad \text{ADF} = -2.64 \qquad R^2 = 0.98$$

DCCC = 0 prior to 1971/4 and DCCC = 1 thereafter. These

Table 9.3 Testing the individual time series for integration

	Levels I(0)		*First difference I(1)*		*Second difference I(2)*	
	DF	*ADF*	*DF*	*ADF*	*DF*	*ADF*
RS	−1.806	−1.809	−7.747	−3.843		
Y	−8.108	−3.079	−15.0	−7.989		
P	−1.352	−1.628	−2.369	−1.143	−16.271	−4.091
ORD	−1.829	−1.929	−6.496	−4.155		
G	−2.019	−1.953	−7.168	−4.215		
RT	−2.131	−2.251	−7.365	−4.385		
M4	0.754	−0.374	−2.816	0.1673	−19.755	−5.66
GFW	3.414	1.649	−2.674	−0.480	−13.353	−6.173

Notes: All variables except interest rates are in log form. The DF and ADF tests are *t* tests for integration that require a significant and negative finding (Dickey and Fuller 1979).

variables clearly do not provide a cointegrating vector as the ADF statistic is below the critical value at the 5 per cent level. Similar problems occurred when the maximum retail rate at banks was used.

Dropping the interest rate term yielded the following.

$$\frac{M}{PY} = -0.02P + 0.87\frac{GFW}{PY} + 0.064\text{DCCC}$$

$$\text{DF} = -6.668 \qquad \text{ADF} = -3.224 \qquad R^2 = 0.975$$

Thus dropping the interest rate terms provides a plausible cointegrating equation. This is a somewhat surprising result as earlier researchers have found significant interest rate effects. It does, however, corroborate the work of Hall *et al.* (1989) who also found that interest rates were not significant in a cointegrating model of M4. To see whether interest rates were perhaps important over earlier periods the equation was estimated over subperiods 1969/1–1980/4 and 1969/1–1975/4, but interest rates were still not found to be significant variables.

The residuals from the above equation were included as the ECM in a final dynamic cointegrating regression which was derived using the general-to-specific modelling strategy:

$$\begin{aligned}\Delta\left(\frac{M}{P}\right) = {} & \text{constant} + \underset{(0.086)}{0.244}\,\Delta\left(\frac{M}{P}\right)_{t-2} - \underset{(0.13)}{0.99}\,\Delta P \\ & + \underset{(0.021)}{0.043}\,Z_{t-1}\end{aligned}$$

$$R^2 = 0.633 \qquad \text{SER} = 0.015 \qquad \text{ARCH (1)} = 0.983$$

$$\text{LM(8)} = 11.93 \qquad \text{LM(4)} = 10.69 \qquad \text{LM(2)} = 0.99$$

LM(4) is a test for fourth-order serial correlation that is valid with a lagged dependent variable; ARCH(1) tests for autoregressive conditional heteroscedasticity; Reset is Ramsey's (1969) test for omitted variables and the Z_t are residuals.

The effects of interest rates at this dynamic stage were again tested but were still found to be insignificant. The results of this cointegration model thus tend to conflict with the standard ECM model estimated earlier. There is therefore considerable doubt as to the validity of the interest elasticities of the demand for M4 equation reported earlier, which may reflect problems of measuring interest elasticities during a period of financial innovation.

9.7 CONCLUSION

The aim of this chapter has been an attempt to evaluate the effect of the abolition of the building societies' recommended rate system and financial innovation on the demand for money function for M4. The main econometric modelling strategies employed in previous research were analysed in Sections 9.2–9.5 and a critique of the underlying methodologies adopted was given. After examination of the main strategies, both an ECM–ADL model and a cointegrating equation were chosen to complement the theoretical specification of the demand for broad money which was established with regard to the likely relevant variables in Chapter 8. A sequential testing-down procedure was used as in the general-to-specific modelling process to arrive at a data-coherent stable final equation, which was then used to explore earlier stated hypotheses.

The final reduced form error-correction equation contains wealth, interest rate, inflation and income variables. Financial innovation is captured through the use of interest rates on high interest easy-access accounts at building societies. The equation passes a number of tests, including the Chow test for parameter stability, and forecasts well in an out-of-sample test.

The fact that income is only included in the form of the error-correction term rather than as a distinct single variable may reflect a reduced importance of income relative to wealth in the non-bank private sector's demand for money. This may be rationalized as the result of money increasingly bearing interest and increasingly being used as a store of wealth.

The importance of high interest easy-access accounts to the overall stability of the equation is important (when this variable is dropped the equation appears to be unstable), but similar results can be obtained by switching this variable with the rate on ordinary shares at building societies. This may also be a reflection of financial innovation, with ordinary shares becoming increasingly liquid and paying a higher real rate of interest in the 1980s. Despite the evidence of earlier research, the total return on gilts (i.e. including expected capital gains) was insignificant in the equation, both on its own and as a differential to building society rates. This may be explained if financial innovation makes the demand for money completely inelastic with respect to long rates of interest, in terms of both the general level of return on gilts and a differential return, although misspecification of the gilts equation cannot be ruled out.

The equation was also unsatisfactory, in the form of insignificant variables when used for forecasting, when the interest differential between Treasury bills and building society high interest easy-access accounts was swapped for the levels of these terms. This may be an indication that levels of interest rates have become of lesser importance in the demand for money function compared with interest rate differentials.

An examination of the effects of financial innovation on the interest elasticity of the differential between the own rate on money and competing rates found that the demand for money has become less sensitive over time to changes in the differential. This contradicts the assertions of some commentators, but may be explained by the fall in the average size of the interest differential over time, which reduces the incentive for shifting out of (interest-earning) money into other interest-earning assets. Thus, the monetary authorities' ability to induce a switch out of money balances into alternative interest-bearing assets appears to have been reduced. An increase in short-term interest rates will have little effect on the interest differential between money and other assets. Thus the error-correction model suggests that controlling the money supply from the demand side (see Chapter 7) is unlikely to be effective. When operating from the demand side, it is unlikely that interest rate differentials will be substantially changed and unlikely that the level of broad money holdings will be reduced (again abstracting from supply-side considerations) when a rise in interest rates is engineered by the monetary authorities. The error-correction model implies that financial innovation has led to a relatively stable pool of balances at banks and building societies that have become increasingly desensitized to interest differentials. In IS–LM terms, the LM curve has become progressively steeper with reduced interest elasticity of money demand.

Given the results of the cointegrating demand for money equation, however, the above conclusions cannot be held. Interest rates were not found to be significant variables in the equation over the period 1969/1–1986/4, or in any subperiods. A tentative rationale is that the effects of interest rates (if any) on the demand for money may be difficult to measure during a period of financial liberalization and innovation.

APPENDIX 9A: DATA SOURCES AND DEFINITIONS

Demand for money equations

M4	Money stock M4, seasonally unadjusted, provided by the Bank of England
Y	Real GDP at factor cost. From *Economic Trends*, Annual Supplement, Table 9
P	Implicit GDP deflator
RT	Rate of interest on three-month Treasury bills. From *Financial Statistics*, Table 13.8
RG	Rate of interest on twenty-year gilts. From *Financial Statistics*, Table S7
RS	Maximum rate of interest (net) on ordinary share accounts and high interest accounts at building societies (average rate over the ten largest societies). From *Building Societies Gazette*
ORD	Net rate of interest on ordinary share accounts. From *BSA Bulletin* and *Compendium of Building Society Statistics*, 6th edn
RB	Maximum rate of interest at banks. From *Financial Statistics*, Table S7, and Midland Bank High Interest Account
GFW	Gross financial wealth of the non-bank private sector. From *Financial Statistics*, Tables 14.1 and E
RN	Rate on mortgages (net of tax). From *BSA Bulletin* and *Compendium of Building Society Statistics*, 6th edn

Capital gains equation

ED	Interest rate on three-month Eurodollars. From *Financial Statistics*, Table 13.3
TFE	Total final expenditure. From *Economic Trends*, Table 14
NFW	Net financial wealth of the non-bank private sector. From *Financial Statistics*, Tables E and 14.1
P	Implicit consumers' deflator
R	Yield on $2\frac{1}{2}$ per cent consols. From *Financial Statistics*, Table 13.3
CG	Capital gains on gilts. From *Financial Times Index of Gilt Prices*
r	Short rate of interest (three-month Treasury bill rate). From *Financial Statistics*, Table 13.8
ML	Total flow of mortgage lending. From *Financial Statistics*, Table 14.4
Y	Real personal disposable income (RPDI). From *Economic Trends*, Annual Supplement, 1989, Table 5
RMO	Rate of interest on building society mortgages (net) measured as $1 + (\text{RM}/100) - (\ln \text{PC}_{-1} - \ln \text{PC}_{-5})$
RCB	Clearing banks' base rate, measured as $1 + (\text{RCB}/100) - (\ln \text{PC}_{-1} - \ln \text{PC}_{-5})$
RMD	Minimum deposit rate on durables

Consumers' expenditure equation

CD	Consumers' expenditure on durables (real), 1980 prices. From *Economic Trends*, Annual Supplement, 1988, Table 27
NLA	Net liquid assets of the personal sector (nominal). From *Financial Statistics*, Tables 9.5 and 10.3
P	Consumers' expenditure deflator (durables), 1980–1. From *Economic Annual Supplement* 1988

10 Econometric evaluation – the consumers' expenditure function

10.1 INTRODUCTION

The emphasis of this chapter is on the evaluation of the consumers' expenditure function. In Section 10.2 error-correction and cointegrating models of consumers' expenditure are developed and estimated in order to test whether or not the ending of the cartel and a greater importance of the 'price' of mortgages, as opposed to mortgage rationing, increased the interest elasticity of expenditure. An increase in the interest elasticity of expenditure would have increased the ability of the monetary authorities to control the growth of the money supply, other things being equal.

10.2 THE INTEREST ELASTICITY OF CONSUMERS' EXPENDITURE

It was recognized in Chapter 7 that the transmission mechanism of monetary control may work through the effects of interest rates on consumers' expenditure. Specifically, the effects of increased interest rates on mortgage holders' expenditure may be a strong form of monetary control (Turnbull 1984: 6).

The argument to be tested in this section is that the greater influence and fluidity of the price of mortgages after the abolition of the cartel and increased mortgage debt of the personal sector as a result of credit liberalization *increased* the interest elasticity of consumers' expenditure. In other words, greater personal sector gearing is likely to have increased the sensitivity of consumers' spending with respect to flexible mortgage interest rates. A rise in the interest elasticity of consumers' expenditure would represent an increase in the efficacy of monetary control, all other things being equal.

Given the earlier conjectures as to the importance of the mortgage market to consumers' expenditure, it was decided to model consumers' expenditure on durable goods rather than non-durable goods. Previous researchers into durables expenditure (see *inter alia* Davidson *et al.* 1978; Davis 1984; Dicks 1988) typically estimate durables functions as

$$CD = f(Y, \text{ML}, \text{NLA}, \text{RMD}) + \text{dummy variables}$$

where CD is the consumers' expenditure on durables (real), *Y* is real personal disposable income (RPDI) or real household disposable income, ML is the flow of mortgage lending, NLA is real net liquid assets of the personal sector and RMD is the minimum deposit rate on durables. Additionally, Dicks (1988) and Cuthbertson (1980) include an interest rate term (clearing banks' base rate minus the annual inflation rate of consumer prices).

The general model estimated here was of the form

$$\begin{aligned} \text{CD} = \; & \text{constant} + \sum_{i=0}^{4} \text{CD}_{-i} + \sum_{i=0}^{4} \text{RPDI}_{-i} + \sum_{i=0}^{4} \text{ML}_{-i} \\ & + \sum_{i=0}^{4} \text{NLA}_{-i} + \sum_{i=0}^{4} \text{RM}_{-i} + \sum_{i=0}^{4} \text{MRAT} + \text{D731} \\ & + \text{D732} + \text{D764} + \text{D792} + \text{D793} \end{aligned}$$

Note that there are a number of innovations in this equation compared with previous researcher's models of consumers' durables expenditure. Specifically, the interest rate on building society mortgages (RM) is included, in the expectation that the cost of mortgages is likely to be a significant determinant of consumers' expenditure. Similarly, the MRAT term which is Meen's (1985) measure of mortgage rationing is included on the grounds that the liberalization of the mortgage market may have affected consumers' spending on durable goods. The dummy variables are for the budgets of 1973 and 1979 which affected expenditure through indirect tax changes (i.e. some expenditure was brought forward to avoid tax changes (Dicks 1988)) and are standard in models of consumers' expenditure (full data definitions and sources are provided in Appendix 9A).

Testing down from the initial general specification, however, it was found that neither RM nor MRAT was significant in the durables equation. As an alternative interest rate variable, the base rate of clearing banks was included (RCB):

$$\begin{aligned} \text{CD} = \; & -\underset{(1.4)}{2.6} + \underset{(0.1)}{0.45}\text{CD}_{t-2} + \underset{(0.48)}{1.04}\text{RPDI}_{t-1} - \underset{(0.06)}{0.11}\text{ML} \end{aligned}$$

$$+ 0.68\text{NLA} - 0.33\text{RCB} + 0.09\text{D731} + 0.05\text{D732}$$
$$(0.18) \quad (0.05) \quad (0.08) \quad (0.09)$$

$$+ 0.068\text{D764} + 0.35\text{D792} - 0.07\text{D793}$$
$$(0.08) \quad (0.08) \quad (0.08)$$

$R^2 = 0.92$ SER = 0.08
AR $F[4, 44] = 4.45$ Normality [2] = 9.74
Reset [1, 47] = 0.54 ARCH $F[4, 40] = 0.13$
Heteroscedasticity [15, 32] = 0.83
All variables are in logarithms.

All the variables apart from some of the dummies are significant. The model does not track well (Figures 10.1–10.3) and there are some problems of normality and autocorrelation (Dicks (1988) also found this to be the case).

The interest elasticity of consumers' expenditure on durables has risen from −0.45 in 1977/4 to −0.51 in 1987/2. It is also noticeable that the interest rate term is insignificant prior to 1980, suggesting that interest rates have recently become an important determinant of consumers' expenditure (Tables 10.1 and 10.2). This would tend to suggest that the effects of interest rates on expenditure have become marginally more powerful over time. It is noticeable, however, that these elasticitics are relatively 'low' and do not imply an especially strong transmission mechanism of monetary policy.

To test the applicability of the consumers' expenditure model derived above a cointegrating equation was developed using the Engle–Granger two-step procedure. Table 10.3 shows the order of integration of the individual time series. Consumers' expenditure, interest rates and income are all I(1) and prices, net liquid assets and the flow of mortgage lending are also I(1) (although they are very close to the critical values for I(2)).

It proved relatively easy to find a cointegrating equation of the levels of the individual time series:

$$\text{CD} = 0.25\,Y + 0.828\text{ML} - 0.789\,P$$

$$\text{DF} = -6.47 \qquad \text{ADF} = -3.62 \qquad R^2 = 0.7$$

The residuals from this equation were used as the error-correction mechanism in a dynamic model which was derived using general-to-specific modelling:

$$\text{CD} = -0.521 - 0.118\text{RM} + 1.08\text{CD}_{t-2} - 0.69\,Z_{t-2}$$
$$(0.319) \; (0.056) \quad (0.04) \quad (0.10)$$

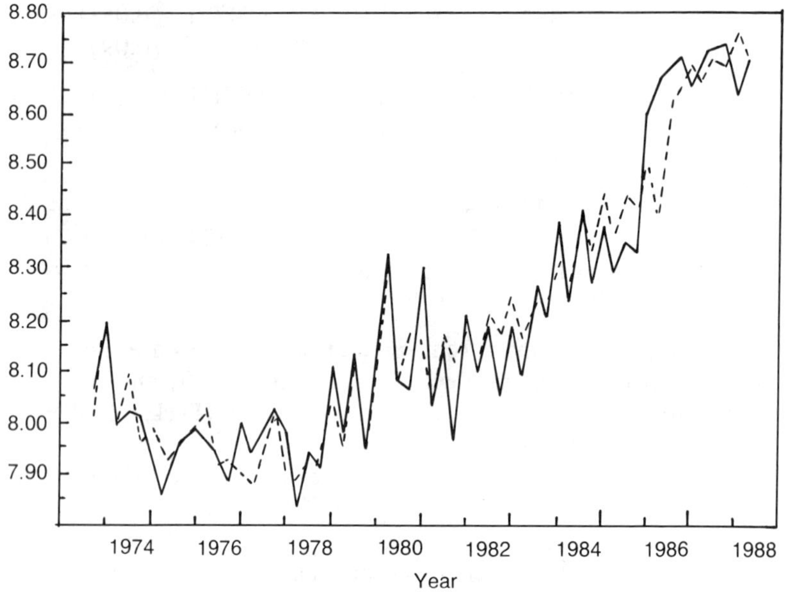

Figure 10.1 Tracking of the consumers' expenditure model: ——, CD; ------, fitted

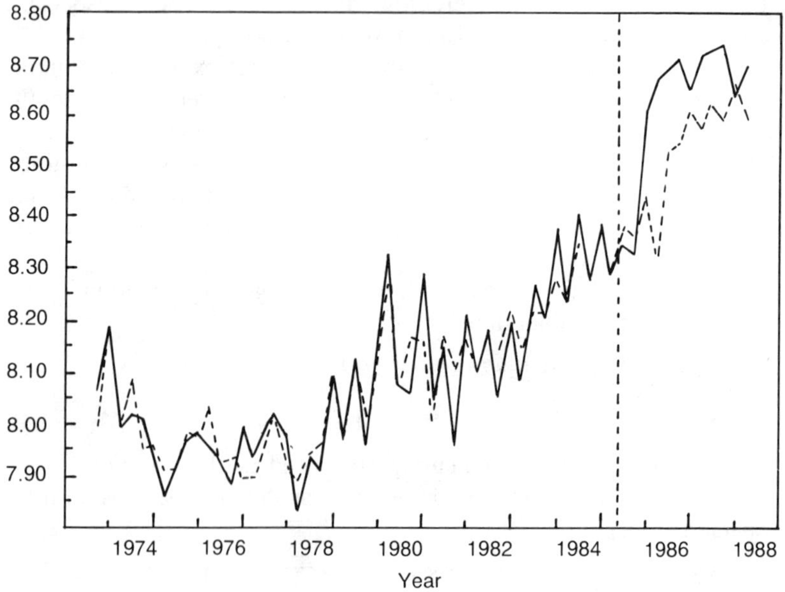

Figure 10.2 Out-of-sample forecast: ——, CD; ------, fitted

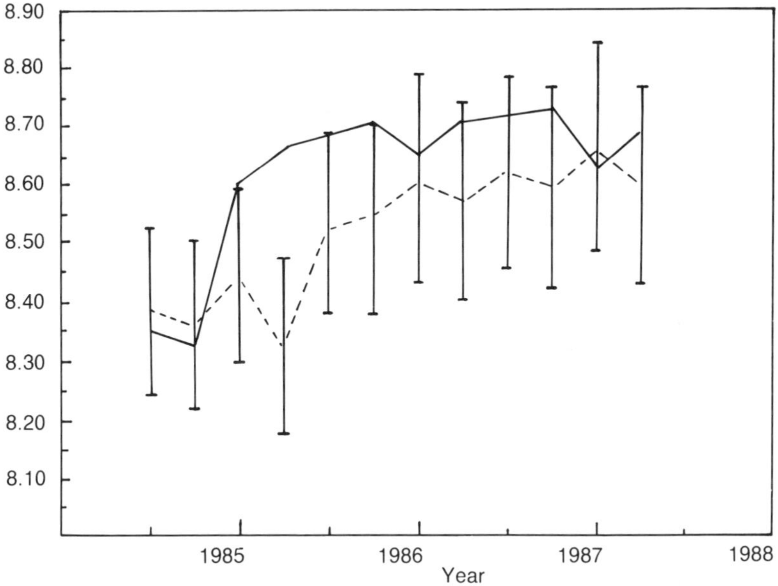

Figure 10.3 Actual and fitted values of quarterly growth in real M4: ——, CD; ------, forecast

$$R^2 = 0.9 \qquad \text{SER} = 0.09 \qquad \text{ARCH} = 0.0007$$

$$\text{LM}(8) = 11.93 \qquad \text{LM}(4) = 3.5 \qquad \text{LM}(2) = 3.03$$

In contrast with the earlier error-correction model, it was found that the interest rate on building society mortgages was significant but that the clearing banks' base rate was not. Interestingly, the dummy variables used earlier were also not significant, nor was the proxy for mortgage rationing.

The equation passes a variety of tests. In particular, Figures 10.4 and 10.5 showing the CUSUMSQ statistic and the one-period-ahead Chow test suggest that the equation is stable (although there is some evidence of instability in 1985/2).

Table 10.4 shows that the interest elasticity of consumers' expenditure fell from −1.5 in the subperiod to 1978 to −0.725 in the period to 1981, and then rose from −0.86 to stabilize around −1.1 to −1.3 over 1983 and 1987. These elasticities are approximately twice the size of those reported earlier, but are in the range reported by Dicks (1988). It is interesting to note that the elasticities reported from this dynamic cointegrating equation follow the same pattern as those of

Table 10.1 Consumer durables expenditure equations

Period	*Constant*	CD_{t-2}	$RPDI_{t-1}$	*ML*	*NLA*	*RCB*	R^2
1972/4–1987/2	−2.56	0.45	1.04	−0.11	0.68	−0.3	0.93
	(1.44)	(0.1)	(0.43)	(0.06)	(0.18)	(0.05)	
1972/4–1986/4	−3.35	0.48	1.10	−0.13	0.75	−0.28	0.92
	(1.5)	(0.1)	(0.48)	(0.07)	(0.18)	(0.05)	
1972/4–1985/4	−3.59	0.49	1.03	−0.15	0.77	−0.28	0.88
	(1.78)	(0.12)	(0.51)	(0.08)	(0.19)	(0.06)	
1972/4–1984/4	−0.02	0.4	1.33	−0.12	0.5	−0.27	0.87
	(1.61)	(0.11)	(0.42)	(0.06)	(0.16)	(0.05)	
1972/4–1983/4	−0.57	0.41	1.32	−0.12	0.55	−0.28	0.83
	(1.9)	(0.12)	(0.44)	(0.07)	(0.18)	(0.05)	
1972/4–1982/4	0.55	0.36	1.29	−0.13	0.49	−0.26	0.78
	(2.0)	(0.12)	(0.45)	(0.07)	(0.19)	(0.05)	
1972/4–1981/4	0.88	0.34	0.31	−0.13	0.47	−0.26	0.74
	(2.23)	(0.14)	(0.47)	(0.08)	(0.21)	(0.07)	
1978/4–1980/4	0.88	0.29	1.35	−0.11	0.5	−0.28	0.74
	(2.83)	(0.16)	(0.49)	(0.08)	(0.28)	(0.1)	
1972/4–1979/4	0.1	0.24	1.0	−0.11	0.6	−0.33	0.80
	(3.1)	(0.15)	(0.5)	(0.07)	(0.3)	(0.17)	
1972/4–1978/4	0.2	0.32	0.94	−0.12	0.56	−0.31	0.69
	(3.5)	(0.18)	(0.47)	(0.07)	(0.3)	(0.18)	
1972/4–1977/4	−0.2	0.2	0.79	−0.07	0.62	−0.35	0.65
	(4.9)	(0.21)	(0.57)	(0.08)	(0.42)	(0.03)	

Table 10.2 Interest elasticity of consumers' expenditure[a]

1987/2	−0.51
1986/4	−0.53
1985/4	−0.54
1984/4	−0.54
1983/4	−0.47
1982/4	−0.41
1981/4	−0.39
1980/4	−0.39
1979/4	−0.44
1978/4	−0.45
1977/4	−0.45

Note: [a]Measured as the coefficient on the interest rate divided by one minus the coefficient on the lagged dependent variable.

Table 10.3 Testing the individual time series for integration

	Levels I(0)		*First difference I(1)*		*Second difference I(2)*	
	DF	*ADF*	*DF*	*ADF*	*DF*	*ADF*
CD	−1.34	−0.62	−15.95	−4.17		
NLA	2.15	−1.04	−5.19	−3.31	−16.35	−5.13
ML	3.71	2.03	−6.84	−3.28	−14.6	−5.42
RCB	−2.33	−3.16	−8.13	−5.17		
RM	−1.93	−1.76	−6.38	−4.19		
Y	−8.11	−3.08	−15.0	−7.98		
P	1.79	1.24	−7.12	−3.19	−12.7	−6.14

Note: All variables except interest rates are in logarithmic form.

the standard error-correction model in terms of a fall in elasticity from 1978 to 1981 and an increase thereafter with subsequent stabilization around 1984–7.

10.3 CONCLUSION

An attempt has been made in this chapter to evaluate earlier stated ideas with regard to the consumers' expenditure function on durables and the demand for credit. A model of consumers' expenditure on durables was developed with income, interest rate, holdings of net liquid assets and mortgage lending variables. It was possible to

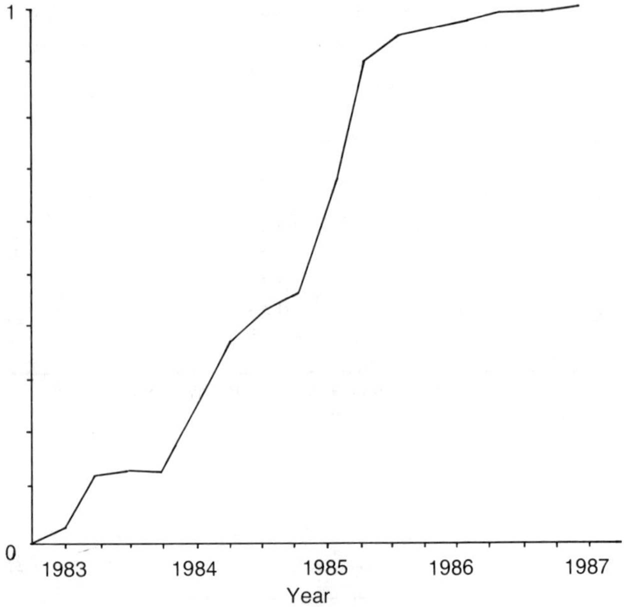

Figure 10.4 CUSUMSQ statistic

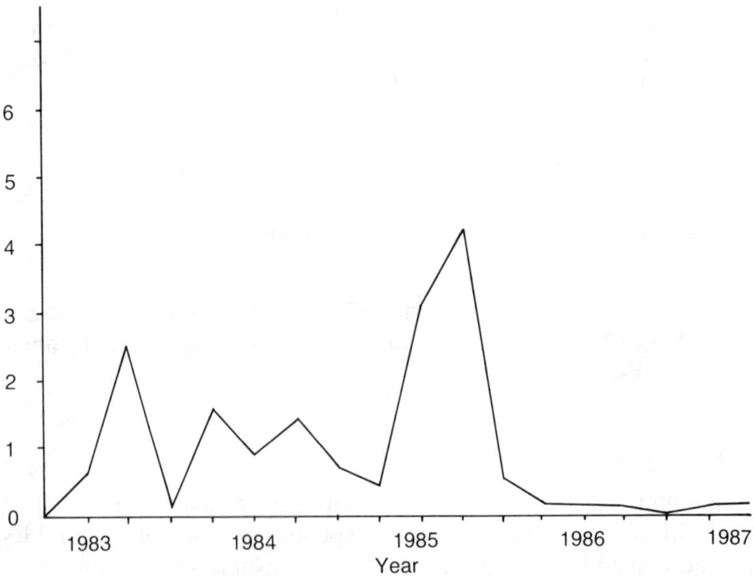

Figure 10.5 Sequential Chow test

estimate both a standard error-correction model and a dynamic cointegrating model for consumers' expenditure.

Building society mortgage rates were significant in the cointegrating equation but not the error-correction model, whilst bank base rates were significant in the error-correction model but not the cointegrating equation. Where the interest rates are significant in each equation they suggest that the interest elasticity has increased over time. The increase in interest elasticity of consumers' expenditure suggests that monetary control working through this route has become more powerful in the 1980s. The evidence from the cointegrating equation tends to imply that the greater fluidity of mortgage interest rates and market-relatedness has led to consumers' expenditure becoming more sensitive to interest rates.

11 The move to a new regime – concluding thoughts

11.1 INTRODUCTION

This book has provided an analysis of the efficiency of monetary policy and monetary control in relation to the activities of building societies and banks. The central thematic core has been that the application of monetary control cannot be separated from the financial system within which it operates and the intermediation activities of the financial institutions that make up that system. An attempt has been made to re-emphasize the importance of an institutionalist approach to monetary control, which reneges against the predominant assumption of the passivity of financial institutions and a static financial system. Indeed, direct parallels have been drawn between the warnings of the institutionalist school over two decades ago that financial innovation reduces the efficiency of monetary control and the recent concern expressed by the monetary authorities over the effects of a changing financial system.

The importance of the institutional system to the manner in which monetary control is conducted cannot be over-emphasized:

> The choice of monetary policy instruments and the evolution of the financial system are inextricably inter-related. The relative importance of banks in total financial intermediation, the size of the financial market, the barriers to entry into banking, the pace and extent of financial innovation, the nature of bank competition and conceptions about how banks react to the use of different policy weapons determine the types of instruments that are given prominence as well as the way they are designed and used.
>
> (Bingham 1985: 103)

In Chapter 2 the central tenets of monetarism and monetary control were analysed and contrasted with those of the opposing Keynesian school. The necessary and sufficient conditions for a monetarist policy of control of the money supply were specified, as was the Keynesian view as to the conduct of monetary policy.

Specifically, it was noted that if monetary aggregates are to be controlled as part of a money supply targeting strategy, it is a necessity that there is a reasonably stable relationship between the policy instrument and the monetary aggregate(s) targeted, a reasonably stable relationship between the monetary aggregate(s) and the ultimate goal and a stable demand for money function. An attempt was made to re-evaluate these traditional paradigms of monetary economics in terms of the increasing recognition of the importance of the financial system to monetary control.

The analysis of the forces determining financial innovation and change by the building societies and banks emphasized the crucial role of regulations, monetary control and the cartel as major constraints and major catalysts. Asymmetric monetary controls, placed on the banking system in the 1970s but not on the building societies, were important in shaping the activities of banks and building societies, and hence a major determinant of both the nature of competition between these financial institutions and the level of financial innovation.

Specific attention was paid to the interaction between the monetary authorities' changes in regulations and monetary controls and the innovatory activities of building societies and banks. It has been emphasized that official actions that induce changes in regulatory and monetary control provisions rarely have a neutral effect upon the structure and operations of financial institutions.

The importance of the mutuality of the building society industry and the recommended rate system has been emphasized in terms of the manner in which these institutional factors shaped the nature of competition between the mix of price and non-price elements, and hence provided a constraint to financial innovation. The cartel had a major effect on the type of competition between banks and building societies and on the level of financial innovation. Price competition was effectively ruled out as a change in interest rates was only carried out by all building societies as a group.

It was pointed out that the operation of the building societies' cartel had the effect of smoothing building society interest rates and created an excess demand for mortgages that tended to vary with changes in general interest rates. The lag in the building society deposit and mortgage interest rates created high excess demand for mortgages when general interest rates were rising, and non-price rationing devices were used to limit mortgage supply. When general market rates were falling, deposit inflows to building societies were strong and mortgage rationing fell. When the cartel was in operation there was thus a limited role for the price of mortgages to determine the supply of mortgages. It was maintained that the abolition of the cartel would lead to more market-related mortgage rates and greater importance of the price of mortgages in equilibrating the supply and demand for house purchase loans.

Portfolio monetary controls on the banking system in the 1970s effectively inhibited the banks from competing for personal sector deposits or from entering the mortgage market on a large scale. The building societies' cartel could only really be operational in combination with this asymmetry of monetary control. Lack of competition for personal sector deposits was reflected in the homogeneous and simple nature of building society and bank accounts.

The abandonment of distorting portfolio monetary controls on the retail banking sector allowed them to redistribute their portfolios towards mortgage lending, increasing the level of competition in this sector and precipitating the breakdown of the building societies' interest rate cartel. The cartel had maintained the building societies' deposit and mortgage interest rates below market clearing levels. Increased competition and the abandonment of the cartel did indeed lead to a change in the interest rate policies of the building societies. Building society interest rates also became less sticky and tended to be market related.

It was argued that the abolition of the cartel had finite stock effects which affected the interpretation of monetary conditions. It was maintained that credit liberalization after the ending of the recommended rate system resulted in a finite portfolio reallocation by the personal sector to regain its desired credit position. This caused problems of interpretation of the growth rates of the monetary aggregates during the period when the stock adjustments occurred, but was not a long-term problem for monetary control. It would also be expected that the relationships between credit and income and money and income were altered in the interim, but may have settled down to a steady state.

Financial innovation by building societies and banks in terms of interest-bearing transactions balances would be expected, it was argued, to produce stock effects which might cause fast growth of one or more monetary aggregates and alter the money–income relationship as balances were moved into the new innovatory accounts. In the long term, however, it would be expected that the money–income relationship would stabilize.

The Radcliffe Report (1959) first drew attention to the significance of non-bank financial intermediaries in relation to the operation of monetary control. The report argued that spending decisions are affected by the broad liquidity position of wealth-holders rather than the possession of money balances (paragraph 389). It concluded that the existence of non-bank financial intermediaries and money substitutes makes the relationship between the money stock and the level of expenditures on goods, services and real assets more uncertain. Now, almost thirty years after the deliberations of the Radcliffe Committee, developments within the UK financial system (and in particular in relation to the activities of retail financial intermediaries) have reached the stage whereby the distinction between bank and non-bank financial intermediaries is largely academic in respect of many aspects of the provision of financial services.

An analysis of the effects of financial innovation on the definition of money in Chapter 5 points to the conclusion that it is no longer possible to distinguish between balances that are for purely transactions or purely investment purposes. This has tended to confuse interpretation of monetary conditions.

The analysis of Chapter 5 suggested that the stock effects of the desire on the part of the personal sector to hold high interest easy-access accounts within their portfolios were a major determinant of the change in the money–income relationship as evidenced by the fall in the velocity of circulation of broad money in the 1980s.

The credit market was analysed in Chapter 6 in terms of finite stock effects and the effects on the growth rates of the monetary aggregates relative to nominal incomes. The effect of credit liberalization of the mortgage market after the ending of the cartel upon the growth of the monetary aggregates was examined. It appears that the credit-side shock of mortgage lending led to a large number of last-time sellers who willingly held their balances in the form of interest-bearing money. This seems to be part of the explanation of the fall in the income velocity of circulation of the broad monetary aggregates. Removal of direct monetary constraints allowed a portfolio reallocation on the part of the personal sector in both money balances and credit. Both were increased faster than nominal incomes to adjust to the portfolio allocation position that would have been previously preferred. In turn, the credit shock did not lead to holdings of unwanted balances as would be expected under buffer stock models.

It has been noted that buffer stock theorists have explained early instability in demand for broad money functions as the result of the non-bank private sector being 'forced off' its demand for money function. This theory may have been relevant for the 1970s, but it has been argued that it is not applicable to the 1980s. Financial innovations by building societies and banks that introduced financial instruments which offered market-related rates of interest meant that, at the time of credit-side shocks, money balances were willingly held rather than being slowly spent over a period of time. This was particularly the case after the banks entered the mortgage market in the 1980s.

The usual duality between the views of endogeneity and exogeneity appears to be a function of the manner in which financial institutions operate, which in turn is heavily dependent upon the panoply of constraints which characterize the market environment at any point in time. The ability of building societies and banks to operate as price setters and quantity takers depended largely upon the degree and nature of regulatory and monetary controls adopted by the monetary authorities. As they were able to operate as price setters and quantity takers, then the money supply process, it is argued, was essentially an endogenous phenomenon. This implies that the money supply is demand driven or credit driven when financial institutions are able to operate in this manner. Given that financial institutions have not always had the opportunity to act as price setters and quantity takers, it appears that the money supply process may at times be exogenous and at times endogenous, depending upon the specific market environment and the institutional activities appertaining at the time.

Alternative monetary control techniques were surveyed in Chapter 7, with particular attention paid to the ability of the monetary authorities to control the money supply through the manipulation of interest rates.

It was argued that in addition to causing stock effects the abolition of the cartel would also have produced more continuing effects, and that the greater fluidity of mortgage interest rates and the increased debt-to-income ratio of the personal sector resulted in an increase in the interest elasticity of consumers' expenditure (although these factors are difficult to separate). This would mean an increase in effectiveness of monetary control working through interest rates, other things being equal.

It was also maintained that interest-bearing transactions balances would lead to a reduction in the interest elasticity of the demand for money. This would mean that the ability of the monetary authorities to control the money supply through the demand side (which was not their stated intention) by inducing money-holders into alternative interest-bearing assets by increasing interest rates would be reduced.

It has also been argued that the building society developments analysed have not in fact altered the technical capacity of monetary base control (MBC). If the authorities can control the reserve base, then there is no reason to suggest that financial innovation and credit liberalization will affect the manner in which MBC works. It is widely held that the effectiveness of MBC depends ultimately on the response of the demand for credit to interest rates. Financial innovation and change does not alter this argument.

In fact, it is possible (although difficult to show empirically, and an attempt is outside the scope of this book) that MBC may be more effective as a result of erosion of the banks' endowment effect through financial innovation and competition. It may not be so profitable now for banks to push up deposit and loan rates to attract funds to swap for reserves, as a greater proportion of deposits pay interest than previously. This is certainly an area for further research.

The standard error-correction demand for money function specified for M4 in Chapter 9 has provided some interesting insights. It appears to show that, if financial innovation in the form of interest-bearing easily accessible balances is explicitly taken into account in the equation, then it is possible to specify a relatively robust and stable function. Dropping the own rate terms led to instability of the equation and poor forecasting, indicating the importance of these factors to the overall model specification, and on this evidence confirming the view that financial innovation has been responsible for the breakdown of the demand for money function. The argument that the demand for money has become insensitive to the general rate of interest was evaluated with variables that both included and excluded the expected capital gains to gilts. There does not appear to be a relationship between the demand for money and the return to gilts in the period 1969–86 or in any of the subperiods investigated. This does not, of course, rule out model misspecification, although it does appear to indicate that the null hypothesis should be accepted. It should be noted that this result is in direct contradiction to that of Grice and Bennett (1981, 1984), although their own doubts as to the robustness of their model cannot be ignored.

The viewpoint that interest-bearing money balances have reduced the interest elasticity of the demand for money (and hence made the LM curve steeper) does appear to be sustainable according to the evidence from the error-correction model. There has been a substantial reduction in the interest elasticity of the demand for money between 1980 and 1987. In terms of monetary control operating from the *demand* side this would tend to imply that an increase in interest rates will have had a reduced effect in inducing money-holders to switch into alternative interest-bearing assets and would suggest a decline in the potency of this form of control.

The overall evidence from the demand for money models is somewhat mixed, however. Significant interest rate effects were not found in the cointegrating equation for the demand for M4. This casts considerable doubt on the above findings, and it cannot be held that the interest elasticity of the demand for money has fallen, nor that financial innovation has led to a temporary change in the money–income relationship.

An analysis of the continuing effects of the abolition of the cartel and flexible mortgage rates on the effectiveness of monetary control working through consumers' expenditure was carried out. Using an error-correction equation it was found that bank rates were significant but that mortgage rates were wrongly signed, whilst in the cointegrating equation mortgage rates were significant but bank base rates were not. Such findings are difficult to rationalize.

The evidence from both models suggests that the interest elasticity of consumers' expenditure has become more sensitive to at least one set of interest rates, and this is backed up by recently reported research. The specific evidence from the cointegrating equation, which is theoretically superior to the error-correction formulation, suggests that there has been a rise in the interest sensitivity of expenditure with respect to mortgage interest rates, and it is argued that this has been caused by more flexible and market-related mortgage interest rates and greater debt-to-income ratios of the personal sector after the abolition of the cartel.

The New Libertarian School approach, which maintains that control of the money supply is only feasible under a certain set of institutional conditions, appears to be over-harsh in its attack upon the tenets of monetary control. The stability of the demand for M4 function would tend to militate against the more extreme assertions of the Legal Restrictions or Libertarian School, *for the time being*. In other words, this particular econometric relationship appears to have remained stable over a variety of regulatory regimes and under extensive financial innovation, which vitiates the claim that a stable demand for money function rests largely on various legal restrictions on money and financial institutions. This does not necessarily mean, of course, that further innovation and re-regulation will not bear out the Libertarian case.

Although a stable demand for money function has been estimated over the period 1969–86 after taking account of financial innovation, this has been done with a considerable degree of hindsight. At a time when institutional conditions are changing and financial innovations are being introduced, it is difficult for the monetary authorities to interpret events. As noted earlier, a correctly specified model may be able to capture the effects of financial innovation, but any model that maintains *ex post* forecasting performance and stability *but is incorrectly specified* may subsequently break down under further changing conditions:

> To say, after the event, that our policy did not work because new assets evolved whose existence affected the outcome of our policies in a way that we could have forecast had we only been able to foresee their invention, may be true, but it is not very helpful in enabling us to do better next time, unless the evolution in question was, as it sometimes can be, the predictable policy outcome of some policy action or other.
>
> (Laidler 1981: 4)

The stock effects of the ending of the cartel and of financial innovation on the growth rates of the monetary aggregates suggests that discretionary policy action is a necessity when such events occur. It may be necessary to rely on a variety of indicators in order to assess monetary conditions. These stock effects do not mean, however, that interest rates will not be an effective form of monetary control.

Indeed, the evidence from the cointegrating equation implies that control by manipulating interest rates to influence consumers' expenditure has become a more powerful model of monetary control.

Where does this leave the operation of monetary policy? It appears that there were major changes in the rationale and operation of the Medium Term Financial Strategy (MTFS) as a result of the effects of financial innovation, and a degree of discretion was necessary in policy actions. Currie noted that there are some who maintain that policy is turning full circle back into a fully discretionary mode:

> Indeed, some have chosen to interpret recent policy pronouncements by the Chancellor as showing that the process of easing has gone so far that the MTFS provides little clear guidance as to the future policy actions beyond a broad commitment to maintain a low and declining inflation rate. There is, therefore, the possibility that further evolution will lead us back to total discretion in policy making albeit with inflation as an over-riding priority.
>
> (1987: 1)

That policy had to be discretionary with regard to a variety of indicators was backed up by the monetary authorities, who nevertheless argued that this represented very little deviation from the original *modus operandi* of the MTFS (Bank of England 1987c: 366).

Finally, it should be emphasized that institutional change and innovation is an on-going process and analysis of monetary developments cannot be divorced from the dynamic financial system within which policy operates.

11.2 MONETARY POLICY AND THE EXCHANGE RATE MECHANISM

The purpose of this brief final section is to make some comments on the impact of the exchange rate mechanism (ERM) on monetary control, and particularly on the continued influence of the interaction between banks/building societies and the personal sector. Although the way in which economic policy is conducted has changed, the importance of the institutional framework and the effects of credit liberalization continue to influence the operation of monetary policy and control.

The underlying rationale of fiscal and monetary policy remains the reduction of inflation. The main objective of economic policy under the ERM is to maintain sterling within its permitted bands, although a target is still set for M0 (the only aggregate still to have a target, of 0–4 per cent in 1991).

The main effect of sterling joining the ERM is that the government only has a marginal influence on UK interest rates. Rates will largely be dictated by the strength of sterling within the ERM bands. This led to pre-entry fears that it would not be possible to cut interest rates without a serious weakening and fall in sterling.

In fact, in February 1991, money flowed out of Deutschmarks and into the dollar, which had started to rise, taking the pressure off sterling. The ERM did not thus immediately prevent interest rate cuts. Indeed, when sterling entered the ERM in October 1990 inflation was 10.9 per cent and short-term interest rates were 15 per cent. One year later, in October 1991, inflation was around 4 per cent and interest rates were down to 10.5 per cent. In January 1992, however, the situation was very different, with sterling near the bottom of its band and the possibility of even higher interest rates to stop it falling further.

Domestic monetary policy is no longer the main control mechanism of inflation. Instead, it is the constraint that inflationary cost and price increases cannot be passed onto overseas markets that curbs rising prices. It could be argued that the move to the ERM does not in fact mean a total recant of the precepts of monetarism, but is merely a shift of emphasis in the way in which monetary policy is carried out, from domestic monetarism to international monetarism. This takes the form of linking the UK economy to the Bundesbank's Germanic form of monetary correctness, something which had already been carried out without official recognition under Chancellor Nigel Lawson.

There is still much debate, however, as to the exact channels through which the ERM operates. Entry into the ERM should make shocks from import prices less likely and at the same time make the reduction of inflation easier. The idea is that wages will slow down quickly as workers and employers are aware of the ERM constraints that the government is operating under and will adjust expectations accordingly. There is the hope that consumption and borrowing will rebound despite the money supply figures, as workers perceive that the rate of wage growth starts to outgrow the rate of inflation. The real money supply will then grow as inflation falls.

It is extremely striking, however, that the supporters of monetarism also maintained that wages, and hence prices, would adjust quickly as a result of the government's anti-inflationary monetary policy. In fact, there is absolutely no evidence that workers and employers take into account either the growth of monetary aggregates or the position of sterling within the ERM when pay bargaining.

It is immediately obvious that the financial system still has a major role to play in the authorities' attempts to control the economy, and that the efficiency of monetary policy still relies on the activities and interaction of the banks, building societies and personal sector.

The impact of interest-bearing transactions balances does indeed seem to have reduced the interest elasticity of the demand for money, as noted above. The reduction in interest rates in 1990 had little effect on the volume of cash balances held by the personal sector, and the ability of the authorities to control the money supply through the demand side by inducing money-holders to spend their balances has been ineffective. So, it appears that it is difficult both to reduce inflation by raising interest rates on alternative assets and also to stimulate the economy by reducing interest rates to stimulate spending.

The personal sector has maintained its holdings of money balances as they became increasingly attractive under the high interest rates of the late 1980s. It is still the case that it is impossible to distinguish between balances that are purely for transactions purposes and balances that are purely for investment purposes, and that this tends to confuse monetary conditions. At the same time, money balances held by companies have fallen and companies have slashed stocks and investment levels, which has led to reductions in employment, output and demand.

The UK economy remained depressed for some time because of the effect of continued high levels of consumer debt, which was the overhang from the liberalization of credit conditions in the 1980s (which was not being paid off until 1991–2), and continuing high interest rates, both of which dampened any prospects of a consumer-led recovery. It would be expected that the observed increase in consumers' interest elasticity of expenditure would mean a quick reaction to the reduction in interest rates in the 1990s, but this did not in fact happen, implying that other factors such as the threat of unemployment and the fall in house prices overwhelmed greater interest sensitivity. The ability to influence the economy through interest rates must be further thrown into doubt.

It may well be the case that the fall in house prices has been a major factor in the reluctance of the consumer to increase expenditure plans. The impact of stagnant turnover in the housing market further hits spending as sales of furniture, furnishings and other household goods that are boosted by house-moving are reduced.

The spectre of unemployment also encourages the personal sector to cut back on expenditure plans, and either to reduce borrowings or at least to stop borrowing.

Although there has been a rise in the interest elasticity of expenditure with respect to mortgage interest rates, the effect of the way in which mortgage rate changes are administered by many building societies cannot be ignored. The impact of only adjusting mortgage rates downwards annually or semi-annually will be to postpone the personal sectors' expenditure plans even further, and push back the expected date of any recovery.

Reductions in interest rates should stimulate the demand for credit, which in turn creates new deposits as banks lend and inflate their balance sheets. The problem with the early 1990s, however, rests on the fact that the banks were severely capital constrained and so found it difficult to lend. Moreover, bank lending rates tended to be extremely sticky in a downwards direction, and many would argue that this was a major factor in prolonging the recession.

Although the money supply figures have been discredited in many ways, it would be inappropriate to ignore their information entirely. Indeed, it may be that, now that the monetary aggregates are not being targeted, Goodhart's law will be reversed, i.e. any aggregate that is not being controlled will revert back to normal patterns and relationships, although the evidence for this is of course unresearched.

In the twelve months to October 1991, M0, the Treasury's preferred indicator, grew at only 1.6 per cent, and by only 0.7 per cent in the three months to October 1991. Perhaps more alarmingly, M4 showed a similar pattern. Over the twelve months to October 1991, M4 grew by only 7.2 per cent and in the three months to October 1991 by 0.9 per cent. These growth rates were by far the lowest since the 1970s, and suggested that the economy had much further to go before recovery was fully underway, if the monetary indicators were to be believed.

It may well be the case that the recession in the UK in the early 1990s was prolonged by the move of sterling into the ERM. This is because interest rates had to remain higher than would otherwise be desired in order to prop up a weakened sterling and maintain it within its ERM limits. Commitment to the ERM also rules out any devaluation of sterling, which might otherwise be tempting, but self-defeating. A fall in sterling would boost the economy but have a large effect on inflation as import prices rise, especially as imports into the UK are around a quarter of total domestic spending.

Many would argue that a consequence of ERM entry has also been a higher exchange rate than would have been expected under other circumstances. This also tends to have an impact on domestic demand and slows down the prospects for economic recovery. In addition, it means that manufacturers find profits squeezed, and the decline in inflation may indeed be faster under the ERM.

Moving into the ERM has not made it any easier to understand or forecast the economy, as the Treasury's poor forecasts (and everyone else's) and the government's increasingly frantic efforts to predict the start of a recovery in 1992 show. Moreover, M4 did not indicate the start of the recession until the second half of 1990, by which time it was becoming obvious for other reasons. It is under this type of scenario that the monetary aggregates need to be closely examined for any information they may contain and any discretionary policy action necessary.

It may be that the only option of the government is to carry out monetary policy in an unrigorous month-by-month manner that takes into account a variety of indicators, including the growth rates of the various money supply figures. Even under the ERM it is still not possible to separate monetary policy from the financial system within which it operates and the intermediation activities of the financial institutions that make up that system.

Notes

2 Monetary control – theory, practice and financial change

1 There is not, of course, only one 'brand' of monetarism. It is not intended in this book to describe the various schools of monetarism in detail. This has been adequately done by Congdon (1978), Budd (1980), Arestis and Riley (1980) and Burton (1982). In this work the terms monetarist and monetarism follow the broad classification suggested by Laidler (1981) in his analysis of the conflicting opinions as to the central points of monetarism (see also Brunner 1970; Johnson 1972).

2 Laidler (1985a) and Cuthbertson (1985) provide a thorough survey of the early theoretical and empirical literature on the demand for money.

3 Despite Friedman's assertion to the contrary, critics have argued that his analysis need be modified only slightly to fit into any neo-Keynesian model. Indeed Johnson (1962) and Patinkin (1969) argue that Friedman's theory of the demand for money is essentially an extension of the Keynesian capital-theoretic analysis of the role of money rather than a reformulation of the quantity theory. Friedman, whilst admitting that Keynes's liquidity preference influenced his work (1970a), has set out his own formal framework (1970b, 1971).

4 The decision between the money supply and interest rates depends not only on the relative stability of the functions but also on the *slopes* of the IS–LM curves (see Courakis 1981: 272 for a full explanation of this). Poole points out that it is suboptimal to use *either* the money supply *or* interest rates as the instrument of monetary policy. A combined policy whereby the money supply is a function of the interest rate is preferable. B. Friedman (1975, 1977), however, has argued that a situation whereby the money supply is the intermediate target to be manipulated by the instrument of interest rates is also suboptimal. This policy is wasteful of additional information that may be helpful in achieving the ultimate target, and also neglects Kareken *et al.*'s (1973) stricture that any variable that cannot be precisely controlled should be used as an 'information variable' rather than a 'surrogate goal of policy' (Lane 1985).

5 See *inter alia* Radcliffe (1959), Tobin (1969), Kaldor (1970) and Robinson (1970). Keynesians were not the only economists to take this view. Laidler (1981: 3) has pointed out that pre-Keynesians also did not believe in an empirically stable demand for money function.

6 Uncertainty is of course present in the precautionary demand for money in terms of uncertainty over the future need to carry out expenditures. Keynes emphasized the uncertainty involved with the speculative demand for money, which is dominated by uncertainty over asset values.
7 The money/bonds distinction is of course an extreme simplification of reality derived from assumptions as to the theory being outlined. There *are* alternatives to holding bonds and there is some debate as to the importance of the money/bonds distinction made by Keynes.
8 Keynes also argued that, at very low rates of interest, all investors are likely to think that rates will rise and so no bonds will be held – the 'liquidity trap'.
9 Most Keynesians would in fact admit that the IS curve is unstable, but not so volatile as the LM curve.
10 Often called the New Classical school.
11 Most economists would probably now argue that the strong form of rational expectations is a special case. Few would deny the importance of rational expectations, however. Indeed, many Keynesian models now embody rational expectations (see Begg 1982; Gale 1982).
12 Budd (1980) points to an apparent dichotomy between the Sargent–Wallace and Friedman analyses. Although reaching the same conclusion, they appear to argue from different premises. Friedman argues that *no one* can forecast the future movements of the economy (therefore it should not be used for stabilization policy), whereas Sargent and Wallace argue that *everyone* can forecast the economy (again it should not be used for stabilization policy). This apparent dichotomy can be rationalized by maintaining that the important factor is that the government's forecasts are no more accurate than anyone else's (Budd 1980: 6) which would appear to satisfy both schools of thought.
13 The monetarist viewpoint on a monetary growth rate rule is buttressed by the belief that active stabilization policies cannot be effective and may in fact be destabilizing. Thus, discretionary policy actions may cause the economy to veer off its path (Friedman 1960: 23).
14 The empirical work of Friedman and Schwartz has been heavily criticized, however. For a critique of Friedman and Schwartz's UK econometric work, see Hendry and Ericsson (1983).
15 The relationships among the monetary aggregates and their components are as follows (Figures in parentheses are amounts outstanding in £ billion at the end of October 1987, as shown in the December 1987 issue of *Financial Statistics*; M0 is actually published as the average amount outstanding for all the Wednesdays in the month):

Notes and coins in circulation with the public (13.7)
AGAA

plus Banks' till money (1.6)
AVAA-AGAA

plus Bankers' balances with the Bank of England (0.2)
AVAC

equals M0 (15.5)
AVAD

plus Private sector non-interest-bearing sterling eight bank deposits (31.2)

AUYA

equals Non-interest-bearing M1 (44.9)

AUYH

plus Private sector interest-bearing retail sterling deposits with banks and building societies and National Savings bank ordinary accounts (137.7)

AUYB

equals M2 (182.6)

AUYC

plus Private sector interest-bearing sterling sight bank deposits (47.0)

AGAD

equals M1 (91.9)

AGAF

plus Private sector sterling time bank deposits (90.0)

AGAG

equals M3 (old £M3) (181.9)

AGAJ

plus Private sector holdings of building society shares and deposits and sterling certificates of deposit (129.1)

AJWK

less Building society holdings of bank deposits and bank certificates of deposit, and notes and coin (13.5)

AUYL

equals M4 (297.5)

AUYM

plus Holdings by the private sector (excluding building societies) of money market instruments (bank bills, Treasury bills, local authority deposits), certificates of tax deposit and National Savings instruments (excluding certificates, SAYE and other long-term deposits (15.0)

AUYR + AVEB

equals M5 (312.5)

AVEE

plus Private sector foreign currency bank deposits (31.0)

AGAK

equals AGAL M3c (212.9)

16 See Chapters 3 and 7 for further analysis of competition and credit control.
17 See Chapter 7 for an examination of the efficacy of direct monetary controls.
18 See also Sayers (1960) and Chapter 5 for a further analysis of the importance of financial change and the definition and meaning of money.
19 Spencer (1986) provides a detailed account of financial innovation and monetary controls, but concentrates exclusively on the period up to 1980 and therefore does not consider building society or bank innovations after that time.
20 See Chapter 5 for a further analysis of financial innovation and distortion of the relative movements of the monetary aggregates.
21 Quoted in Goodhart (1984).

3 Building society and bank developments, 1970–9

1 Simons (1936) was one of the first economists interested in the interaction between financial innovation and the monetary system.
2 For broad overviews of financial innovation in the UK see Fforde (1983b) and, for a somewhat earlier perspective, Greenbaum and Heywood (1971). For the USA see Broaddus (1985), Lindsey (1982), Porter *et al.* (1979), Pierce (1983) and Simpson (1984). For Canada see Freedman (1983) and Lucas (1983).
3 On the broad issues relating to the recent evolution and growth of the UK building societies sector, see Boddy (1980), Fforde (1983b) and Boleat (1986). See Cleary (1965) for an earlier perspective and Bellman (1927) for a historical picture.
4 The Building Societies Act 1986 has of course superseded this Act (see Chapter 4).
5 This is confirmed by the variety of objective functions expounded in econometric models of building society behaviour. See Dodds (1981) for a survey of the literature on building society modelling.
6 The ability of the building society movement to operate a cartel explicitly exempt from the Restrictive Trade Practices Act 1976 is an example of the privileged position building societies occupied as major providers of home loans. See Boleat (1986: 175–7) for a review of the historical development of the cartel.
7 Between September 1971 and January 1981, each bank was required to hold at least 12½ per cent of its eligible liabilities in the form of reserve assets. The reserve asset ratio was reduced to 10 per cent in January 1981, temporarily reduced to 8 per cent for most of March and April 1981 and abolished in August 1981. Reserve assets comprised the following:

   (a) balances at the Bank of England (other than special or supplementary deposits);
   (b) British government and Northern Ireland Treasury bills;
   (c) secured money at call with London discount market institutions;
   (d) British government stocks with a residual maturity of less than one year;

(e) local authority bills eligible for re-discount at the Bank;
(f) commercial bills eligible for re-discount at the Bank (i.e. eligible bank bills) up to a maximum of 2 per cent of eligible liabilities.

8 Between 1971 and 1980, eligible liabilities mainly comprised the following:

(a) all sterling deposits, of an original maturity of two years or under, from UK residents (other than banks) and overseas residents (other than overseas offices);
(b) all sterling deposits of whatever term from the UK banking sector *net* of sterling claims (including non-reserve asset lending to listed discount market institutions);
(c) all sterling certificates of deposit issued, of whatever term, less any holdings of such certificates;
(d) the bank's net deposit liability, if any, in sterling to its overseas offices;
(e) the bank's net liability, if any, in currencies other than sterling.

9 A full account of the supplementary special deposits scheme is found in Bank of England (1982b).

10 It was possible, however, for lenders and borrowers to be brought together outside the banking sector. Such 'disintermediation' occurred when large corporate customers borrowed through the use of an acceptance rather than an advance, under which a bank would agree to accept and guarantee bills issued by the customer. These bank bills were close substitutes for certificates of deposit in terms of liquidity, marketability and default risk, yet, as they were only a contingent liability of an accepting bank, they were represented for accounting purposes as off-balance-sheet items and hence excluded from the IBELs definition and from £M3. (See Chapter 7 for further analysis of disintermediation activities.)

11 Through the composite tax rate scheme, the Inland Revenue collects directly from building societies and retail banks the amount of tax revenue which would be paid in aggregate by the individual depositors on their interest receipts if they were received gross and the basic rate of income tax applied to all tax-paying depositors. Thus, as some deposits have always earned incomes below the minimum income tax threshold, the composite rate of tax has always been somewhat below the basic rate of income tax.

4 Re-regulation, competition and innovation by building societies and banks, 1980–90

1 Gilchrist (1986) provides a straightforward analysis of the overall regulatory changes with respect to building societies. For interesting analyses of the monetary authorities' views as to the changing activities of building societies, see Richardson (1978), Davis and Saville (1982), Richardson (1983) and Drayson (1985).

2 Of seven major innovations introduced in the USA, Hester argues that all were induced by previous monetary policy decisions by the authorities. Simons warned of the dangers of ignoring institutional change as far back as 1936. Akhtar (1983) outlines the main broad categories of financial change in the USA, the UK, Canada, Japan, France, Germany and Italy as being

(a) the increasing use of interest-sensitive funds by banks and other financial institutions,
(b) variable rate lending or borrowing and maturity shortening,
(c) the growth of financial markets and of marketable financial instruments,
(d) the changing shape of retail banking and
(e) the diversification of sources of financial services.

3 In fact, once they had reached their desired portfolios the retail banks employed a number of rationing devices on their mortgage lending. Many borrowers had to maintain an account for a minimum period to qualify for a mortgage, and restrictions were placed on the maximum amounts banks were willing to lend as a proportion of property value or as a multiple of income. Of course, these are phenomena more normally associated with the building society industry.

4 The Green Paper *Building Societies: A New Framework* (July 1984) had recommended the abolition of the cartel, deeming it to be anti-competitive, whilst its removal would encourage 'the free play of market forces which would ensure the best deal for savers and borrowers'.

5 Financial innovations are alleged to occur in 'clusters' or 'swarms' (Podolski 1985, 1986) as one financial innovation acts as the catalyst for another. It does seem that in practice one financial innovation will trigger off another, particularly in the form of a competitive innovation from a competing financial institution. The evidence as to 'swarms' of financial innovations is not clear cut, however.

6 It may be significant that a building society (the Nottingham) was the first institution to offer a full home banking service in conjunction with the Bank of Scotland.

7 Indeed, Niehans (1982) considers that declining transactions costs are the major determinant of financial innovation, although this hypothesis is not adequately substantiated. It is possible to illustrate the effects of technological advances upon product variety and product mix by using a product matrix (see figure opposite) (Lewis 1987). The bottom of the matrix is the product complexity axis whilst the vertical axis shows the breadth of the product line. The former runs from standardized services to individually tailored requirements. The latter shows the variety of products offered, ranging from high to low. It is argued that technological advances allow the product matrix to shift to the right, increasing the complexity and variety of products on offer as a result of low and declining costs.

8 It is interesting to note that it is not only the retail banks which will have to re-evaluate their strategies. The Halifax Building Society, the only one amongst the big six societies to eschew a paper-based transmission service in favour of electronic-based systems, has announced that it is re-exam-

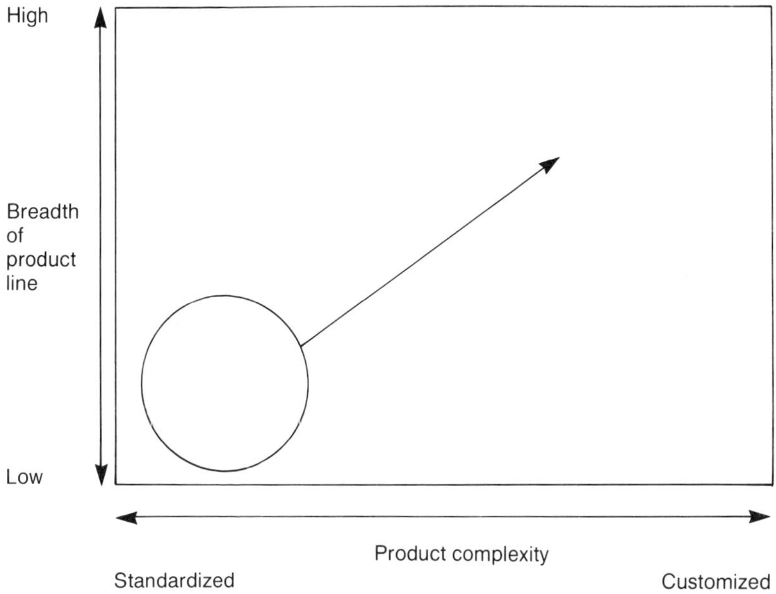

Figure 4.11n Impact of technology upon the product matrix for financial institutions
Source: Lewis 1987

ining its policy in the light of other building societies offering interest-bearing cheque accounts.

9 The Stow Report (1979) examined the need for societies to adopt wholesale funding. The general conclusion was that traditional sources of funds would be adequate but it was suggested that issuing certificates of deposit would provide building societies with more flexibility. The Phillips Report (B. Phillips 1980) examined wholesale funding in more detail and concluded that building society certificates of deposit would help to stabilize lending and allow societies to operate with lower liquidity ratios. The report did recognize that, although in principle there were no restrictions on societies' raising funds in the wholesale markets, they were effectively precluded by the fact that they were required to pay interest net of tax at the composite rate (the tax being unclaimable). The Stow and Phillips Reports were written at a time when building society retail rates were generally below other rates. The change in rates such that retail rates were in general above wholesale rates gave an impetus to use wholesale markets on a far greater scale than as envisaged by the reports.

10 For earlier evidence see Gough (1979, 1981), Gilchrist and Rothwell (1980), Barnes and Dodds (1981) and Barnes (1985).

11 There are two further aspects to the societies' endowment effect. First, interest is only credited to investors' accounts every six or twelve months

and, of course, additional interest is only earned on the original interest from the date of crediting. Building societies will thus tend to have a pool of interest-free funds that has not yet been credited to investors' accounts. This is particularly important during periods of high interest rates.

Second, building societies will tend to make greater provision for composite rate tax during periods of high interest rates. Until these funds are paid to the government (normally quarterly) these interest-free funds can be profitably invested.

12 See Drake and Llewellyn (1988) for a detailed analysis of the conversion to PLC debate.

13 With respect to capital adequacy requirements, the BSC has stated that building societies will eventually come under the Bank for International Settlements proposals for a minimum risk–assets ratio of 8 per cent. This represents a major turn towards regulatory convergence (see Llewellyn 1988b) in that banks, PLC societies and mutual societies will be regulated on equal terms for capital measures, but retains asymmetry in terms of the degree to which mutual and PLC societies can diversify.

5 Financial innovation and the monetary aggregates

1 Sayers was one of the major authors of the Radcliffe Report.

2 See also Coghlan (1977, 1978b).

3 The Building Societies Association has recently argued that building society accounts are primarily used for investment purposes (Building Societies Association, 1983c), but with the introduction of interest-bearing cheque accounts there are an increasing number of accounts that combine both transactions and investment services.

4 Hadjimichalakis (1982) examines the effects of payment of interest on money upon the operation of monetary control in a US context. As much of the analysis concentrates upon the effects of the lifting of Regulation Q, the conclusions are not strictly transferable to the UK.

5 It has been suggested that a solution to the breakdown of the money–income relationship may be to specify the monetary aggregates in Divisia index form (Barnett 1978; Barnett *et al.* 1984; Spindt 1984). The present monetary aggregates give equal weight to all asset components, whereas a Divisia monetary aggregate would weight assets according to their 'money' services or 'user costs' (the difference between a benchmark asset and the asset's yield). Although this seems intuitively plausible, the new aggregates would be difficult for economic agents to understand and, moreover, Mills (1983) reports that it is not possible, according to his research, to specify a demand for money equation for a broad Divisia aggregate.

6 See Mills (1983) and Bailey *et al.* (1982) for analyses of the information content of the monetary aggregates in the UK in terms of their ability to 'explain' nominal income statistically.

7 See Bordo and Jonung (1981) for an international perspective of the trends in the income velocity of circulation of money.

6 Competition, mortgage lending and the money–income relationship

1 Two factors have particularly increased the demand for home-ownership in the 1980s. First, the government has actively encouraged home-ownership through the sale of council houses. Second, demographic changes have played a part. The 'baby boom' of the early 1960s had led to a large number of first-time buyers in the early 1980s.

2 Hacche (1974), however, argues that there may have been a shift or successive shifts of the demand function because of events unique to 1971 and 1972, leading to a higher level of desired money balances than previous experience would have predicted. In particular, it is possible that, as a result of changes introduced by competition and credit control (see Chapter 2) and the subsequent increase in banks' competitiveness, interest-bearing 'money' may have increased in attractiveness relative to other financial assets. Following this particular hypothesis, Hacche (1974) argues that the demand for M3 may have been affected by the rate of interest on wholesale time deposits and certificates of deposit.

Hacche employed four different own rate variables in order to ascertain whether or not they could explain the 'shift' towards interest-bearing money. He found that including the certificate of deposit (CD) rate provided equations which adequately fit the data to the end of 1972. He offered the explanation that:

> the importance of the C.D. rate to the results may to a large extent be a reflection of the transition to the changed money-market environment, and in particular of adjustment to the growing market in C.D's.
> (1974: 296)

Artis and Lewis allow for the growth of the CD market post-1971 by utilizing definitions of money which do not include CDs, i.e. M1 and M3 minus CDs. They note that both these definitions produce results no better than those for M3 (conventionally defined) and therefore, according to this evidence, allowance for CDs cannot explain the forecasting error. More formally, Artis and Lewis use a variable which they claim will measure both interest rate competition before 1971 and also any greater competitiveness of bank interest rates after 1971. They split the money stock M3 into components of interest-bearing deposits (see Artis and Lewis 1974: Appendix 4), and a weighted average of the rates on these deposits is then used. Artis and Lewis conclude that the inclusion of this 'own' rate still results in an unstable demand for broad money.

It is possible also to criticize Hacche's measure of the own rate because of his assumption that there is no interest rate competition between banks, accepting houses and overseas and other banks prior to competition and credit control (Artis and Lewis 1976: 150). The consequence of employing an own rate of zero prior to 1971 and the CD rate post-1971 is analogous to utilizing a dummy variable in the equations. This will therefore exaggerate the importance of the CD (own rate) after 1971.

3 Milbourne cogently argues that the buffer stock model is unlikely to be applicable to a narrow definition of money such as M1 (the focus of

much of the econometric research into buffer stocks) and suggests that, if the buffer stock is applicable at all, it is relevant to a broader definition of money (see also Goodhart 1984: 267).

4 As Milbourne notes, a crucial element of the buffer stock model is the exogeneity of supply-side shocks. This is essential since a central tenet of monetarism is the assumption that the money supply process is independent of the factors which determine the demand for money. There are reasons, however, for supposing that changes in bank lending (i.e. supply-side shocks) are largely demand determined, particularly in recent years. Re-intermediation following the abandonment of the supplementary special deposits scheme can only be rationalized as demand determined, particularly in view of the high interest rates charged on advances (Bank of England 1988b). The implication of an endogenous money supply for the applicability of the buffer stock model will not be pursued here, however. The argument that financial innovation invalidates much of the buffer stock model applies whether or not the money supply is exogenous or endogenous.

7 Financial innovation and the effectiveness of monetary control

1 'Monetary base' here refers to that group of liabilities of the central bank over which they are believed to have control. It is assumed here that this includes notes and coins held by the banks and bankers' balances held at the Bank of England. See Goodhart (1984: 203–4) for the relative merits of inclusion of various central bank liabilities in the base money definition. See Foot *et al.* (1979), Congdon (1980) and Lewis (1980a) for general critiques of MBC.

2 The MBC debate is traditionally centred on the monetary system. In view of the noted similarity between banks and building societies, and a presumed wish of the authorities to bring building societies under the aegis of an MBC policy, certain technical changes would need to be made.

8 Financial innovation, the demand for money, the demand for credit and the consumption function

1 See Artis and Lewis (1974, 1976), Hacche (1974), Hendry and Mizon (1978), Coghlan (1978), Hendry (1979), Grice and Bennett (1981, 1984), Judd and Scadding (1982), Laidler (1985a) and Cuthbertson (1987).

2 See Boughton (1979, 1981a) for a survey of the econometric research into the demand for money in OECD countries.

3 Budd and Holly's final equation takes the form:

$$\Delta\left(\frac{M}{P}\right)_t = \underset{(1.49)}{-0.0162} + \underset{(2.81)}{0.1806}\,\Delta\left(\frac{M}{P}\right)_{t-1}$$

$$- \underset{(5.30)}{0.1166} \left(\frac{M}{PY}\right)_{t-2} - \underset{(3.90)}{0.0212}\, \text{rs}_t$$

$$- \underset{(4.34)}{0.0861}\, (\text{rL} - \text{rL}_{t-2}) + \underset{(1.59)}{0.0286}\, (\text{rbd} - \text{rs})_t$$

$$- \underset{(11.25)}{0.6181}\, \Delta P_t + \underset{(4.84)}{0.3123}\, \Delta P_{t-1} + \text{dummies}$$

$R^2 = 0.768$ SEE = 2.22% LM(3) = 1.67

M is sterling M3, P is the price level, Y is real income, rs is the short interest rate, rL is the long interest rate and rbd is the rate of interest on bank deposits. Four dummy variables were included, two for the two World Wars, one for a change in data source in 1967 and one for the period 1921–55 when, according to Friedman and Schwartz, there was a shift in liquidity preference (although this last dummy variable was dropped from the final equation). The general-to-specific methodology was used (see Chapter 9). LM(3) is a Lagrange multiplier test for autocorrelation of the residuals. All the variables are in logarithmic form (including the interest rates). Figures in parentheses are t statistics.

4 Johnston's final equation for total personal sector holdings of liquid assets was

$$\frac{z_l}{P} = \underset{(4.18)}{-0.48} - \underset{(3.31)}{0.041} \frac{z_1/P_{t-1}}{\text{TW}/P_{t-4}} + \underset{(14.21)}{0.81} \frac{WAQ}{P} + \underset{(4.36)}{0.079} \frac{y}{P}$$

$$+ \underset{(2.61)}{0.65}\, (r_{z_1})_{t-2} - \underset{(2.03)}{0.46}\, (r_{z_1})_{t-3} \underset{(2.32)}{-0.22}\, (r_L + \text{ECG})_{t-1}$$

$$- \underset{(6.59)}{0.38}\, r_s\, (1 - \text{TAX})$$

$R^2 = 0.91$ DW = 2.17 SEE = 0.49%

LM(1) = 0.5 LM(4) = 6.1

Hendry = 24.1 Chow = 4.8

estimation period: 1967/4–1982/4

where z_1 has been given above, WAQ/P is personal sector real gross acquisitions of financial wealth, P is the consumer expenditure deflator, y is personal disposable income, ECG is an estimate of expected capital gains, r_{z1} is the average return on the aggregate z_1, r_s is a general measure of market interest rates, the three-month inter-bank rate, and r_L is a long-term interest rate, the gross redemption yield on twenty-year gilts. The general-to-specific methodology was used. All variables (except interest rates) are in logarithmic form.

5 Johnston's model of total debt of the personal sector takes the form:

$$\Delta\left(\frac{TD}{P}\right) = \underset{(1.73)}{0.78} - \underset{(3.92)}{0.27}\left(\frac{TD}{P}\right)_{t-1} - \underset{(1.89)}{0.22}\left(\frac{TD}{P}\right)_{t-3}$$

$$+ \underset{(5.28)}{0.33}\left(\frac{TD}{P}\right)_{t-4} + \underset{(2.26)}{0.01}\,(r_{bsa})_{t-1} - 0.008\,(r_{bsa})_{t-4}$$

$$- \underset{(2.28)}{0.005}r_s\,(1-\text{TAX})_{t-4} - \underset{(3.74)}{0.015}\,r_m\,(1-\text{TAX})$$

$$- \underset{(5.72)}{0.48}\left(\frac{Y}{P}\right)_{t-2} - \underset{(2.28)}{0.48}\,\Delta\,P_{t-3} + \underset{(5.62)}{0.14}\,\text{Ph}_{t-1}$$

$$- \underset{(3.87)}{0.0013}\,\text{XSMD} - \underset{(3.95)}{0.0013}\,\text{XSMD}_{t-1}$$

$$- \underset{(0.65)}{0.006}\,\text{DC1} - \underset{(2.25)}{0.017}\,\text{DC2} - \underset{(0.12)}{0.001}\,\text{DC3}$$

$$+ \underset{(7.13)}{0.242}\,\frac{NW}{P} + \underset{(4.44)}{0.041}\,\text{DCCC}$$

$R^2 = 0.82$ DW = 1.82 SEE = 1.03%

LM(1) = 0.6 LM(4) = 18.1 Hendry = 8.5

The corset dummy variables are as follows: DC1 = 1 for 1974/1–1975/1 and is zero otherwise; DC2 = 1 for 1976/4–1977/3 and is zero otherwise; DC3 = 1 for 1978/3–1980/2 and is zero otherwise. DCCC is a dummy for competition and credit control taking the value 1 after 1971/3. TD is personal sector financial debt, P is the consumer expenditure deflator, Y is personal disposable income, Ph is an index of house prices at the completion stage, XSMD is a measure of excess mortgage demand, NW is net financial wealth, r_{bsa} is the quarterly average building society deposit rate (net of basic rate tax) and r_s is the quarterly average three-month inter-bank rate. All variables except interest rates are in logarithmic form.

6 The wealth series is constructed from national balance sheet data (see Reid 1978; Pettigrew 1980).

7 Following Grether and Maddala (1973).

8 Grice and Bennett's final function is of the form:

$$\frac{M}{P} = -1.2445 + \underset{(7.60)}{0.772}\,\Delta\left(\frac{GW}{P}\right) - \underset{(2.09)}{0.276}\left(\frac{GW}{P}\right)_{t-3}$$

$$+ \underset{(4.07)}{0.470}\left(\frac{GW}{P}\right)_{t-4} + \underset{(4.36)}{0.742}\left(1 + \frac{REV}{GW}\right)_{t-2}$$

$$+ \underset{(2.01)}{0.184} \left(1 + \frac{REV}{GW}\right)_{t-5} + \underset{(5.93)}{0.369} \frac{TFE}{P}$$

$$- \underset{(3.49)}{0.181} \left(\frac{TFE}{P}\right)_{t-3} - \underset{(2.88)}{0.145} \left(\frac{TFE}{P}\right)_{t-5}$$

$$- \underset{(2.87)}{0.00859} \Delta_2 \text{ RM} + \underset{(3.48)}{0.000734} \text{ RMRGEG}$$

$$- \underset{(2.42)}{0.000406} \text{ RMRGEG}_{t-1} + \underset{(1.93)}{0.000212} \text{ RMRGEG}_{t-5}$$

$$+ \underset{(3.00)}{0.0183} \text{ CCCDUM} + \underset{(5.45)}{0.0395} \text{ CRISIS}$$

$$+ \sum_{i=1}^{3} D_i + \underset{(17.54)}{0.970} \left(\frac{M}{P}\right)_{t-1} + \underset{(4.10)}{0.493} \left(\frac{M}{P}\right)_{t-3}$$

$$- \underset{(5.82)}{0.929} \left(\frac{M}{P}\right)_{t-4} + \underset{(3.60)}{0.330} \left(\frac{M}{P}\right)_{t-5}$$

where $D_1 = -0.0458$ (6.95), $D_2 = -0.0273$ (5.26), $D_3 = -0.0250$ (3.74), $R^2 = 0.9971$, SEE = 0.598%, M = M3 (non-bank private sector), GW is non-bank private sector gross financial wealth, REV is cumulated revaluations, TFE is total final expenditure at current prices, P is the price index for TFE (1975 = 1.00), RM is the post-tax rate of return to M3 and RMRGEG is the post-tax rate of return to gilts including expected capital gains. All variables except interest rates are in logarithmic form. The general-to-specific methodology was used.

9 Their cointegrating equations take the form:

$$\frac{M}{PY} = -0.71 \, \Delta^4 \, P + 0.72 \frac{W}{PY} - 0.2\text{SND} + 0.1\text{DCCC}$$

where P is the log of the GDP deflator, Y is the log of real GDP, W is the log of the total financial wealth of the personal sector, ND = min [Δ (log of FT Share Index)], SND = $\sum_{i=0}^{7} \text{ND}_{t-i}$, DCCC = 0 prior to 1971/4 and 1 thereafter. The final equation was

$$\Delta \text{ (M4)} = \underset{(4.8)}{0.016} + \underset{(5.2)}{0.512} \, \Delta \text{ (M4)}_{t-1} - \underset{(2.4)}{0.15}\text{RES}_{t-1}$$

where RES is the residuals from the levels regression.

10 Weale's estimated equation is:

$$S_{it} = \sum_{j=3}^{6} y_{ij} \log P_j + \beta_i \left[\log \frac{W_t}{P_t^*}^* - \log e_t \right.$$
$$+ \sum_{j=1}^{5} V_{ij} S_{jt-1} + X_{i1} \varepsilon_1 + X_{i2} \varepsilon_2 + X_{i3} \varepsilon_3 + \alpha_i$$

where S_{it} is the share of asset i, S_{jt-1} is the holding of asset j in the previous period, W_t is total short-term asset holdings at the end of period t, P_j is the price of asset j, P_t^* is the asset price index, e_t is expenditure in period t and ε_1, ε_2 and ε_3 are seasonal dummies. The equation is estimated by three-stage least squares for the period 1967/2–1981/3. The assets tested are notes and coin, bank sight deposits, bank time deposits, Savings Bank deposits, building society deposits and local authority deposits.

11 Currie and Kennally's final equation takes the form:

$$\begin{aligned}
\Delta_{QD} = \; & \underset{(5.7)}{-2.62} + \underset{(11.1)}{0.917}\,\Delta\,QW_t - \underset{(3.3)}{0.774}\,\Delta\,QW_{t-1} \\
& \underset{(3.6)}{-0.893}\,\Delta\,RPI_{t-1} + \underset{(2.9)}{0.121}\,\Delta\,QCE_{t-1} \\
& \underset{(5.6)}{+0.250}\,\Delta\,QCE_{t-2} + \underset{(4.6)}{0.226}\,\Delta\,QCE_{t-3} \\
& \underset{(1.1)}{+0.486}\,ROWN_{t-2} - \underset{(4.0)}{0.152}\,QD_{t-2} \\
& \underset{(4.8)}{+0.159}\,QW_{t-4} + \underset{(4.1)}{0.236}\,QCE_{t-4} - \underset{(6.0)}{0.029}\,SD1 \\
& \underset{(3.0)}{+0.001}\,TIM
\end{aligned}$$

$R^2 = 0.95$ $\quad$ SEE = 0.59%
LM(4) = 5.3 $\quad$ XSQ = 16.2

All variables except interest rates are in logarithms. The general-to-specific methodology was used where QD is the sum of building society deposits and sight and time bank deposits of the personal sector, divided by the consumers' expenditure deflator, QW is permanent wealth of the personal sector (divided by the consumers' expenditure deflator), QCE is a measure of transactions expenditure (divided by the consumers' expenditure deflator), ROWN is the weighted average own rate of interest on liquid assets minus the rate of return on a competing non-liquid financial asset (2½ per cent consols), SD1 is a seasonal dummy variable, RPI represents inflation, TIM is a time trend variable, LM(4) is the Lagrange multiplier test for serial correlation and XSQ is the eight-period forecast test.

12 Dicks' durables consumption function takes the form:

$$\text{CD} = \underset{(6.8)}{1.074}\ \text{YDLH} - \underset{(5.0)}{0.656}\ \text{RR} - \underset{(5.3)}{0.005}\ \text{RMD}_{t-1}$$

$$+ \underset{(3.7)}{0.125}\left(\frac{ML}{PC}\right)_{t-1} + \underset{(2.4)}{0.206}\left(\frac{NLAJ}{PC}\right)_{t-1} - \text{constant}$$

$$+ \text{dummies}$$

$$R^2 = 0.988$$

Numbers in parentheses are t values. All variables are in logarithms. The estimation period was 1963/3–1985/4. YDLH is real household disposable income in 1980 prices, RR = (1 + clearing banks' base rate) − (PC_{t-1} − PC_{t-5}), PC is the consumers' expenditure deflator (1980 = 1), RMD is the effective minimum deposit rate on durables, ML is the flow of mortgage loans (nominal) and NLAJ is personal sector net liquid assets (nominal).

13 Dicks' non-durables consumption function takes the form

$$\text{CND} = \underset{(6.7)}{0.534}\ \text{CND}_{t-1} + \underset{(4.7)}{0.340}\ \text{CND}_{t-2} + \underset{(3.0)}{0.116}\ \Delta\ \text{YDLH}$$

$$+ \underset{(6.4)}{0.196}\ \Delta\ \text{YDLH}_{t-1} + \underset{(-)}{0.119}\ \text{YDLH}$$

$$+ \underset{(2.8)}{0.008}\left(\frac{RNFWJ}{YDLH}\right)_{t-1} - \underset{(2.7)}{0.0614}\ \text{RR}_{t-1} + \text{constant}$$

$$+ \text{dummies}$$

$R^2 = 0.997$ estimation period: 1967/4–1985/2

where CND is real consumers' expenditure on goods and services, RNFWJ = *NFWJ*/PC, NFWJ is personal sector net financial wealth (nominal) and PC is the consumers' expenditure deflator (1980 = 1).

9 Econometric evaluation

1 For general critiques of the econometricians' approach to the estimation of the demand for money see Leamer (1978, 1983), Sims (1980), Cooley and LeRoy (1981), Leamer and Leonard (1983) and McAcleer *et al.* (1985).

2 That capital gains or losses may occur can be explained by the activities of the Bank of England in the gilts market (Fisher 1973). Gilts markets are not efficient, it is argued, because of the authorities' control of short rates and because of the policy of 'leaning into the wind' (Grice and Bennett 1984). It is possible, therefore, that prices may at times not fully reflect expected capital gains or losses to gilts as the prices may not be those which an unhindered market would normally establish.

3 Mizon suggests a test to evaluate whether or not the equation can be accepted as a specialization of its corresponding general form:

$$F(r, T-K) = \frac{\mathrm{SSE}^{\mathrm{R}} - \mathrm{SSt}^{\mathrm{u}}}{\mathrm{SSt}^{\mathrm{u}}} \frac{T-K}{r}$$

where $\mathrm{SSE}^{\mathrm{R}}$ is the residual sums of squares in the restricted equation, $\mathrm{SSt}^{\mathrm{u}}$ is the residual sums of squares in the unrestricted equation, T is the number of observations, r is the number of restrictions and K is the number of explanatory variables in the unrestricted case.

References

Akhtar, M.A. (1983) 'Financial innovations and their implications for monetary policy: an international perspective', Economic Papers 9, Bank for International Settlements, December.

Allen, W.A. (1983) 'Recent developments in monetary control in the UK', in L.H. Meyer (ed.) *Improving Money Stock Control*, Norwell, MA: Kluwer-Nijhoff, pp. 97–123.

Anderson, G.J. and Hendry, D.F. (1984) 'An econometric model of United Kingdom building societies', *Oxford Bulletin of Economics and Statistics* 46 (3): 185–210.

Arestis, P. and Riley, J. (1980) 'Monetarism: the principal issues and areas of disagreement', *British Review of Economic Issues* 2 (6): 51–69.

Artis, M.J. (1974) 'Monetary policy in the 1970's in the light of recent developments', in H.G. Johnson and A.R. Nobay (eds) *Issues in Monetary Economics*, Oxford: Oxford University Press.

—— (1978) 'Monetary policy – Part II', in F.T. Blackaby (ed.) *British Economic Policy 1960–1974*, Cambridge: Cambridge University Press.

—— (1982) 'Recent developments in the theory of demand management', in M.J. Artis *et al.* *Demand Management, Supply Constraints and Inflation*, Manchester: Manchester University Press.

—— (1988) 'The 1988 budget and the MTFS', *Fiscal Studies* 9 (2): 14–29.

Artis, M.J. and Currie, D.A. (1981) 'Monetary and exchange rate targets', in A.S. Courakis and R.L. Harrington (eds) *Monetarism: Traditions, Theory and Policy*, London: Macmillan.

Artis, M.J. and Lewis, M.K. (1974) 'The demand for money: stable or unstable?', *The Banker* 124: 239–47.

—— (1976) 'The demand for money in the UK, 1963–73', *The Manchester School* 44: 147–81.

—— (1981) *Monetary Control in the UK*, Oxford: Philip Allan.

Artis, M.J. and Nobay, A.R. (1969) 'Two aspects of the monetary debate', *National Institute Economic Review* August: 33–51.

Artis, M.J., Kiernan, E. and Whitley, J.D. (1973) 'The effects of building society behaviour on housing investment', in M. Parkin and A.R. Nobay (eds) *Contemporary Issues in Economics*, Manchester: Manchester University Press, pp. 37–62.

Atkinson, P. and Chouraqui, J.-C. (1986) 'The formulation of monetary policy: a reassessment in the light of recent experience', OECD Department of Economics and Statistics, March.

Baba, Y., Hendry, D.F. and Starr, R.M. (1987) 'US money demand, 1960–1984', Discussion Paper, Nuffield College, Oxford.

Bailey, R.W., Driscoll, M.J., Ford, J.L. and Mullineux, A.W. (1982) 'The information content of monetary aggregates in the UK', *Economics Letters*: 61–7.

Bain, A.D. (1986) 'Causes of change and innovation in the mix of financial instruments: the U.K. experience', in D.E. Fair (ed.) *Shifting Frontiers in Financial Markets*, Amsterdam: Martinus Nijhoff.

Bain, A.D. and McGregor, P.G. (1985) 'Buffer stock monetarism and the theory of financial buffers', *The Manchester School* 53: 385–403.

Bank of England (1971) 'Competition and credit control', *Bank of England Quarterly Bulletin* 11 (2): 189–94.

—— (1972) 'Bank lending: the Governor's letter to the banking system', *Bank of England Quarterly Bulletin* 12 (3): 327.

—— (1973) 'Does the money supply really matter?', Speech by the Governor of the Bank of England, *Bank of England Quarterly Bulletin* 13 (2): 193–202.

—— (1977) 'The adoption of monetary targets', *Bank of England Quarterly Bulletin* 17 (2): 150–5.

—— (1978a) 'Reflections on the conduct of monetary policy', *Bank of England Quarterly Bulletin* 18 (1): 31–7.

—— (1978b) 'Transactions demand for money', *Bank of England Quarterly Bulletin* 18 (1): 48–60.

—— (1980a) 'Background note on methods of monetary control', *Bank of England Quarterly Bulletin* 20 (4): 428–9.

—— (1980b) 'Review of monetary developments', Speech by the Governor of the Bank of England, *Bank of England Quarterly Bulletin* 20 (4): 457–9.

—— (1981a) 'The financial scene in the 1970's', Speech by the Governor of the Bank of England, *Bank of England Quarterly Bulletin* 21 (1): 71–6.

—— (1981b) 'Main economic and monetary developments', *Bank of England Quarterly Bulletin* 21 (3): 313–25.

—— (1981c) 'Monetary control - provisions', *Bank of England Quarterly Bulletin* 21 (3): 347–50.

—— (1981d) 'Monetary control - next steps', *Bank of England Quarterly Bulletin* 21 (1): 38–9.

—— (1982a) 'Monetary policy in the year ahead', *Bank of England Quarterly Bulletin* 22 (1): 6–25.

—— (1982b) 'The supplementary special deposits scheme', *Bank of England Quarterly Bulletin* 22 (1): 74–85.

—— (1982c) 'The role of the Bank of England in the money market', *Bank of England Quarterly Bulletin* 22 (1): 86–94.

—— (1982d) 'Transactions balances - a new monetary aggregate', *Bank of England Quarterly Bulletin* 22 (2): 224–5.

—— (1982e) 'Bank lending, monetary control and funding policy', *Bank of England Quarterly Bulletin* 22 (3): 403.

—— (1982f) 'Composition of monetary and liquidity aggregates, and associated statistics', *Bank of England Quarterly Bulletin* 22 (4): 530–7.

—— (1982g) 'Recent changes in the use of cash', *Bank of England Quarterly Bulletin* 22 (4): 519–29.

—— (1983a) 'Setting monetary objectives', *Bank of England Quarterly Bulletin* 23 (2): 200–8.

—— (1983b) 'Competition, innovation and regulation in British banking', *Bank of England Quarterly Bulletin* 23 (3): 363–76.

—— (1983c) 'The nature and implications of financial innovation', *Bank of England Quarterly Bulletin* 23 (3): 358–62.

—— (1984a) 'Changing boundaries in financial services', *Bank of England Quarterly Bulletin* 24 (1): 40–5.

—— (1984b) 'The business of financial supervision', Lecture by the Deputy Governor of the Bank of England, *Bank of England Quarterly Bulletin* 24 (1): 46–50.

—— (1984c) 'Changes to monetary aggregates and the analysis of bank lending', *Bank of England Quarterly Bulletin* 24 (1): 78–82.

—— (1984d) 'Some aspects of UK monetary policy', *Bank of England Quarterly Bulletin* 24 (4): 474–81.

—— (1984e) *The Development and Operation of Monetary Policy, 1960–1983*, Oxford: Oxford University Press.

—— (1985a) 'Operation of monetary policy', *Bank of England Quarterly Bulletin* 25 (1): 24–35.

—— (1985b) 'Changes in the structure of financial markets: a view from London', *Bank of England Quarterly Bulletin* 25 (1): 75–9.

—— (1985c) 'Problems of monetary policy and change in the city', *Bank of England Quarterly Bulletin* 25 (4): 534–6.

—— (1986a) 'The U.K. approach to financial regulation', *Bank of England Quarterly Bulletin* 26 (1): 48–50.

—— (1986b) 'Financial change and broad money', *Bank of England Quarterly Bulletin* 26 (4): 499–507.

—— (1986c) 'Developments in monetary policy and in the City's markets', *Bank of England Quarterly Bulletin* 26 (4): 508–9.

—— (1986d) 'Structural change in housing finance', *Bank of England Quarterly Bulletin* 26 (4): 528–31.

—— (1987a) 'Measures of broad money', *Bank of England Quarterly Bulletin* 27 (2): 212–19.

—— (1987b) 'The financial behaviour of the U.K. personal sector 1976–85', *Bank of England Quarterly Bulletin* 27 (2): 223–33.

—— (1987c) 'The instruments of monetary policy', *Bank of England Quarterly Bulletin* 27 (3): 365–70.

—— (1988a) 'Personal credit in perspective', *Bank of England Quarterly Bulletin* 28 (1): 48–50.

—— (1988b) 'The financial behaviour of industrial and commercial companies, 1970–86', *Bank of England Quarterly Bulletin* 28 (1): 75–82.

Barclays Review (1987) 'UK monetary review', August, 5–7.

Barnes, P.A. (1980) 'Break up the building societies cartel – yes, but how?', *Accountancy* 91 (1044), August: 56.

—— (1985) 'U.K. building societies – a study of the gains from merger', *Journal of Business Finance and Accounting* 13 (1), Spring: 75–91.

Barnes, P.A. and Dodds, J.C. (1981) 'Building society mergers and their size–efficiency relationship: a comment', *Applied Economics* 13 (4): 531–4.

Barnett, W.A. (1978) 'The user cost of money', *Economics Letters* 1: 145–9.

Barnett, W.A., Offenbacher, E.K. and Spindt, P.A. (1984) 'The new Divisia monetary aggregates', *Journal of Political Economy* 42 (6): 1049–85.

Barr, D.G. and Cuthbertson, K. (1989) 'Econometric modelling of the financial decisions of the UK personal sector: preliminary results', *Bank of England Discussion Papers*, Technical Series, No. 22, February.

Barrell, R. (1985) 'The demand for money: problems and issues', *Economic Review* January: 10–13.

Bean, C. (1986) 'The estimation of "surprise" models and the "surprise" consumption function', *Review of Economic Studies* 53 (4): 497–516.

Begg, D.K. (1982) *The Rational Expectations Revolution in Macro-economics: Theories and Evidence*, Oxford: Philip Allan.

—— (1987) 'Recent British fiscal policy: placing the MTFS in context', in P. Minford (ed.) *Monetarism and Macro Policy*, London: Institute of Economic Affairs.

Bellman, H. (1927) *The Building Society Movement* London: Methuen.

Bennett, A. (1986) 'Expenditure, wealth, and the rate of interest', *Economic Modelling* January: 72–80.

Benson, W.J. (1978) 'London clearing banks' evidence to the Wilson Committee', *National Westminster Bank Quarterly Review* May: 2–7.

Bernanke, B.S. and Blinder, A.S. (1988) 'Credit, money and aggregate demand', *American Economic Review, Papers and Proceedings* 78 (2): 435–45.

Bingham, T.R.G. (1985) *Banking and Monetary Policy*, Paris: OECD.

Black, F. (1970) 'Banking and interest rates in a world without money', *Journal of Bank Research* 1 (3): 8–28.

Blaug, M. (1980) *The Methodology of Economics*, Cambridge: Cambridge University Press.

Blinder, A.S. and Stiglitz, J.E. (1983) 'Money, credit restraints and economic activity', *American Economic Review, Papers and Proceedings* 73 (2): 297–302.

Boddy, M. (1980) *The Building Societies* London: Macmillan.

Boleat, M.J. (1979) 'Banks and building societies – controls are not the answer', *The Banker* 129 (641), July: 55–61.

—— (1980) 'Competition between banks and building societies', *National Westminster Bank Quarterly Review* November: 43–57.

—— (1986) *The Building Society Industry* London: Allen & Unwin.

Bootle, R. (1984) 'Origins of the monetarist fallacy – the legacy of gold', *Lloyds Bank Review* July: 16–37.

Bordo, M.D. and Jonung, L. (1981) 'The long-run behaviour of the income velocity of money in five advanced countries, 1870–1975: an institutional approach', *Economic Inquiry* 19, January: 96–116.

Borooah, V.K. and Sharpe, D.R. (1986) 'Aggregate consumption and the distribution of income in the United Kingdom: an econometric analysis', *Economic Journal* 96: 449–66.

Boughton, J.M. (1979) 'The demand for money in major OECD countries', *OECD Economic Outlook*, Occasional Studies, January: 35–57.

—— (1981a) 'Recent instability of the demand for money: an international perspective', *Southern Economic Journal* 47 (3): 579–97.

—— (1981b) 'Money and its substitutes', *Journal of Monetary Economics* 8: 375–86.

Brainard, W.C. (1964) 'Financial intermediaries and a theory of monetary control', *Yale Economic Essays* 4 (1): 431–82.

Bristol & West (1987) 'Impact of competition on ordinary share accounts', *Factual Background* Autumn: 6–8.

Broaddus, A. (1985) 'Financial innovation in the United States – background, current status and prospects', *Economic Review, Federal Reserve Bank of Richmond* 71, January/February: 2–22.

Brunner, K. (1970) 'The monetarist revolution in monetary theory', *Weltwirtschaftliches Archiv* 105 (1): 1–30.

Brunner, K. and Meltzer, A.H. (1963) 'The place of financial intermediaries in the transmission of monetary policy', *American Economic Review* 53 (2): 372–83.

—— (1988) 'Money and credit in the transmission process', *American Economic Review, Papers and Proceedings* 78 (2): 446–51.

Budd, A. (1980) 'Recent developments in monetarism', *British Review of Economic Issues* November: 1–10.

Budd, A. and Dicks, G. (1980) 'The budget, the PSBR, and the money supply', *Economic Outlook*, London Business School, February.

Budd, A. and Holly, S. (1986) 'Does broad money matter?', *Economic Outlook*, London Business School, June, pp. 16–22.

Building Societies Association (1972) 'Do building societies have tax advantages?', *Building Society Affairs* January: 2.

—— (1978) Evidence submitted by the Building Societies to the Committee to Review the Functioning of Financial Institutions (Wilson Committee), October.

—— (1979) 'The taxation of building society interest', *BSA Bulletin* 17, January.

—— (1980) 'Building society shares and deposits and the money supply', *BSA Bulletin* 22, April: 32–5.

—— (1983a) 'Building societies and taxation', *BSA Bulletin* 33, January: 16–20.

—— (1983b) *The Future Constitution and Powers of Building Societies*, London: Building Societies Association.

—— (1983c) 'Transactions or savings: how do people use their building society share accounts?', *BSA Bulletin* 35, July: 23–5.

—— (1988) 'The secondary mortgage market', *BSA Bulletin* 56, October: 13–20.

Buiter, W.H. (1984) 'Allocative and stabilization aspects of budgetary and financial policy', Discusison Paper 42, Centre for Economic Policy Research.

Burton, J. (1982) 'The varieties of monetarism and their policy implications', *The Three Banks Review* June: 14–31.

Cagan, P. (1979) 'Financial developments and the erosion of monetary controls', in W. Fellner (ed.) *Contemporary Economic Problems*, American Enterprise Institute.

Cagan, P. and Schwartz, A.J. (1975) 'Has the growth of money substitutes hindered monetary policy?', *Journal of Money, Credit and Banking* 7 (2): 137–59.

Chetty, V.K. (1969) 'On measuring the nearness of near-monies', *American Economic Review* 59: 270–81.

Clarke, M. (1986) *Regulating the City – Competition, Scandal and Reform*, Milton Keynes: Open University Press.

Clayton, G. (1962) 'British financial intermediaries in theory and practice', *Economic Journal* 72: 869–86.

Clayton, G. *et al.* (1974) 'An econometric model of the U.K. financial sector: some preliminary findings', in H.G. Johnson and A.R. Nobay (eds) *Issues in Monetary Economics*, Oxford: Oxford University Press, pp. 323–61.

Cleary, E.J. (1965) *The Building Society Movement*, London: Elek.

Clower, R. (1967) 'A reconsideration of the microfoundations of monetary theory', *Western Economic Journal* 6, December: 1–8.

Cobham, D. (1981) 'Definitions of domestic credit expansion for the United Kingdom', *Journal of Economic Studies* 8 (3): 65–78.

—— (1984) 'Convergence, divergence and realignment in British macroeconomics', *Banca Nazionale del Lavoro Quarterly Review* 149: 159–76.

—— (1988) 'A disequilibrium monetarist approach to the assessment of monetary control regimes', *British Review of Economic Issues* 10 (22): 1–22.

Cochrane, D. and Orcutt, G.H. (1949) 'Applications of least squares regression to relationships containing auto-correlated error terms', *Journal of the American Statistical Association* 44 (245): 32–61.

Coghlan, R.T. (1977) 'Analysis within the "new view"', *Journal of Money, Credit and Banking* 9: 410–27.

—— (1978a) 'A transactions demand for money', *Bank of England Quarterly Bulletin* March: 48–60.

—— (1978b) 'A new view of money', *Lloyds Bank Review* 129: 12–27.

—— (1980) *The Theory of Money and Finance*, London: Macmillan.

Coghlan, R.T. and Sykes, C. (1980) 'Managing the money supply', *Lloyds Bank Review* 135: 1–13.

Coleby, A.L. (1983) 'The bank's operational procedures for meeting monetary objectives', *Bank of England Quarterly Review* 23, June: 209–15.

Committee of London Clearing Banks (1977) Evidence by the CLCB to the Committee to Review the Functioning of Financial Institutions (Wilson Committee).

Congdon, T. (1978) *Monetarism: An Essay in Definition*, London: London Centre for Policy Studies.

—— (1979) 'Building societies are already within the framework of monetary control', *Building Societies Gazette* April: 358–60.

—— (1980) 'Should Britain adopt monetary base control', *The Banker* 130 (648), February: 31–7.

—— (1982) *Monetary Control in Britain*, London: Macmillan.

Cooley, T.F. and LeRoy, S.F. (1981) 'Identification and estimation of money demand', *American Economic Review* 71 (5): 825–44.

Cooper, J.C.B. (1980) 'Economies of scale in the U.K. building society industry', *Investment Analyst* January: 31–7.

Cottrell, A. (1985) 'The endogeneity of money and money-income causality', *Scottish Journal of Political Economy* 33 (1): 2–27.

Courakis, A.S. (1978) 'Serial correlation and a Bank of England study of the demand for money: an exercise in measurement without theory', *Economic Journal* 88: 537–48.

—— (1981) 'Monetary targets: conceptual antecedents and recent policies in the U.S., U.K. and W. Germany', in A.S. Courakis (ed.) *Inflation, Depression and Economic Policy in the West*, London: Mansell, pp. 259–357.

Currie, D.A. (1982) 'The monetarist policy rule: a critique', *Banca Nazionale del Lavoro Quarterly Review*: 335–346.

—— (1987) 'Options for UK macroeconomic policy', *Oxford Review of Economic Policy* 3 (3): 1–8.

Currie, D. and Kennally, G. (1985) 'Personal sector demand for liquid deposits in the U.K.', Discussion Paper 100, National Institute of Economic and Social Research.

Currie, D. and Levine, P. (1986) 'Time inconsistency and optimal policies in deterministic and stochastic worlds', *Journal of Economic Dynamics and Control* 10: 191–9.

Cuthbertson, K. (1980) 'The determination of expenditure on consumer durables', *National Institute Economic Review* 102, November: 63–77.

—— (1984) 'Techniques of monetary control in the United Kingdom', *Journal of Economic Studies* 11 (4): 46–68.

—— (1985) *The Supply and Demand for Money*, Oxford: Basil Blackwell.

Cuthbertson, K. and Taylor, M.P. (1987) 'The demand for money: a dynamic rational expectations model', *Economic Journal*, Conference Papers, 97: 65–76.

Darnell, A.C. (1987) 'General to specific modelling: a methodological perspective', Mimeo, University of Durham.

Davidson, J.E.H., Hendry, D.F., Srba, F. and Yeo, S. (1978) 'Econometric modelling of the aggregate time-series relationship between consumers expenditure and income in the United Kingdom', *Economic Journal* 88: 661–92.

Davidson, P. (1972) 'A Keynesian view of Friedman's theoretical framework for monetary analysis', *Journal of Political Economy* 80 (5): 846–82.

Davidson, P and Weintraub, S. (1973) 'Money as cause and effect', *Economic Journal* 83: 1117–32.

Davies, G. and Davies, M. (1981) *Building Societies and their Branches – A Regional Economic Survey*, London: Franey.

Davis, E. (1982) 'The consumption function in macroeconomic models: a comparative study', Technical Paper 1, Bank of England.

—— (1984) 'A recursive model of personal sector expenditure and accumulation', Technical Paper 6, Bank of England.

Davis, E.P. and Saville, I.D. (1982) 'Mortgage lending and the housing market', *Bank of England Quarterly Bulletin* 22 (3): 390–8.

Davis, K.T. and Lewis, M.K. (1982) 'Can monetary policy work in a deregulated capital market?', *Australian Economic Review* 1st Quarter: 9–21.

Dennis, G.E.J. (1981) *Monetary Economics*, London: Longman.

Desai, M. (1981) *Testing Monetarism*, London: Pinter.

Desai, M. and Low, W. (1987) 'Measuring the opportunity for product innovation', in M.de Cecco (ed.) *Changing Money*, Oxford: Basil Blackwell, pp. 112–40.

Dickey, D.A. and Fuller, W.A. (1979) 'Distribution of the estimation for autoregressive time series with a unit root', *Journal of the American Statistical Association* 74: 427–31.

Dicks, M.J. (1988) 'The interest elasticity of consumers' expenditure', *Bank of England Discussion Papers*, Technical Series, No. 20, December.

Dodds, J.C. (1981) 'Modelling the portfolio behaviour of British building societies – a survey', *Managerial Finance* 7 (3): 12–26.

Dornbusch, R. (1976) 'Expectations and exchange rate dynamics', *Journal of Political Economy* 84 (6): 1161–76.

Dow, C. (1987) 'A critique of monetary policy', *Lloyds Bank Review* October: 20–32.

Dow, J.C.R. (1958) 'The economic effect of monetary policy 1945–57', *Principal Memoranda of Evidence*, vol. 3, *Committee on the Working of the Monetary System*, London: HMSO, 1960, pp. 76–105.

Dow, J.C.R. and Saville, I.D. (1988) *A Critique of Monetary Policy*, Oxford: Clarendon Press.

Drake, L.M. (1986) 'Economies of scale in the building society industry', Research Paper 26, Loughborough University Banking Centre.

—— (1988) 'Conversion to PLC status for building societies', Research Paper 53, Loughborough Banking Centre.

Drake, L. and Llewellyn, D.T. (1988) 'Conversion to PLC', series of articles in *Chartered Building Societies Institute Journal*.

Drayson, S.J. (1985) 'The housing finance market: recent growth in perspective', *Bank of England Quarterly Bulletin* 25 (1): 80–91.

Driscoll, M.J. and Ford, J.L. (1980) 'The stability of the demand for money function and the predictability of the effects of monetary policy', *Economic Journal* 90: 867–84.

Duck, N.W. and Sheppard, D.K. (1978) 'A proposal for the control of the U.K. money supply', *Economic Journal* 88: 1–17.

Durbin, J. (1954) 'Errors in variables', *Review of the International Statistical Institute* 1 (1): 23–32.

Easton, W.W. (1985) 'The importance of interest rates in five macroeconomic models', Discussion Paper 24, *Bank of England*.

Engle, R.F. (1982) 'Autoregressive conditional heteroskedasticity, with estimates of variance of United Kingdom inflation', *Econometrica* 50: 987–1008.

Engle, R.F. and Granger, C.W.J. (1987) 'Co-integration and error-correction: representation, estimation and testing', *Econometrica* 55 (12): 251–76.

Fama, E.F. (1980) 'Banking in the theory of finance', *Journal of Monetary Economics* 12: 7–28.

Fand, D. (1970) 'Monetarism and fiscalism', *Banca Nazionale del Lavoro Quarterly Review* September: 127–38.

Feige, E.L. and Pearce, D.K. (1977) 'The substitutability of money and near-money: a survey of the time series evidence', *Journal of Economic Literature* 15 (2): 439–68.

Ferber, R. (1973) 'Consumer economics: a survey', *Journal of Economic Literature* 11 (4): 1303–42.

Fforde, J.S. (1983a) 'Setting monetary objectives', *Bank of England Quarterly Bulletin* 23 (2): 200–8.

—— (1983b) 'Competition, innovation and regulation in British banking', *Bank of England Quarterly Bulletin* 23 (3).

Fisher, D. (1973) 'The speculative demand for money: an empirical test', *Economica* 40 (158): 174–9.

Fisher, G. (1968) 'The demand for money in Britain: quarterly results 1951 to 1967', *The Manchester School* 36: 239–344.

Fisher, I. (1911) *The Purchasing Power of Money* New York: Macmillan (revised edition 1922).

Foot, M.D.K.W., Goodhart, C.A.E. and Hotson, A.C. (1979) 'Monetary base control', *Bank of England Quarterly Bulletin* 19 (2): 149–59.

Frazer, P. and Vittas, D. (1980) 'Competition in retail banking', *The Banker* 130 (648): 47–51; 130 (649): 35–9.

—— (1983) 'The forces of change in retail banking', *The World of Banking* 1 (4).

Freedman, C. (1983) 'Financial innovation in Canada: causes and consequences', *American Economic Review, Papers and Proceedings* 73 (2): 101–6.

Friedman, B.M. (1975) 'Targets, instruments and indicators of monetary policy', *Journal of Monetary Economics* 1: 443–73.

—— (1977) 'The inefficiency of short-run monetary targets for monetary policy', *Brookings Papers on Economic Activity* 2: 293–346.

—— (1982) 'The roles of money and credit in macroeconomic analysis', in J. Tobin (ed.) *Macroeconomics, Prices, and Quantities*, Oxford: Basil Blackwell, pp. 161–99.

—— (1983) 'Monetary policy with a credit aggregate target', in K. Brunner and A.H. Meltzer (eds) *Money, Monetary Policy and Financial Institutions*, Carnegie-Rochester Conference Series on Public Policy 18, pp. 117–47.

Friedman, M. (1948) 'A monetary and fiscal framework for economic stability', *American Economic Review*, 38: 245–64.

—— (1953) *Essays in Positive Economics*, Chicago, IL: University of Chicago Press.

—— (1956) 'The quantity theory of money – a restatement', in M. Friedman (ed.) *Studies in the Quantity Theory of Money*, Princeton, NJ: Princeton University Press.

—— (1959) 'The demand for money: some theoretical and empirical results', *Journal of Political Economy* 67 (4): 327–51.

—— (1960) *A Programme for Monetary Stability*, New York: Fordham University Press.

—— (1970a) 'The counter-revolution in monetary theory', Occasional Paper 33, Institute of Economic Affairs.

—— (1970b) 'A theoretical framework for monetary analysis', *Journal of Political Economy* 78, March/April: 193–238.

—— (1971) 'A monetary theory of nominal income', *Journal of Political Economy* 79, March/April: 323–7.

—— (1980) 'Memorandum on monetary policy in Treasury and Civil Service Committee', *Memoranda on Monetary Policy*, Series 1979–80, London: HMSO.

—— (1984) 'Lessons from the 1979–82 monetary policy experiment', *American Economic Review, Papers and Proceedings* 74 (2): 397–400.

Friedman, M. and Meiselman, D.I. (1963) 'The relative stability of monetary velocity and the investment multiplier in the U.S., 1897–1958', *Commission on Money and Credit, Stabilization Policies*, Englewood Cliffs, NJ: Prentice Hall, pp. 165–223.

Friedman, M. and Schwartz, A.J. (1963) *A Monetary History of the United States, 1867–1960*, National Bureau of Economic Research.

—— (1970) Monetary Statistics of the United States: Estimates, Sources, Methods, New York: Columbia University Press for the National Bureau of Economic Research.

—— (1982) *Monetary Trends in the U.S. and the U.K.*, Chicago, IL: Chicago University Press.

Gale, D. (1982) *Money: In Equilibrium*, Welwyn Garden City: J. Nisbet.

Gibson, N.J. (1970) 'The significance of financial intermediaries for economic policy', Hobart Paper 39, *Institute of Economic Affairs.*

Gilbert, C.L. (1986) 'Professor Hendry's econometric methodology', *Oxford Bulletin of Economics and Statistics* 48: 283–307.

Gilchrist, D. (1986) 'Deregulation: implications for British building societies', in D.E. Fair (ed.) *Shifting Frontiers in Financial Markets*, Amsterdam: Martinus Nijhoff.

Gilchrist, D. and Rothwell, S. (1980) 'Mergers of medium societies should mean more efficiency', *Building Societies Gazette* 212 (1350), January: 20–2.

Godley, W. and Cripps, F. (1983) *Macroeconomics*, New York: Oxford University Press.

Goodhart, C.A.E. (1975) *Money, Information and Uncertainty*, London: Macmillan.

—— (1981) 'Problems of monetary management: the U.K. experience', in A.S. Courakis (ed.) *Inflation, Depression and Economic Policy in the West*, London: Mansell, pp. 111–43.

—— (1984) *Monetary Theory and Practice: The U.K. Experience*, London: Macmillan.

—— (1986a) 'Financial innovation and monetary control', *Oxford Review of Economic Policy* 2 (4): 79–102.

—— (1986b) 'The implications of shifting frontiers in financial markets for monetary control', in D.E. Fair (ed.) *Shifting Frontiers in Financial Markets*, Amsterdam: Martinus Nijhoff.

Goodhart, C.A.E. and Crockett, A.D. (1970) 'The importance of money', *Bank of England Quarterly Bulletin* 10 (2): 159–98.

Gordon, R.J. (1984) 'The short-run demand for money: a reconsideration', *Journal of Money, Credit and Banking* 16: 403–34.

Gough, T.J. (1979) 'Building society mergers and the size–efficiency relationship', *Applied Economics* 11 (2): 185–94.

—— (1981) 'Building society mergers and the size–efficiency relationship: a reply', *Applied Economics* 13 (4): 535–8.

—— (1982) *The Economics of Building Societies*, London: Macmillan.

Gough, T.J. and Taylor, T.W. (1979) 'The building society price cartel', Hobart Paper 83, Institute of Economic Affairs, July.

Gowland, D. (1978) *Monetary Policy and Credit Control*, London: Croom Helm.

Gramley, L.E. (1982) 'Financial innovation and monetary policy', *Federal Reserve Bulletin* 68 (7): 393–400.

Granger, C.W.J. and Newbold, P. (1974) 'Spurious regression in econometrics', *Journal of Econometrics* 2: 111–20.

Greenbaum, S.I. and Heywood, C.F. (1971) 'Secular change in the financial

services industry', *Journal of Money, Credit and Banking* 3 (2): 571–89.
Greene, M. (1981) 'Will technology undermine today's monetary control techniques?', *The Banker* 131 (666), August.
Green Paper (1980) *Monetary Control*, Cmnd 7858, London: HMSO, March.
—— (1984) *Building Societies: A New Framework*, Cmnd 9316, London: HMSO.
Grether, D.M. and Maddala, G.S. (1973) 'Errors in variables and serially correlated disturbances in distributed lag models', *Econometrica* 41 (2): 225–62.
Grice, J. and Bennett, A. (1981) 'The demand for £M3 and other aggregates in the United Kingdom', Treasury Working Paper 20.
—— (1984) 'Wealth and the demand for £M3 in the United Kingdom 1963–78', *The Manchester School* 52 (3): 239–71.
Griffiths, B. and Wood, G.E. (eds) (1981) *Monetary Targets*, New York: St Martin's Press.
—— (eds) (1984) *Monetarism in the U.K.*, London: Macmillan.
Gurley, J.G. and Shaw, E.S. (1955) 'Financial aspects of economic development', *American Economic Review* 45 (4): 515–38.
—— (1956) 'Financial intermediaries and the saving–investment process', *Journal of Finance* 11 (2): 256–76.
—— (1960) *Money in a Theory of Finance*, Washington, DC: Brookings Institution.
Hacche, G.J. (1974) 'The demand for money in the United Kingdom: experience since 1971', *Bank of England Quarterly Bulletin* 14 (3): 284–305.
Hadjimichalakis, M.G. (1982) *Monetary Policy and Modern Money Markets*, New York: Lexington Books.
Hall, M.J.B. (1983) *Monetary Policy since 1971, Conduct and Performance*, London: Macmillan.
Hall, R.E. (1982) 'Monetary trends in the United States and the United Kingdom: a review from the perspective of new developments in monetary economics', *Journal of Economic Literature* 20, December: 1552–6.
Hall, S.G. (1986) 'An application of the Granger and Engle two-step estimation procedure to UK aggregate wage data', *Oxford Bulletin of Economics and Statistics* 48 (3): 229–40.
Hall, S.G., Henry, S.G.B. and Wilcox, J.B. (1989) 'The long-run determination of the U.K. monetary aggregates', Discussion Paper 41, Bank of England.
Harrington, R. (1974) 'The importance of competition for credit control', in H.G. Johnson and A.R. Nobay (eds) *Issues in Monetary Economics*, Oxford: Oxford University Press, pp. 548–66.
Hendry, D.F. (1979) 'Predictive failure and econometric modelling in macroeconomics', in P. Ormrod (ed.) *Modelling the Economy*, London: Heinemann.
—— (1985) 'Monetary economic myth and econometric reality', *Oxford Review of Economic Policy* 1: 72–84.
—— (1988) 'The encompassing implications of feedback versus feedforward mechanisms in econometrics', *Oxford Economic Papers* 40: 132–49.
Hendry, D.F. and Anderson, G.J. (1977) 'Testing dynamic specification in small simultaneous systems: an application to a model of building society

behaviour in the United Kingdom', in M.D. Introligator (ed.) *Frontiers in Quantitative Economics*, vol. 3, Amsterdam: North-Holland, pp. 361–83.

Hendry, D.F. and Ericsson, N.R. (1983) 'Assertion without empirical basis: an econometric appraisal of "Monetary Trends ... in the U.K." by M. Friedman and A. Schwartz', Paper 22, Panel of Academic Consultants, Bank of England.

Hendry, D.F. and Mizon, G. (1978) 'Serial correlation as a convenient simplification, not a nuisance: a comment on a study of the demand for money by the Bank of England', *Economic Journal* 88: 549–63.

Hendry, D.F. and Richard, J.F. (1982) 'On the formulation of empirical models in dynamic econometrics', *Journal of Econometrics* 20: 3–33.

—— (1983) 'The econometric analysis of time series', *International Statistical Review* 51: 111–63.

—— (1987) *Recent Developments in the Theory of Encompassing*, 20th Anniversary Volume, CORE.

Herbert, G. (1984) *Money and the Financial System*, Harlow: Longman.

Hester, D.H. (1981) 'Innovations and monetary control', *Brookings Papers on Economic Activity* 1: 141–200.

—— (1982) 'On the adequacy of policy instruments and information when the meaning of money is changing', *American Economic Review, Papers and Proceedings* 72 (2): 40–4.

—— (1987) 'On the empirical detection of financial innovation', in M. de Cecco (ed.) *Changing Money*, Oxford: Basil Blackwell, pp. 77–111.

Hicks, J.R. (1967) *Critical Essays in Monetary Theory*, Oxford: Clarendon Press.

Holmans, A.E. (1986) 'Flows of funds associated with house purchase for owner-occupation in the U.K. 1977–1984 and equity withdrawal from house purchase finance', Government Economic Service Working Paper 92.

Holtrop, W. (1959) *Radcliffe Committee*, Minutes of evidence, Q11818.

Hood, W. (1987) 'The allocation of U.K. personal sector liquid assets', Government Economic Service Working Paper 94, February.

Hotson, A.C. (1979) 'The forecasting and control of bank lending', Paper presented at Money Study Group Conference on Monetarism, Oxford, September.

Hubbard, R.G. and Judd, K.L. (1986) 'Liquidity constraints, fiscal policy and consumption', *Brookings Papers on Economic Activity* 1: 1–60.

Jackson, R. and Sutton, J. (1982) 'Imperfect capital markets and the monetarist black box: liquidity constraints, inflation, and the asymmetric effects of interest rate policy', *Economic Journal* 92: 108–28.

Jao, Y.C. (1983) 'A libertarian approach to monetary theory and policy', Discussion Paper 23, Department of Economics, University of Hong Kong, November.

Jarque, C.M. and Bera, A.K. (1980) 'Efficient tests for normality, homoskedasticity, and serial independence of regression residuals', *Economics Letters* 6: 255–9.

Johansen, S. (1988) 'Statistical analysis of cointegrating vectors', *Journal of Economic Dynamics and Control* 12 (2/3): 231–54.

Johnson, C. (1986) 'Moving the goalposts', *Lloyds Bank Bulletin*, January.

Johnson, H.G. (1962) 'Monetary theory and policy', *American Economic Review* 52 (3): 336–84.

—— (1968) 'Problems in efficiency in monetary management', *Journal of Political Economy* 76 (5): 971–90.

—— (1972) *Further Essays in Monetary Economics*, London: Allen & Unwin.

Johnston, R.B. (1984) 'The demand for non-interest-bearing money in the U.K.', Government Economic Service Working Paper 66, London: HMSO, February.

—— (1985) 'The demand for liquidity aggregates by the UK personal sector', Treasury Working Paper 81, June.

Jones, D. (1984) 'Electronic banking', *The P.A. Journal for Management* 1 (1): 30–4.

Jonson, P.D. and Parkin, R.W. (1986) 'On some recent developments in monetary economics', Research Discussion Paper 8605, Reserve Bank of Australia, August.

Judd, J.P. and Scadding, J.J. (1982) 'The search for a stable money demand function', *Journal of Economic Literature* 20 (3): 993–1023.

Judge, G. (1983) 'The stability of behavioural relationships and their empirical estimates', *British Journal of Economic Issues* 5 (12): 1–14.

Kaldor, N. (1970) 'The new monetarism', *Lloyds Bank Review* 97, July: 1–17.

—— (1980) 'Monetarism and U.K. monetary policy', *Cambridge Journal of Economics* 4: 293–318.

Kane, E.J. (1977) 'Good intentions and unintended evil', *Journal of Money, Credit and Banking* 9, February: 55–69.

—— (1981) 'Accelerating inflation, technological innovation and the decreasing effectiveness of banking regulation', *Journal of Finance* 36 (2): 355–67.

—— (1983) 'Policy implications of structural changes in financial markets', *American Economic Review, Papers and Proceedings*, 73 (2): 96–100.

Kareken, J., Muench, T. and Wallace, N. (1973) 'Optimal open-market strategy: the use of information variables', *American Economic Review* 63 (1): 156–72.

Kaufman, A.G. (1969) 'More on an empirical definition of money', *American Economic Review* 59, March: 78–87.

Kavanagh, N.J. and Walters, A.A. (1966) 'Demand for money in the UK, 1877–1961', *Oxford Bulletin of Economics and Statistics* 28, May: 93–116.

Kearney, C. and MacDonald, R. (1985) 'Public sector borrowing, the money supply, and interest rates', *Oxford Bulletin of Economics and Statistics* 47 (3): 249–73.

Keynes, J.M. (1923) *A Tract on Monetary Reform*, London: Macmillan.

—— (1936) *The General Theory of Employment, Interest and Money*, London: Macmillan.

Khan, M.S. (1974) 'The stability of the demand for money function in the US, 1901–1965', *Journal of Political Economy* 82 (6): 1205–19.

Kiviet, J.F. (1986) *Testing the Specification of the Linear Regression Model*, Amsterdam: University of Amsterdam Press.

Koning, J.H. (1986) 'Financial innovation and monetary aggregate targeting',

in D.E. Fair (ed.) *Shifting Frontiers in Financial Markets*, Amsterdam: Martinus Nijhoff.
Laidler, D.E.W. (1969) 'The definition of money: theoretical and empirical problems', *Journal of Money, Credit and Banking* 1: 508–25.
—— (1971) 'The influence of money on economic activity: a survey of some current problems', in G. Clayton *et al.* (eds) *Monetary Theory and Policy in the 1970's*, Oxford: Oxford University Press.
—— (1973) 'Monetarist policy prescriptions and their background', *The Manchester School* 41: 59–71.
—— (1977) *The Demand for Money: Theories and Evidence*, New York: Dun-Donnelly.
—— (1978) 'Money and money income: an essay on the transmission mechanism', *Journal of Monetary Economics* 4: 151–91.
—— (1980) 'The demand for money in the United States – yet again', Carnegie-Rochester Conference Series on Public Policy 12, pp. 219–271.
—— (1981) 'Monetarism: an interpretation and an assessment', *Economic Journal* 91: 1–28.
—— (1982) *Monetarist Perspectives*, Oxford: Philip Allan.
—— (1984) 'The "buffer stock" notion in monetary economics', *Economic Journal* 94, Supplement: 17–34.
—— (1985a) *The Demand for Money*, 3rd edn, New York: Harper & Row.
—— (1985b) 'Monetary policy in Britain: successes and shortcomings', *Oxford Review of Economic Policy* 1 (1): 35–43.
—— (1986) 'What do we really know about monetary policy', *Australian Economic Papers* June: 1–16.
Laidler, D.E.W. and Parkin, J.M. (1970) 'The demand for money in the United Kingdom, 1955–67: preliminary estimates', *The Manchester School* 38: 187–208.
Lancaster, K. (1982) 'Innovative entry: profit hidden beneath the zero', *Journal of Industrial Economics* 31: 41–56.
Lane, T.D. (1985) 'The rationale for money-supply targets: a survey', *The Manchester School* 53 (2): 179–207.
Lavoie, M. (1984) 'The endogenous flow of credit and the post Keynesian theory of money', *Journal of Economic Issues* September: 771–97.
Lawson, N. (1986) 'Broad money and credit', Reported in *Financial Times* 17 October.
Lawson, T. (1983) 'Different approaches to econometric modelling', *Cambridge Journal of Economics* 7: 77–84.
Leamer, E.E. (1978) *Specification Searches: ad hoc Inference with Non-experimental Data*, New York: Wiley.
—— (1983) 'Let's take the con out of econometrics', *American Economic Review* 73: 31–44.
Leamer, E.E. and Leonard, H.B. (1983) 'Reporting the fragility of regression estimates', *Review of Economics and Statistics* 65: 306–17.
Leigh-Pemberton, R. (1979) 'Banks, building societies and personal savings', *National Westminster Bank Quarterly Review* May: 2–10.
—— (1986) 'Shifting frontiers in financial markets: their causes and consequences', in D.E. Fair (ed.) *Shifting Frontiers in Financial Markets*, Amsterdam: Martinus Nijhoff.
Lewis, M.K. (1980a) 'Is monetary base control just interest rate control in

disguise?', *The Banker* 130: 35–8.
—— (1980b) 'Rethinking monetary policy', *Lloyds Bank Review* 137, July: 41–60.
—— (1981) 'Understanding the monetary control debate', *Economics* Autumn: 69–73.
—— (1987) 'The provision of retail financial services', *International Journal of Bank Marketing* 5 (2): 33–46.
Lindsey, D.E. (1982) 'Recent monetary developments and controversies', *Brookings Papers on Economic Activity* 1: 245–71.
Llewellyn, D.T. (1979a) 'Do building societies take deposits away from banks?', *Lloyds Bank Review* 131, January: 21–34.
—— (1979b) 'End of the U.K. exchange control: the monetary implications', *The Banker* December: 43–7.
—— (1980) 'Can monetary targets influence wage bargaining?', *The Banker* January: 49–53.
—— (1982) 'How will the building societies meet the challenge from the banks?', *Bankers Magazine* July: 16–17.
—— (1985a) *The Evolution of the British Financial System*, Gilbart Lectures on Banking, London: Institute of Bankers.
—— (1985b) 'The changing structure of the U.K. financial system', *The Three Banks Review* 145, March: 19–34.
—— (1986a) 'Regulation and myth', *Banking World* May: 37–9.
—— (1986b) 'The regulation and supervision of financial institutions', Gilbart Lectures on Banking, London: Institute of Bankers.
—— (1987a) 'Banks and building societies: the competitive environment', Paper given at the Association of Banking Teachers Conference, May.
—— (1987b) 'Competition and the regulatory framework', *National Westminster Bank Quarterly Review* August: 4–13.
—— (1988a) 'The challenge from the building societies', *Banking World* July: 32–5.
—— (1988b) 'Future regulatory arrangements for building societies', Research Paper 54, Loughborough University Banking Centre.
—— (1988c) 'Financial innovation: a basic analysis', Research Paper 56, Loughborough University Banking Centre, November.
Llewellyn, D.T. and Drake, L.M. (1987) 'The balance of wholesale and retail funding', Research Paper 33, Loughborough University Banking Centre, January.
Llewellyn, D.T. and Kearney, C. (1984) 'The British monetarist experiment: a preliminary assessment', *Economics* Spring: 15–22.
Llewellyn, D.T., Dennis, G.E.J., Hall, M.J.B. and Nellis, J.G. (1982) *The Framework of U.K. Monetary Policy*, London: Heinemann.
Lucas, R.E. (1972) 'Expectations and the neutrality of money', *Journal of Economic Theory* 4: 103–24.
—— (1976) 'Econometric policy evaluation: a critique', in K. Brunner and A.M. Meltzer (eds) *The Phillips Curve and Labour Markets*, Carnegie-Rochester Conference on Public Policy 1, pp. 19–46.
Lucas, R.E. and Sargent, T.J. (1981) *Rational Expectations and Econometric Practice*, London: Allen & Unwin.
Lucas, R.F. (1983) 'Financial innovation and the control of monetary aggregates: some evidence from Canada', Working Paper 11, 57, National

Bureau of Economic Research, June.
Lynne-Evans, J. (1988) 'Adjustment modelling and the stability of the demand for money function', *British Review of Economic Issues* 10 (23), Autumn: 49–76.
McAleer, M., Pagan, A.R. and Volker, P.A. (1985) 'What will take the con out of econometrics?', *American Economic Review* 75: 293–313.
McCallum, B.T. (1976) 'Rational expectations and the natural rate hypothesis: some consistent estimates', *Econometrica* 44 (1): 43–52.
—— (1984) 'Monetarist rules in the light of recent experience', *American Economic Review, Papers and Proceedings* 4 (2): 388–91.
McClam, W.D. (1978) 'Targets and techniques of monetary policy in Western Europe', *Banca Nazionale del Lavoro Quarterly Review* 31, March: 3–27.
McLeod, A.N. (1984) *The Principles of Financial Intermediation*, New York: University Press of America.
McMahon, C.W. (1981) 'Changing structure of intermediation and the implications for policy', *Journal of the Institute of Bankers* 102, February: 3–7.
Mason, W.E. (1976) 'The empirical definition of money: a critique', *Economic Enquiry* 14, December: 525–38.
Mayer, T. (1975) 'The structure of monetarism', *Kredit and Kapital* 8: 191–218.
—— (1982) 'Financial innovation – the conflict between micro and macro optimality', *American Economic Review, Papers and Proceedings* 72 (2): 29–34.
Meen, G.P. (1983) 'Identifications of excess mortgage demand and the mortgage interest rate', Mimeo, University of Melbourne, November.
—— (1985) 'An econometric analysis of mortgage rationing', Government Economic Service Working Paper 79, July.
Meltzer, A.H. (1963) 'Demand for money: the evidence from the time series', *Journal of Political Economy* 71: 219–46.
—— (1969a) 'Controlling money', *Federal Reserve Bank of St Louis Review* 51: 16–24.
—— (1969b) 'Money, intermediation and growth', *Journal of Economic Literature* 7 (1): 27–56.
Midland Bank (1978) 'The banking sector and monetary policy', *Midland Bank Review*, Winter.
Milbourne, R. (1986a) 'Re-examining the buffer-stock model of money', *Economic Journal* 97, Supplement: 130–42.
—— (1986b) 'Financial innovation, deregulation and the redefinition of the monetary aggregates', Working Paper 91, Centre for Applied Economic Research, *The University of New South Wales*, September.
Miller, M. (1981) 'Monetary control in the U.K.', *Cambridge Journal of Economics* 5: 71–9.
Miller, M.H. and Orr, D. (1966) 'A model of the demand for money by firms', *Quarterly Journal of Economics* 80 (3): 413–42.
Miller, S.M. (1986) 'Financial innovation, depository institution, deregulation and the demand for money', *Journal of Macroeconomics* 8: 279–96.
Mills, T.C. (1978) 'The functional form of the U.K. demand for money', *Journal of the Royal Statistical Society Series C* 27: 52–7.
—— (1983) 'Composite monetary indicators for the United Kingdom:

construction and empirical analysis', Technical Discussion Paper 3, Bank of England, May.
Mills, T.C. and Wood, G.E. (1977) 'Money substitutes and monetary policy in the U.K. 1922–1974', *European Economic Review* 10: 19–36.
Minsky, H.P. (1957) 'Central banking and money market changes', *Quarterly Journal of Economics* 81 (2): 171–84.
Mizon, G.E. (1984) 'The encompassing approach in econometrics', in D.F. Hendry and K.F. Wallis (eds) *Econometrics and Quantitative Economics*, Oxford: Basil Blackwell.
Mizon, G.E. and Hendry, D.F. (1980) 'An empirical application and Monte Carlo analysis of tests of dynamic specification', *Review of Economic Studies* 49: 21–45.
Monopolies Commission (1968) *House of Commons Paper 319*, July.
Moore, B.J. (1979) 'The endogenous money stock', *Journal of Post-Keynesian Economics* 2 (1): 49–70.
—— (1983) 'Unpacking the post-Keynesian black box', *Journal of Post-Keynesian Economics* 5 (4): 537–56.
—— (1988) *Horizontalists and Verticalists*, Cambridge: Cambridge University Press.
Moore, B.J. and Threadgold, A.R. (1980) 'Bank lending and the money supply', Discussion Paper 10, Bank of England.
Morgan, E.V. (1969) 'The essential qualities of money', *The Manchester School* 37, September: 237–48.
—— (1988) 'The role of building societies in a changing financial environment', Graham Bannock and Partners.
Muth, J.F. (1961) 'Rational expectations and the theory of price movements', *Econometrica* 29, July: 315–35.
National Board for Prices and Incomes (1966) *Rate of Interest on Building Society Mortgages* Report 22, Cmnd 3136, London: HMSO.
—— (1967) *Bank Charges* Report 1.34, Cmnd 3292, London: HMSO, May.
Nellis, J.G. and Thom, R. (1983) 'The demand for mortgage finance in the United Kingdom', *Applied Economics* August: 521–9.
Niehans, J. (1982) 'Innovation in Monetary Policy', *Journal of Banking and Finance* 6: 9–28.
Odling-Smee, J. and Riley, C. (1985) 'Approaches to the PSBR', *National Institute Economic Review* 113: 65–80.
Pagan, A.R. (1984) 'Model evaluation by variable addition', in D.F. Hendry and K.F. Wallis (eds) *Econometrics and Quantitative Economics*, Oxford: Basil Blackwell.
Paish, F.W. (1958) 'The future of British monetary policy', *Principal Memoranda of Evidence*, vol. 3, *Committee on the Working of the Monetary System*, London: HMSO, 1960, pp. 182–8.
Parkin, M. (1975) 'Where is Britain's inflation going?', *Lloyds Bank Review* July: 1–13.
—— (1978) 'A comparison of alternative techniques of monetary control under rational expectations', *The Manchester School* 46 (3): 252–87.
Patinkin, D. (1961) 'Financial intermediaries and the logical structure of monetary theory', *American Economic Review* 51 (1–2): 95–116.
—— (1969) 'The Chicago tradition, the quantity theory and Friedman',

Journal of Money, Credit and Banking 1, February: 46–70.

Peasnell, K.V. and Ward, C.W.R. (1985) *British Financial Markets and Institutions*, London: Prentice Hall International.

Pettigrew, C.W. (1980) 'National and sector balance sheets for the United Kingdom', *Economic Trends* 325: 82–100.

Phillips, A. (1981) 'Competition and regulation in financial markets: concluding observations', in A. Verheirstraeten (ed.) *Competition and Regulation in Financial Markets.*

Phillips, B. (1980) *Report on the Working Group on Marketable Securities*, London: Building Societies Association.

Pierce, D.G. and Shaw, D. (1974) *Monetary Economics: Theories, Evidence and Policy*, London: Butterworths.

Pierce, J.L. (1982) 'How regulations affect monetary control', *Journal of Money, Credit and Banking* 14 (4) Part 2: 775–95.

—— (1983) 'Did financial innovation hurt the great monetarist experiment?', *American Economic Review, Papers and Proceedings*, 74 (2): 392–6.

Pigou, A.C. (1917) 'The value of money', *Quarterly Journal of Economics* 32, November: 38–65.

Podolski, T.M. (1985) 'Control of a monetary quantity: constraint or contumacy', *British Review of Economic Issues* 7 (17): 1–37.

—— (1986) *Financial Innovation and the Money Supply*, Oxford: Basil Blackwell.

Poole, W. (1970) 'Optimal choice of monetary policy instruments in a simple stochastic macro model', *Quarterly Journal of Economics* 84: 197–216.

Popper, K.R. (1972) *Conjectures and Refutations*, 4th edn, London: Routledge.

Porter, R.D., Simpson, T.D. and Mauskopf, E. (1979) 'Financial innovation and the monetary aggregates', *Brookings Papers on Economic Activity* 1: 213–29.

Price, L.D.D. (1972) 'The demand for money in the United Kingdom: a further investigation', *Bank of England Quarterly Bulletin* 12 (1): 43–55.

Radcliffe Committee (1959) *Report on the Working of the Monetary System*, Cmnd 827, London: HMSO.

Ramsey, J.B. (1969) 'Tests for specification errors in classical linear least squares regression analysis', *Journal of The Royal Statistical Society Series B* 31: 350–71.

Reid, D.J. (1978) 'Personal sector balance sheets', *Economic Trends* 291: 97–107.

Reifler, W.W. (1959) Memoranda of Evidence, *Radcliffe Committee*, vol. 1.

Revell, J. (1978) 'Competition and regulation of banks', *Bangor Occasional Papers in Economics* 14.

—— (1986) 'Implications of information technology for financial institutions', in D.E. Fair (ed.) *Shifting Frontiers in Financial Markets*, Amsterdam: Martinus Nijhoff.

Revell, J. and Barnes, P. (eds) (1984) 'The new technology and financial institutions', *Managerial Finance, Special Edition* 10 (1).

Richardson, G. (1978) 'The building societies in a changing financial environment', Speech by the Governor of the Bank of England, 18 May 1978, *Bank of England Quarterly Bulletin* 18 (2): 245–9.

—— (1983) 'The future of building societies: a central banker's view', Speech by the Governor of the Bank of England, *Bank of England Quarterly Bulletin* 23 (2): 216–20.

Robinson, J. (1970) 'Quantity theories old and new', *Journal of Money, Credit and Banking* November: 504–12.

Rose, H. (1978) 'The competition for deposits and the impact of monetary policy', *Institute of Bankers* November: 1–19.

—— (1986) 'Change in financial innovation in the UK', *Oxford Review of Economic Policy* 2 (4): 18–40.

Rowan, D.C. and Miller, J. (1979) 'The demand for money in the United Kingdom 1963–1977', Discussion Paper in Economics and Econometrics 7902, Southampton University.

Rybczynski, T.M. (1984) 'The U.K. financial system in transition', *National Westminster Bank Quarterly Review* November: 26–42.

—— (1986) 'Shifting financial frontiers: implications for financial institutions', in D.E. Fair (ed.) *Shifting Frontiers in Financial Markets*, Amsterdam: Martinus Nijhoff.

Salmon, M. (1982) 'Error correction mechanisms', *Economic Journal* 92: 615–629.

Sargan, J.D. (1964) 'Wages and prices in the U.K.: a study in econometric methodology', reprinted in D.F. Hendry and K.F. Wallis (eds) *Econometrics and Quantitative Economics*, Oxford: Basil Blackwell, 1984.

—— (1980) 'Some tests of dynamic specification for a single equation', *Econometrica* 48: 879–97.

Sargent, T.J. and Wallace, N. (1975) 'Rational expectations, the optimal monetary instrument and the optimal money supply role', *Journal of Political Economy* 83 (2): 241–54.

—— (1976) 'Rational expectations and the theory of economic policy', *Journal of Monetary Economics* 2, April: 169–83.

—— (1982) 'The real bills doctrine versus the quantity theory', *Journal of Political Economy* 90 (6): 1212–36.

Savage, D. (1979) 'Monetary targets and the control of the money supply', *National Institute Economic Review* 9, August: 44–52.

—— (1980) 'Some issues of monetary policy', *National Institute Economic Review* 91, February: 78–85.

Saving, T.R. (1967) 'Monetary policies and indicators', *Journal of Political Economy* 75, Supplement: 446–56.

Sayers, R.S. (1960) 'Monetary thought and monetary policy in England', *Economic Journal* 70: 710–24.

Silber, W.L. (1975a) 'Towards a theory of financial innovation', in W. Silber (ed.) *Financial Innovation*, Lexington, MA: Lexington Books, pp. 53–86.

—— (ed.) (1975b) *Financial Innovation*, Farnborough: Lexington Books/ D.C. Heath.

—— (1983) 'The process of financial innovation', *American Economic Review, Papers and Proceedings* 73 (2): 89–95.

Simons, E.C. (1947) 'The relative liquidity of money and other things', *American Economic Review*, 37, Supplement: 308–11.

Simons, H.C. (1936) 'Rules versus authorities in monetary policy', *Journal of Political Economy* 44: 1–30.

Simpson, T.D. (1984) 'Changes in the financial system: implications for

monetary policy', *Brookings Papers on Economic Activity* 1: 249–72.
Sims, C.A. (1980) 'Macroeconomics and reality', *Econometrica* 48: 1–18.
Smith, D. (1978) 'The demand for alternative monies in the U.K.: 1924–77', *National Westminster Bank Quarterly Review* November: 35–48.
Smith, W.L. (1959) 'Financial intermediaries and monetary controls', *Quarterly Journal of Economics* 73 (4): 533–53.
Smithin, J.N. (1984) 'Financial innovation and monetary theory', *The Three Banks Review* December: 26–38.
Spanos, A. (1984) 'Liquidity as a latent variable – an application of the mimic model', *Oxford Bulletin of Economics and Statistics* 46 (4): 125–43.
—— (1986) *Statistical Foundations of Econometric Modelling*, Cambridge: Cambridge University Press.
Spencer, P.D. (1981) 'A model of the demand for British Government stocks by non bank residents 1967–77', *Economic Journal* 91: 938–60.
—— (1986) *Financial Innovation, Efficiency and Disequilibrium*, Oxford: Clarendon Press.
Spindt, P.A. (1984) 'Modelling the money multiplier and the controllability of the Divisia monetary quantity aggregates', *Review of Economics and Statistics* 2, May: 314–19.
Sprenkle, C.M. and Miller, M.H. (1980) 'The precautionary demand for narrow and broad money', *Economica* 47, November: 407–21.
Stiglitz, J.E. and Weiss, A. (1981) 'Credit rationing in markets with imperfect competition', *American Economic Review* 71 (1): 393–410.
Stow, R. (1979) *Mortgage Finance into the 1980's*, London: Building Societies Association.
Taylor, M.P. (1987) 'Financial innovation, inflation and the stability of the demand for broad money in the United Kingdom', *Bulletin of Economic Research* 39 (3): 225–33.
Thygesen, N. (1986) 'What monetary targets in an evolving financial system? An introductory address', in D.E. Fair (ed.) *Shifting Frontiers in Financial Markets*, Amsterdam: Martinus Nijhoff.
Tobin, J. (1956) 'The interest-elasticity of transactions demand for cash', *Review of Economics and Statistics* 38 (3): 241–7.
—— (1963) 'Commercial banks as creators of money', in D. Carson (ed.) *Banking and Monetary Studies*, Homewood, IL: Irwin, pp. 408–19.
—— (1969) 'A general equilibrium approach to monetary theory', *Journal of Money, Credit and Banking* 1, February: 15–29.
—— (1970) 'Money and income: *post hoc ergo propter hoc*', Quarterly Journal of Economics 84, May: 301–17.
—— (1983a) 'Financial structure and monetary policy', *Kredit and Kapital* 16: 155–71.
—— (1983b) 'Monetary policy: rules, targets, shocks', *Journal of Money, Credit and Banking* 15 (4): 506–18.
Tobin, J. and Brainard, W.C. (1963) 'Financial intermediaries and the effectiveness of monetary controls', *American Economic Review* 53 (2): 393–412.
Treasury and Civil Service Committee (1980) *Memoranda on Monetary Policy*, vols 1 and 2, London: HMSO.
Turnbull, P. (1984) 'Mortgage lending and consumers' expenditure', *Investment Analyst* 72, April: 3–6.

Turnbull, S.P. (1979) 'Building societies and monetary policies – equality in misery', *BSA Bulletin*, September.

Vaciago, G. (1985) 'A note on credit aggregates as targets or indicators of monetary policy', *Banca Nazionale del Lavoro Quarterly Review* June: 155–71.

Vittas, D. and Frazer, P. (1980) 'Competition in retail banking', *The Banker* February: 47–51.

Wagner, J.R. (1974) 'Reflections on the interest rate elasticity of the demand for money', *Economic Journal* March: 156–8.

Wallace, N. (1983) 'A legal restrictions theory of the demand for "money" and the role of monetary policy', *Federal Reserve Bank of Minneapolis Quarterly Review* Winter: 1–7.

Wallis, K.F. (1974) 'Seasonal adjustment and relations between variables', *Journal of the American Statistical Association* 69: 18–31.

Walters, A. (1986) *Britain's Economic Renaissance: Margaret Thatcher's Reforms 1979–1984* Oxford: Oxford University Press.

Weale, M. (1986) 'The structure of personal sector short-term asset holdings', *The Manchester School* 2, June: 141–61.

White, H. (1980) 'A heteroskedasticity-consistent covariance matrix estimator and a direct test for heteroskedasticity', *Econometrica* 48 (4): 817–38.

White, L.H. (1984) 'Competitive payments systems and the unit of account', *American Economic Review* 74 (4): 649–712.

Williams, D., Goodhart, C.A.E. and Gowland, D.H. (1976) 'Money, income and causality: the U.K. experience', *American Economic Review* 66 (3): 417–23.

Wills, H.R. (1982) 'The simple economics of bank regulation', *Economica* 49: 249–59.

Wilson Report (1980) *Committee to Review the Functioning of Financial Institutions*, Cmnd 7937, London: HMSO.

Wood, G.E. (1979) 'Cash base control of the money supply – its institutional implications', *The Banker* July: 37–43.

—— (1985) 'Where next in U.K. monetary policy?', *The Banker* 135 (718), December: 32–5.

Wood, J.H. (1981) 'Financial intermediaries and monetary control', *Journal of Monetary Economics* 8: 145–63.

Yeager, L. (1968) 'Essential properties of the medium of exchange', *Kyklos* 21: 45–69.

Zawadski, K.F. (1981) *Competition and Credit Control*, Oxford: Basil Blackwell.

Index